THE HIRSCH HERITAGE

נחלת צבי

The Collected Writings

SAMSON RAPHAEL HIRSCH

The Collected Writings
VOLUME III

JEWISH SYMBOLISM

Published for the
Rabbi Dr. Joseph Breuer Foundation
and the
Samson Raphael Hirsch Publications Society

Philipp Feldheim, Inc.
New York — Jerusalem

Library of Congress Catalog Number: 84–60015

ISBN 0–87306–924–2
Copyright © 1984 by
Rabbi Dr. Joseph Breuer Foundation
2nd edition 1988

Philipp Feldheim, Inc.
200 Airport Executive Park
Spring Valley, NY 10977

Feldheim Publishers Ltd.
POB 6525/Jerusalem, Israel

Printed in the United States of America

In tribute to our parents

JACQUES AND HANNA SCHWALBE

*Whose wisdom, dignity and love
guide us always*

Gaby and Harold Goldblatt
Peter Schwalbe
Robert and Jane Schwalbe
Vicky and Michael Nathan

Table of Contents

Part Two
Analysis of the Symbolic Character
of Specific Laws and Institutions

MILAH

TSITSITH

TEFILLIN

THE SANCTUARY

BASIC CONCEPTS

Acknowledgements

The editors wish to express their appreciation to—

Dr. Paul Forchheimer, a talmid of the late Rav Dr. Joseph Breuer זצ״ל, and an exponent of and adherent to the Hirschian "Torah im Derech Eretz" ideal, for his translation of the German original;

Gertrude Hirschler for editing the translation manuscript;

Ralph Levy, Jerusalem, for permission to adapt the translation by his late father, Dr. Isaac Levy ז״ל, of the essay on the Shmone Esre and for providing to the Rabbi Dr. Joseph Breuer Foundation his father's English version of "Symbolism" which aided in the preparation of this volume;

Philipp Feldheim and Yitzchak Feldheim for their personal involvement in the publication of this volume.

The staff of Simcha Graphic Associates for their continued co-operation and expertise.

Marc Breuer
Jacob Breuer
Meta Bechhofer
Elliott Bondi

Introduction

In his *Nineteen Letters* and in the *Horeb,* Rabbi Samson Raphael Hirsch divides the mitzvoth into six categories. One of these categories is edoth, defined as "Symbolic observances representing truths which form the basis of Israel's life." By the performance of these edoth, we are to bring to mind and impress upon ourselves the essential ideas which these mitzvoth represent. The classic example of a symbolic mitzva is tsitsith, about which the Torah commands וראיתם אתו וזכרתם את כל מצות ה' ועשיתם אתם.

Clearly, a deep understanding of the relationship between the symbol (ציצת) and the truth it represents (כל מצות ה') is required for the proper fulfillment of the mitzva.

An indispensable part of the performance of edoth is reflection along definite lines of thought, which serves to attach the physical symbol to the abstract idea.

R. Hirsch's explanation of טעמי המצות, the significance and purpose of mitzvoth, comprise large portions of his *Commentary* on the *Torah* and of *Horeb.* However, it is his extensive "Basic Guidelines for Jewish Symbolism" (*Gesammelte Schriften* Vol.III) which presents the principles of his system of analysis. This is followed by an elaborate exposition of four mitzvoth — mila, tsitsith, tefillin and mishkon — in which it is shown how every nuance of the mitzva reflects symbolic meaning.

In prefacing this volume on symbolism, one must emphasize that, while it is permissible and even encouraged to elucidate the meaning of the mitzvoth, explanations can never affect the practice of the law. R. Hirsch's own clarification to the study of טעמי המצות is found in a footnote to the eighteenth letter of his *Nineteen Letters:*

> One word here concerning the proper method of Torah investigation. Two revelations are open before us; that is, nature and the Torah. In nature, all phenomena stand before us as indisputable facts, and we can only endeavor a posteriori to ascertain the law of each and the connection of all. Abstract demonstration of the truth, or rather, the probability of theoretical explanations of the

acts of nature, is an unnatural proceeding. The right method is to verify our assumptions by the known facts, and the highest attainable degree of certainty is to be able to say: "The facts agree with our assumption" — that is, all the phenomena observed can be explained according to our theory. A single contradictory phenomenon will make our theory untenable. We must, therefore, acquire all the knowledge possible concerning the object of our investigation, and know it, if possible, in its totality. If, however, all efforts should fail in disclosing the inner law and connection of phenomena revealed to us as facts in nature, the facts remain, nevertheless, undeniable and cannot be reasoned away.

The same principles must be applied to the investigation of the Torah. In the Torah, even as in nature, God is the ultimate cause. In the Torah, even as in nature, no fact may be denied, even though the reason and the connection may not be understood. What is true in nature is true also in the Torah; the traces of divine wisdom must ever be sought. Its ordinances must be accepted in their entirety as undeniable phenomena, and must be studied in accordance with their connection to each other, and the subject to which they relate. Our conjectures must be tested by their precepts, and our highest certainty here also can only be that everything stands in harmony with our theory.

In nature, the phenomena are recognized as facts, though their cause and relationship to each other may not be understood, and are independent of our investigation. So, too, the ordinances of the Torah must be law for us, even if we do not comprehend the reason and the purpose of a single one. Our fulfillment of the commandments must not depend on our investigations. Only the commandments belonging to the category of edoth, which are designed to impress emotional and intellectual life, are incomplete without such research.

As mentioned in the previous volume of this series, the task of translating the German literary style of the last century into modern English is formidable. To clarify the original, yet preserve its style, certain textual liberties have been taken and some redundancies have been eliminated.

In addition, R. Hirsch's treatise on the שמונה עשרה (*Gesammelte Schriften,* Vol. IV), in which he explains its symbolic meaning, is included in the current volume.

The Hirschian system of interpreting symbolism has become an integral part of Torah learning. Thus, it was the wish of the late Rav Dr. Joseph Breuer זצ״ל that this fundamental work be made accessible to the English-speaking public to enhance the knowledge and understanding of the teachings of Rabbi Samson Raphael Hirsch.

Part One

Basic Guidelines
for a Jewish Symbolism

Introduction to the Study of Symbolism

The purpose of the present study is to draw up guidelines for a science which, if properly understood, might perhaps provide the basis for solving one of the most complex problems of Jewish knowledge. It is our intention to define the concept and function of a Jewish symbolism, and to show the methods for achieving this end. But first we shall analyze the purpose of symbolism as such and then, from the nature of symbolism, attempt to derive the prerequisites for a proper approach to such a study.

Natural Symbolism.

A study of symbols can serve a two-fold purpose:

a) to teach the rules for expressing abstract concepts; i.e., for finding appropriate, tangible means to express such concepts;

b) to teach the rules for understanding symbols; i.e., for deriving from these symbols an understanding of the concepts that these physical symbols are meant to express. The subject of the present study is the last-named aspect of symbolism—how to interpret symbols and how to derive from a symbol the idea which it is intended to express.

The ability to express ideas by physically perceptible signs, or symbols, is as natural and as necessary to man as are the ability and the urge to communicate ideas by means of spoken, audible words. Indeed, it is not too bold to suggest that the beginnings of language derive from a kind of auditory symbolism. Thus, it is appropriate to

3

inquire into the natural connection between sounds and the idea those sounds are intended to convey.

All of us use a natural symbolism that requires no special study to understand it. Yet, an analysis of this symbolism may well teach us the value inherent in the symbol as a reinforcement of the spoken word. The bodily gestures with which we accompany our words and which, indeed, we often permit to take the place of words, are simply a natural symbolism which we practice and which we certainly would not want to do without. Whether we want to say "Yes" or "No," whether we want to express agreement or disagreement, approval or criticism, respect or contempt, joy or sorrow, friendship or love, we could not express even half of what we feel unless we add appropriate gestures to our verbal communication. Indeed, in some instances a bodily gesture alone might be sufficient. I am apt to forget quickly the farewells bidden in mere words. But the silent handclasp with which my friend took leave of me, which for a moment united us physically, making a bond that he would have liked to preserve forever—this gesture, which brought home to me in full measure the sadness my friend felt at parting from me, I will never forget.

Symbols in Human Communication

In the preceding paragraph we referred to our bodily gestures as "natural symbolism." To be sure, many of the bodily gestures through which we express our thoughts, or with which we supplement our verbal expressions of thoughts, are part of man's very nature. Such gestures would, perhaps, include the side-to-side movement of the head with which we express negation, or the up-and-down nod with which we express affirmation. A closer investigation of this peculiarity would fall within the realm of human physiology. However, there is no doubt that many gestures which appear natural to us are only conventional and therefore vary from one ethnic group to another. But even such "conventions" can be interpreted as conventional to a limited extent only, in much the same manner as languages may be characterized as conventional because of their diversity.

These differences can be clearly explained as the results of natural differences in ethnic character. Hence such natural differences may represent the deeper natural basis for variations in linguistic expression. Therefore, a physiological study of ethnographic differences in human bodily gestures could make a significant contribution to the understanding of ethnic characteristics. Even the two most natural of all bodily gestures, tears and laughter, are functionally interchangeable at the climax of the emotions they express. We know the laughter of grief and the tears of joy. Precisely the deepest grief may cause an outbreak of laughter, while the pinnacle of joy may bring tears.

However, such bodily sign language does not yet satisfy our need for physical acts to express our thoughts and emotions. The spoken word and the gestures that accompany it, or substitute for it, are ephemeral and fleeting. If we want to dwell at some length on the expression of a particular thought or emotion, or to give these expressions a measure of permanence, we must resort to other means. The desire to spend more time on the expression of a thought or an emotion gives rise to a symbolic act. The intention to perpetuate a thought or an emotion results in a gesture that we call symbolic.

The greeting we accord a friend on his arrival, and the manner in which we see him off when he departs, along with most of the acts connected with solemn observance of rejoicing or mourning, are symbolic acts. They are sequences of physically perceptible gestures, all of which express one and the same idea, one and the same emotion. The wreath with which we pay tribute to the memory of a poet, the ring which a friend gives us as a keepsake, any object which we dedicate to the lasting remembrance of a thought or an emotion thus becomes endowed with symbolic meaning. It becomes a symbol, an object which, whenever we look at it, will evoke in us a specific thought, a specific emotion, or a specific chain of thoughts and emotions. Our domestic and civic lives move largely within the sphere of such symbolic signs and actions.

Most of the symbolic phenomena we have considered thus far are subjective in character. They do not express an objective concept, or a declaration, or a judgment based on intellect, as much as they demonstrate our attitudes and emotions toward a specific person, subject or idea. However, as we shall see, symbols do not serve merely to supplement or to accentuate our verbal interjections. There are areas and functions even in the objective expression of logical concepts and

judgments for which verbal language, spoken or written, is not sufficient, and one must resort to a symbolization of these concepts and
judgments. Everywhere and in every age, nations in their political
lives, and even more so in their religious lives, have used symbolic
expressions of concepts and judgments to attain their particular
purposes. Pictures, symbolic signs and emblems are employed by a
society to express ideas, truths, doctrines or principles which are to be
adopted by that society and which are to serve as a bond through
which that society becomes one united whole. The adoption and
activation of these ideas are expressed by specific symbolic acts.
National colors and emblems, pictures or images, altars, sacrifices and
ceremonies, which set the stage for the political and religious life of the
nations, are all part of this symbolism.

If we recall the instances in which thus far we have noted symbols
as supplements to, or substitutes for, the spoken word, it will not be
difficult for us to analyze the unique functions of the symbol which
place the symbol alongside spoken or written language and may even
give the former priority over the latter.

First of all, what is it that lends such force to bodily gestures, the
natural symbolism of our bodily movements, when these movements
are made to accompany, or to replace, words? Why does a word have a
much greater impact on me when it is accompanied by an appropriate
movement of the body? What is it that endows a silent handclasp, a
wordless twinkle of the eye, a raising of the brow, a shrug of the
shoulders, in short, any symbolic bodily expression, with an impact
infinitely more profound than that of the most clear, distinct verbal
language uttered by the lips alone, without the participation of any
other part of the speaker's body? The answer lies precisely in the fact
that the rest of the speaker's body goes into action along with his lips.
If the words are uttered by the lips alone, who is to say whether they
truly come from the speaker's heart, that they do not merely reflect
cold calculation with the human aspect totally uninvolved? On the
other hand, if speech is joined by bodily movements, then every move,
every shrug of the shoulder, every pressure of the hand shows that the
speaker has engaged his entire body, his entire being, to support the
words he is uttering. It then becomes clear that the entire personality

of the speaker lives in the words pronounced by his lips, that the thoughts and the emotions he expresses truly pervade his whole person. Such gestures mean that we have devoted the best of our energies, of the spiritual and physical aspects of our personality, to the thoughts and emotions we mean to demonstrate and this is the magic inherent in the symbolism of bodily movements.

It is their impact and value that acted as prime factors in introducing the symbol and the symbolic acts as means of expression whenever a fact, a doctrine, a verity or a principle of obvious importance was to be demonstrated. This is true especially where the awareness and acknowledgment of such teachings or truths are to be realized by a mass of people, a collective entity or a nation. In such instances, a mere recording of that fact or doctrine is not considered sufficient; it is not enough to express it only in words. Instead, throughout history, the means employed to perpetuate such verities or principles has been the symbol. The awareness and acceptance of these truths or tenets were enshrined in specific, appropriate symbolic acts, which the collective entity, or the nation, was summoned to perform at specified, recurring periods.

The more aware a nation is of its unity, and the more this unity is borne by specific spiritual principles, the more prominent will be the place of symbols and symbolic acts in its political and religious life. Conversely, if a people's sense of unity is weak, if they do not feel bound together by a common history or by a common purpose, if they attach no meaning to their own unique ethnic characteristics, if the nation accords first place instead to the personal concerns, ideas and aspirations of the individual, then symbols and symbolic acts will increasingly vanish from that nation's political and religious life. In that case, too, the awareness of commonly held principles, and practical cooperation to translate these principles into reality, will also cease in that nation. This fact has been documented in history, both ancient and modern.

As we have already noted, symbols and symbolic acts have an advantage over words in that the actions they entail engage the entire person, and do so for a longer time than would the mere spoken word. But they have two additional advantages: a) symbols employed, or symbolic acts performed, by hundreds of thousands of individuals at the same time underscore their sense of unity and uniformity and their recognition and acknowledgment of the teachings and principles that hold them together; b) by accompanying us throughout our lives, regardless of our momentary concerns, symbols serve us as constant reminders of the ideas they represent—an advantage that can never be attained by the spoken word, or even by the written word.

On the one hand, then, symbols and symbolic acts have definite advantages over language in that they require a greater investment of time and effort, and in that they set forth their meaning with deliberate sameness. As a result, their impact upon us will be greater than that of the word, spoken or written. On the other hand, they suffer from a manifest disadvantage with regard to one element basic to any exchange of ideas: the element of clarity. Therefore, when we are presented with a symbol intended to convey to us specific ideas, we have the problem of finding the right method to help us discern the precise idea whose expression is the sole purpose of our symbol. The proper approach and method to be employed in the interpretation of a symbol can be derived only from the unique character of the symbol itself and from the relationship between the symbol and its meaning.

Symbols are signs taken from the range of physically perceptible objects and phenomena for the purpose of representing certain ideas and concepts. However, the symbolic meaning of these objects or phenomena is not derived from their original nature. Their symbolic significance is based solely on their selection as a vehicle for a given idea because they have a certain relationship or association with that idea. Only by virtue of having been thus selected can they express that idea. They derive their symbolic significance solely from the intention of the one who instituted the symbol and employed it for that stated purpose.

There are thousands of forget-me-nots blooming along the roadside. But only that one flower which my friend picked as we parted and which, without uttering a word, he pinned to the lapel of my coat, has become a symbol, telling me, "Forget me not." Even a handclasp, that symbolic bodily gesture with a natural eloquence all its own, derives its meaning only from the intention of the one who clasped my hand.

Without that intention, the meaning of the handclasp would not go beyond the physical sensation of pressure. Only my knowledge of the intention of the one whose act produced this physical sensation, lets me interpret the handclasp as a symbol with a special message for me.

Therefore, the first prerequisite for our understanding of a symbol is that we must ascertain its intent. We must make certain that the one who chose that particular object or phenomenon as a symbol really intended it to express a specific idea. As long as we are in doubt about the intent, we have no basis for interpreting that object or phenomenon as a symbol, and we have no right to define it in terms of anything else but its original and primary meaning.

Image of the Symbol

In view of the foregoing, our first question must always be: Is the object or the phenomenon which we see before us a symbol, or must we interpret it simply in terms of its original and primary meaning? Only after we have resolved this preliminary question, only after we have the certainty that this particular object or phenomenon is intended to express some idea, thought, truth or doctrine, may we start to search for the ideas which the one who originally vested that object or phenomenon with symbolic meaning intended to communicate through that symbol. Without the certainty that we are indeed dealing with a symbol, any attempt on our part to interpret it, no matter how ingenious, will only be an exercise in arbitrary, trifling sophistry, without value or objective reality.

To answer this question we must, first of all, examine the object or phenomenon as such, looking for clues as to whether it should be understood simply in terms of its primary meaning, or whether it must be viewed in terms of symbolic meaning. We must examine it also in the context of the time and environment in which it occurs. Thus, for instance, if we see an anchor at the waterfront, we will interpret it simply in terms of its primary physical characteristics; i.e., as an anchor. But if that anchor is so small or made of such material that it can have no practical use for a ship, we will immediately realize that its purpose must be something other than that usually associated with such an instrument. If we see an anchor suspended over the door of a chandler's shop, it is obviously just the emblem of a business concern.

If we see an anchor depicted on a seal, along with a map and a mariner's compass, we will interpret it as the badge of a ship's captain. Only if it appears in connection with certain other emblems will we interpret an anchor as a symbol of hope. If we see before us a pictorial representation of a serpent, a bee, a dog, a horse or any other part of nature, only additional information about the artist's intention, and about the time and environment in which the work was created, can help us determine whether the picture was intended simply to represent an object as such, or whether it was meant to symbolize a specific idea.

But even if we have satisfied ourselves that a given object or act does indeed have a symbolic meaning, this rarely means that we will also recognize, at once, and beyond the shadow of a doubt, the idea which this symbol is meant to express. The symbolic meaning of the object or phenomenon in question is not dependent upon its primary, physical features but solely upon a choice or intent imposed upon it from without. Precisely for this reason, in most cases, the symbol, considered by itself, will admit of many possible interpretations, but only one of these interpretations will be correct; namely, the one envisioned by him who chose this particular object or phenomenon as a symbol in the first place.

Let us return once again to the simplest, most natural bodily gesture—the handclasp. If I know nothing more about it than that A has shaken hands with B, that handclasp is open to any number of interpretations. Appreciation, felicitations, sympathy, farewell, welcome, friendship, a promise—how many different thoughts can this common, natural symbol express! The same variety of interpretations is possible for any symbol. Yet, in the case of each symbol, only one of these interpretations will be correct. The problem we face in each instance is: From among all the ideas the symbol could express, how do we find the one idea which the symbol is really intended to communicate?

If we bear in mind that the significance of any symbol is only that which is conferred upon it by the choice and purpose of the one who instituted it, then we must immediately come to the following conclusion: A symbol can be interpreted only by taking into account the person who chose it, the person to whom it is addressed, and the time and place of its origin. In other words, a symbol can be analyzed only in the context of its own local and historical background. Any attempt to explain a symbol outside this context cannot be called a genuine search for truth. Only if I study a symbol in this context can I probe into the intentions of its originator, and only an understanding of these intentions can lead me to discover the true meaning of the symbol.

If I do not know the person who has just shaken my hand, if he does not know me, if I do not know of any relationship—past, present or future—between him and myself and also cannot assume such knowledge on his part, then his handclasp, this simplest and most natural of symbolic acts, will continue to be open to many possible interpretations. For this very reason, its true meaning will remain a mystery to me forever. Even a handclasp can be understood only in the context of its personal implications, and of the time and place at which it was exchanged. If this is so, how could I dare attempt to interpret a symbol far more distant, far more alien to me, in terms of anything else but that context?

Even a written text can be properly understood only if one considers the person of the writer, the person for whom the communication was intended, and the time and place in which the text was written. Furthermore, within the text itself, every sentence, every clause, indeed every single word, can and must be analyzed only in the framework of the whole, if it is to be correctly understood. Anything can be read into a sentence taken out of context. Even a written text, which is almost the immediate symbolic representation of the spoken word, can be understood correctly only if it is examined in the proper context. The study of a symbol offers an even greater variety of possible interpretations. Hence, it is all the more mandatory upon us to study symbols only in their proper context.

Take a pictorial representation of a serpent. Is it meant simply to depict the reptile as it appears in nature? Or is it, as in Genesis 3, 14, intended to symbolize the earth, or temptation? Is it to be understood as a tool of sorcery or fortunetelling, or, in general, as a symbol of cunning, cleverness or shrewdness? Does it specifically denote the art of healing? Or does it, by some other implication, symbolize the "bite" of a guilty conscience?

What about the picture of a bee? Is it meant simply to depict a winged insect as it appears in nature? Or is it to be interpreted as the symbol of sweetness, or of nourishment in general? Or—in view of the intoxicating effect of honey—should it be understood as symbolizing ecstasy? Or, perhaps, are we to understand this pictorial representation of a bee as a symbol of industry and diligence?

What of the dog? Is it merely a zoological depiction of the canine species? Or is it a symbol of hunting, vigilance, faithfulness, or perhaps, conversely, of filth or shamelessness? Or could it symbolize—as often in ancient texts—the constellation of Sirius,* which implies life and fertility?

What of the picture of a horse? Is it merely intended to show that animal in its natural pose? Or is it an emblem of chivalry? Or—in view of its swiftness—is it meant to symbolize running water?

What of the sun? Descending each night as it seems into the netherworld, should it be taken to symbolize the judge of the netherworld and of death?

We can gain clarity about all these queries only if we first seek to establish, independently of the pictorial representation, the intention of the one who executed the picture, and the context of time and place in which the picture originated.

Indeed, depending on him who devised it, and on the person to whom it is addressed, one and the same symbol or symbolic act may represent two diametrically opposed concepts. The father who, on his deathbed, presented first a bundle of arrows to his sons, and then gave them each arrow separately, one at a time, to break, meant to impress upon his sons that there is strength in unity. He so sought to admonish them to pull together as brothers. But if a man such as Machiavelli were to give the same arrows, first in a bundle and then each separately, one arrow at a time, to one of his charges, he would have demonstrated in a most graphic manner the truth of his principle "divide and conquer," thereby cautioning him most impressively against tolerating unity and harmony among his subjects and among his peers.

Ambiguity of the Symbol

When studied in its own, historical and local context, a symbol loses much of the ambiguity that it offers when examined out of

---

* The brightest star in the constellation Canis Major (Dog Star)

context. In most instances, such a study in context narrows the number of possible interpretations to a few specific ideas. The more thorough one's knowledge of the personalities involved, and of the historical and local background of the symbol, the smaller the number of possible interpretations. Our approach will then become less hesitant and there will be less danger of error. Hence, before studying any symbol, we must acquire as thorough a knowledge as possible of the personalities and the local and historical background relevant to the symbol.

Now if the originator of the symbol did not present it in silence but accompanied it with words, if he did not offer it in isolation but associated it, in a specific context, with other factors that are either enunciated or designated by symbols of their own, the circle around the symbol we are studying will become smaller and smaller, and our inquiry will take an increasingly steady and sure direction.

The choice of a given object or act as the symbolic expression of an idea will always be guided by the relationship of that object or act to the idea it is meant to express. If, then, the field of vision within which we must search for the meaning of the symbol is narrowed down as much as possible, we will have to search within these boundaries for that particular sphere or sequence of ideas which is somehow associated with the symbolic object under scrutiny. Such an association may be physical, social or historical. It may be based on some natural characteristic of the symbolic object, on its sociological significance, or on some historical event through which that object first attained prominence. In many instances, the word for that object, in the language in which the idea to be expressed was originally conceived, may be used as a metaphor, and that metaphorical expression may become quite popular and generally understood. The meaning of a symbol can therefore be discerned with any degree of reliability only if careful consideration has been given to all of the following pertinent factors: personal, historical and local context; words that accompanied the institution of the symbol; associations with other factors; the physical, social or historical significance of the symbolic object; the metaphorical meaning of the name of the object in light of its linguistic background.

A final prerequisite for arriving at an authentic explanation of the symbol is a careful analysis of the symbolic object or act in all its essential aspects.

Any interpretation obtained by this method must be subjected to rigorous testing to determine whether the object or act which we have found to be of symbolic character will indeed satisfy the criteria which the originator of the symbol had in mind. These criteria are as follows: the essential features of the symbol, seen against the background of the personalities involved, and of local and historical conditions; explanatory words that accompanied the institution of the symbol; and any other circumstances associated with the symbol. Even the most clever, ingenious explanation must be rejected as soon as it is found to be at variance with any one of these essential aspects of the symbol. Any assumption regarding the meaning of the symbol can be defended only if it can explain and justify all the aspects of the symbol in uncontrived harmony, so that they may be understood as deriving from one and the same higher thought.

In the final analysis, this is the method that must guide any responsible interpretation of a written text. Ten commentators may offer ten different interpretations for one and the same text, but we will accept as correct only that one interpretation which duly takes into account and explains all the linguistic peculiarities of the words and sentences, and the contexts and associations in which they occur.

It will not be possible for us to reach any conclusion with mathematical certainty. However, we will categorically reject any obvious misinterpretation. We will be able to qualify our acceptance of an interpretation with the statement that, after a most painstaking analysis, all the factors that had to be considered have made it appear that our assumption might be the correct one.

The Symbol as a Message

Foremost among the conditions we have set down for the analysis of a symbol is the requirement that the symbol must be considered in association with both the person who instituted it and the person to whom it is addressed. This requirement has far-reaching significance in the analysis of a symbol.

By studying the personality who instituted the symbol, we will discover the trend of thought from which arose the intention to convey an idea through the symbol under consideration.

By studying the personality to whom the symbol is addressed we will ascertain the frame of mind within which the initiator of the symbol can expect the symbol to be understood. The message inherent in the symbol can be perceived only in a sphere of thought which the communicator of the symbol knows to be already established among those to whom the message of the symbol is addressed. No symbol is capable of conveying to its recipient a truth that is completely new to him. It can give added dimension to a concept with which he is already familiar. The person to whom the symbol is addressed must already have some knowledge of the symbolic object and the idea it is intended to symbolize, but it has not yet occurred to him that there may be a connection between the two. In that case the symbol serves to show the object and the idea, both of which he is familiar with, in an interrelation which up to that point had been unknown to him. This is the highest degree of new thought that a symbol can convey. However, no symbol is capable of conveying the meaning of an object or of an idea that is still foreign to the recipient. The recipient of the symbol must work on his own to ascertain its message, and for this reason he can search for its meaning nowhere else but within the range of ideas with which he is already familiar. A symbol cannot reveal to him an idea that is outside his sphere of thought. Rather, each symbol must have reference to an idea already known to him. Thus, *symbols cannot serve to reveal concepts that are completely unknown to the recipient.*

We must remember that the usefulness of a message-symbol does not lie in the clarity and preciseness of its content, but in the fact that symbols provide a mechanism of continuous activity for the acceptance, the imprinting and the retention of the ideas the symbols intend to convey. We should readily understand that the purpose of communication by means of symbols is not to reveal previously unknown truths but only to impress upon the recipient, in a manner more profound and enduring than mere words, truths that have already been made known to him earlier.

But just as the contents of a symbol presuppose that the recipient is familiar with their subject matter, telling him nothing new, so, too, he who instituted the symbol must assume that the recipient is familiar with the physical, social or historical features of the symbolic object, as related to the idea which that object is intended to symbolize. Thus, he who instituted the symbol can illustrate his idea symbolically only through objects whose relationships to the idea are within the conceptual realm of those who should assimilate that particular idea through that specific symbol.

All these preliminary observations should convince us that symbolism, a study of the symbols prevalent in a given society, must not be considered open territory for arbitrary speculation, loose banter and random conjecture. On the contrary, the study of symbolism must be undertaken most earnestly and seriously. Any assumption that something is indeed a symbol and that such is its interpretation can, and indeed must, be subjected to a most searching scientific scrutiny.

After these preliminary observations we shall now proceed to the main topic of our investigation: an attempt to draw up guidelines to a Jewish symbolism.

Jewish Symbolism in History and Law

In our introductory observations we have analyzed the essence and the specific character of the symbol, and the communication of ideas through symbolic signs and acts. From these preliminary investigations we have developed the following ground rules:

1) The symbolic significance of an object or of an act is never intrinsic but always metaphoric; i.e., it derives from the intentions of the one who instituted that object or act as a symbol.

2) When an object or an act is assigned a symbolic role, several of its aspects must be taken into consideration. Symbolic meaning may be attached to the natural, social or historical aspects of that object or act.

3) The symbolic meaning of an object or an act may vary depending on the presumed intention of the one who instituted that object or act as a symbol, on the ideology presumed for the one to whom the message of the symbol is addressed, and on the historical and local identification of the symbolic object or act.

4) Therefore, in seeking to establish the symbolic role of any object or act, and also the meaning and intended message of the symbol, one

must take into account the natural, social and historical aspects of the symbol, particularly its connection with the person who instituted it and the person to whom its message is addressed. Local and contemporary factors must likewise be considered.

5) Symbols can never reveal ideas or facts that were completely unknown before. Symbols can only demonstrate new relationships between known ideas and facts and thus serve to commit these ideas and facts to renewed and lasting remembrance.

With these guiding principles in mind we shall now proceed to an examination of Jewish symbolism; i.e., to an analysis of the symbols and symbolic acts instituted and prescribed by Jewish religious law for its adherents.

At the very outset of our study we find ourselves faced with a curious situation: our proposed project will encounter misgivings from two diametrically opposed points of view, rejecting the legitimacy of our study. They will assert, more or less emphatically, that there are no symbols in Judaism. The objects and actions entailed in the observance of Jewish Law, they insist, are devoid of symbolic meaning, and therefore any attempt to set up a science of Jewish symbolism would be un-Jewish from the start.

The reason for these objections is that the symbolic interpretation of the ritual objects and activities in Jewish Law has often been undertaken on an irresponsible and superficial manner. Clever—and not-so-clever—minds have considered it an open field, subject to no controls whatsoever, where anyone may take liberties with the ordinances of Divine Law.

Moreover, there are those who, believing that a given Divine law has only symbolic value, consider themselves exempt from its observance, claiming that once one knows the message inherent in the act, the act itself can be discarded as an empty shell. As a result of such abuses, truly conscientious servants of God's Law have become suspicious of any attempt at a symbolic interpretation of Divine laws. They would rather abstain altogether from such ventures than expose themselves and the holy Laws of God to the dangers of such speculations.

Indeed, opposition to any attempt at establishing a Jewish symbolism has come also from entirely different quarters: from the modernists who consider the observance of Jewish Law a nuisance. A

large number of our contemporaries had boldly cast aside in practice
what they regarded as a cumbersome vestige and now clamored for a
new scientific theory that would justify their defection. Such a theory
was not long in coming. All the commandments in the Law of God
that seemed irksome were now labled as irrelevant, meaningless formalities to which God, Who had instituted these ordinances, could not
possibly have attributed such great importance. Historical and local
considerations were invented which, it was claimed, might have
motivated the Legislator in another age but which had become totally
irrelevant to our own time and to the conditions under which we live
today. This soothed the conscience of those who had already broken
with so many sacred, God-ordained duties. Naturally, the propaga-
tors of such a theory must have found most uncomfortable and incon-
venient the opposing claim that underscores the most solemn earnest-
ness with which God, in His Law, demands the observance of precisely
those ordinances which many wanted to dismiss as cumbersome
trifles. This counterclaim insists that these so-called formalities have a
meaning which raises them high above all changes of time and place
because the ideas which permeate them are eternal.

The modernists considered it so essential for their purposes to
negate the existence of symbolism in the Divine Law of Judaism that
the brilliant author of a very recent "History of The Jews," which
moves within the ideology of such theories, actually says there, in all
seriousness:

> Symbolism, as I see it, is a characteristic peculiar to Chris-
> tianity as distinct from Judaism. Moreover, in Christianity
> itself, it is not a product stemming from Judaism but an
> element adopted from Hellenism. As a matter of fact, one
> could say that whatever in Judaism is, or appears to be,
> symbolism is in fact of pagan, Greek or Christian origin.*

* Graetz, H., Geschichte der Juden von der ältesten Zeit bis zur Gegenwart, Vol. XII,
pg. 151.

In view of all the foregoing, we must make certain that the proposed subject of our research is real. We must answer this question: Is there, indeed, a Jewish symbolism? Does the Law of God contain regulations which we are justified in interpreting as symbolic signs or acts and which we therefore may, indeed must, analyze for their symbolic content?

Symbols in Jewish History

Now, therefore: Is there, indeed, a Jewish symbolism? And, more specifically, is there a symbolism inherent in Jewish Law? Are we entitled, or even compelled, to assume that God, in His Law, has ordained the preparation of specific objects and the performance of specific acts, in order that these objects and acts should serve to help us remember and continually bear in mind specific ideas and truths? After all, this is actually the connotation of all symbols and symbolic acts. But before we go any further, let us examine that part of Divine revelation which lies outside the Law as such, so that we may determine whether or not we find any indication that God employs symbols and symbolic acts as instruments for communicating ideas. An unbiased analysis of this preliminary question will demonstrate that the answer is definitely in the affirmative.

In nearly every decisive manifestation of God's sovereignty, intended for the training of mankind in general and of Israel in particular, up to the time of Israel's selection and the giving of the Law, we see that the Word of God never occurs by itself. The truth of God's Word—the banner for all future times—is never entrusted to mere words. The word is supported by symbols and symbolic acts that make for a far greater impact and more enduring retention. Later when Israel, by its failure to observe the Law, forfeited its position and became increasingly ripe for a time of trials and sufferings, God called upon men, as messengers of His Word, to introduce this new era of affliction. And we see that the call they received, and the truths they had to convey to the nation, were both communicated through symbols and symbolic acts.

God's Covenant with Mankind

One world had been destroyed, and there was now a new world. The Creator, Judge and Father of the world wished to establish a new covenant with man and all living creatures associated with man on earth. Henceforth there was to be a new order; another way was to be found to overpower the evil that grew rampant from human egotism. Never again was the evil of man to cause the destruction of all living things on earth; never again was it to place a curse on the total development of the earth as the soil of mankind. From that time on, planting and harvesting, cold and heat, summer and winter, day and night were to run their course on earth undisturbed. Never again was a flood to come down upon the earth and plunge it into primeval night. This promise and covenant was given to Noah at the threshold of the ark, and he was to hand it down to all future generations. At that moment God directs Noah's attention to the heavens, shows him the rainbow and says to him: "This is the sign of the covenant! My bow, which I have set in the cloud, shall henceforth be a sign of the covenant between Myself and the earth!" (Gen. 9, 13) The rainbow, then, becomes an אות, a symbol.

Abraham, Bearer of God's Word

The history of mankind's development and education continues. Having been given the earth anew, mankind very soon forgets to look to God as the sole mainstay and uniting force of human society. Society seeks support from within its own self, from its own cunning, its own inventiveness and its own power to control the forces of nature and mankind. Men said: We shall make a name not for God but for *ourselves*—נעשה לנו שם—and create a monument to our own greatness that will reach into the heavens (Gen. 11, 4). But God frustrated their undertaking at its very start and dispersed them over the globe, each to struggle alone against the forces of nature and against each other. God then chose for Himself one man who, in the midst of all this selfishness and thirst for glory, had recognized His Name once more, and He said to him: לך לך, Go your own way! Renounce all other ties and follow Me! While all the others group themselves into nations so that, together, they may unfold their strength, you are to become a nation through Me and thereby become a monument to My greatness and My almighty power among men who worship their own greatness and might. And so Abraham tore himself free from all his other ties and followed the One God. He walked among men and built altars for this One God of his, and summoned men to rally around the name of God. But he had grown old and had yet to see the initial phase of the future nation that God had promised him: his first son. True, he had walked among men as a living protest against all the enterprises in which men engaged in his day, and God had protected him; indeed, He had made him victorious even over kings flushed with past victories. But of what good had all this been for the salvation of mankind? Abraham walked the earth without offspring. With his death, what had been mankind's guiding light would die out like a bright meteor. "My God and Lord! What can You give me, seeing that I go about childless?" (Gen. 15, 2) Thereupon God led him outside and said to him: "Look upon the sky and count the stars if you are able to count them! *Thus* shall your seed be." (V. 5) Did not God, then, appoint the stars as symbols for the origin and the future of the nation that God had promised to establish from Abraham's seed? How great is the significance of that one word: "Thus!"

Let us continue: Not only like the stars was this nation to be directly dependent on the Word of God for its existence and its numbers, not only would it be said of this nation some day that "He Who numbers each one of the stars also calls each one by its name," (Psalms 147, 4) but this nation was also to be given a territory on earth. It was to receive the land on which its progenitor had walked as a stranger. But Abraham wanted to know: במה אדע כי אירשנה? (Gen. 15, 8) If we understand this question correctly, Abraham, as the progenitor of the future nation, meant to ask God on behalf of that nation-to-be: How would this nation know when the time had come for it to take possession of the land? What dimensions, what power would his descendants have to attain before they could undertake to conquer this land? Abraham wants an answer, so that the future nation, his descendants, will know how to recognize the time when, in accordance with God's decree, it will be sufficiently strong and mature to embark on such a momentous undertaking. God's answer to Abraham's question במה אדע is ידוע תדע. It will not happen in the near future as you imagine; know that only the fourth generation will find itself in this land again.

Three generations will languish in an alien land, without a home, without freedom, without power to resist their oppressors. They will have to serve as slaves, and they will be tormented for four hundred years. But ultimately I shall judge also the nation whom they will serve; only after that will they go forth into freedom, rich in possessions. Only the fourth generation will return here, because Israel's possession of its land is dependent on whether the nation develops its moral greatness. If the nation loses its moral stature, it will also lose its land. At this point, the iniquity of the original inhabitants of the land is not yet complete.

This was God's answer to the father of the future nation. But this spoken answer is preceded by acts, visions and experiences. These happenings appear to be merely symbolic communications of the great message that is subsequently to be detailed through the word. This is the message destined to form the foundation for the strength and faith of the nation that is to mature in an unparalleled four centuries of suffering. "How am I to recognize when I am ready to take possession?" the forefather had asked. And God's answer was: "Bring me three times a calf, and three times a goat, and three times a ram, and one turtle dove and one pigeon." (V. 9) Abraham brought all these to God, split each of them in the middle, placing each half opposite its corresponding half. But he did not split the birds. Then vultures descended upon the carcasses, but Abraham drove them away. When the sun was about to set, Abraham fell into a deep sleep. And a dark, great fear came upon him. And God said to Abraham: "By this shall you know that your seed will be an alien in a land that is not theirs. They will have to serve them, and they will be tormented for four hundred years. But I shall also judge the nation whom they will serve, and after that they will go forth with great wealth. You will go in peace to your fathers and will be buried at a ripe old age. But they will return here in the fourth generation, for the iniquity of the Emorite is not yet complete." (Gen. 15, 13–16) After the sun had gone down and total darkness had descended, there was a smoking furnace, and a flame of fire passing between the pieces. On that day God made a covenant with Abraham: "To your seed have I given this land, from the river of Egypt to the great river, the river Perath; the Kenite, the Kenizzite, and the Kadmonite, the Hittite, the Perizzite and the Rephaim; the Emorite, the Canaanite, the Girgashite and the Jebusite." (V. 18–20)

If we consider this event, even only in its most obvious manifestations, together with the words that accompanied it, we see here once again symbols in the form of most diverse phenomena, supporting the spoken word. We have here symbolic signs, symbolic acts, a symbolic experience, and we see Abraham during the night live through—in anticipation—all the horrors of the dark centuries through which his nation will have to pass. Hence, this was another instance of Divine communication through the use of symbols.

The Future Nation: "Be Whole"

Let us continue. The forefather has been promised the nation and the land. He was already ninety-nine years old, and his wife eighty-nine, when the scion who was to be the bearer of this promise was begotten. But even as the original inhabitants of the promised land will lose the land only because they had forfeited their moral stature, so, too, the fulfillment of the promise, the emergence of the nation and its possession of the land were to be dependent on Israel's attaining and maintaining its moral greatness. The resolve to achieve this end, and the acceptance of this obligation, were to precede the birth of the first scion. A year prior to Isaac's birth, God appeared to Abraham and said to him: "Conduct yourself before Me and be whole." (Gen. 17, 1)

In that momentous utterance God expressed the full extent of this moral condition for the survival and prosperity of the promised nation. התהלך לפני! Conduct yourself before Me. Do so without any inducements from the outside, indeed, if need be, even in opposition to all outside influences, והיה תמים and be "whole." The adjective תמים "whole" (or "perfect") is the most flagrant antithesis to רע‏, "broken."* Be whole! Let all the aspects of your life, physical and spiritual, all of your character, be governed freely by one principle; subordinate yourself entirely, unconditionally, to the One sole God. This is the condition for the survival and prosperity of the promised nation, this the obligation in the Divine covenant to be assumed by Abraham and his people. Abraham fell upon his face and dedicated himself completely to the fulfillment of this obligation. However, the mission that was to be the everlasting foundation for the spiritual

---

* See Commentary Genesis 6,5; 21,11. רע (root רעע) broken, in contrast to תמים whole, perfect.

and moral development of the nation in every aspect of its life was not
to be entrusted to the spoken word alone. "Now then," thus God
concluded the verbal announcement of His covenant, "circumcise the
flesh of your foreskin, so that it may become the sign of the covenant
between Me and you. Thus My covenant upon your body shall
become an everlasting covenant, and an uncircumcised male who does
not circumcise the flesh of his foreskin, his soul shall be eliminated
from the community of its people; he has broken My covenant!" (Gen.
17, 11–14) Is not the circumcised foreskin a symbol, and circumcision
a symbolic act? Are both not אות ברית, symbol of the covenant that calls
out to everyone who bears it upon his flesh the eternal admonition:
התהלך לפני והיה תמים!

Abraham's Descendants

Let us continue. Abraham dies in peace and is buried at a happy,
ripe old age. But with his death, the foretold era of suffering already
becomes manifest. The sun begins to move toward eventide. Isaac
must contend with the molestations of the Philistines, and his home
life is saddened by discord between his offspring. Finally, Jacob
appears, in a dual role. He is both "Jacob" and "Israel," the "holder
of the heel" and "the victor of God," bequeathing both names and
both roles—victim and victor—to the future nation. We see Jacob,
poor and helpless, setting out as a fugitive from his father's home;
what awaits him is servitude in the household of his scheming uncle.
Yet, it is through this same Jacob that God's covenant and promise,
which until now had been upheld only by a few lone men, would
receive an entire family group as bearers. This family group would
constitute the next phase in the development of the future nation.
Jacob journeys forth to get himself a wife fit to help establish this
calling, to nurture the first seed for the establishment of the future
family. There is, however, one error in his past that presages the trials
he will have to undergo in order to make atonement and to cleanse
himself. We read in Midrash Tanchuma: "The tears that Esau had to
shed because of Jacob have fed us with the bread of weeping and with
the full cup of tears." "Jacob fled to the fields of Aram, and Jacob had

to serve for his wife and to become a shepherd in order to get his wife."
(Hosea 12, 13) He goes forth to establish a home, and his first resting
place for the night is a rock!

The sun has set upon him. He finds himself detained at the border
of the Promised Land. He takes some of the rocks from the place,
arranges them as a headrest and goes to sleep in that place. He has a
dream. He beholds a ladder set on the ground with its top reaching to
heaven. He sees angels of God's justice ascending and descending on
it, and he beholds God in His quality of mercy standing beside him,
saying, "I am 'ה, the God of your father Abraham and the God of your
father Isaac. The ground upon which you are sleeping I shall give to
you and to your seed. Your seed will be like the dust of the earth. You
shall spread out to the west and to the east, to the north and to the
south, and all the generations of the earth shall be blessed through you
and through your seed. Behold, I am with you and I shall protect you
wherever you go. And I shall bring you back to this land, for I shall
not forsake you until I have done all that I have promised to you."
(Gen. 28, 13–15)

Jacob awakens from his sleep and says: "So God is in this place,
and I did not know it!" And he is afraid and says: "How awesome is
this place! This is none other than a house of God, and this is the gate
of Heaven." (V. 17)

In the morning Jacob arises, takes the rock that was his headrest
and sets it up as a monument. He pours oil upon the rock and names
the place "House of God." He then makes a vow, saying: "If God will
be with me and will protect me upon this way on which I am walking,
and if He will give me bread to eat and clothing to wear, and I will
return in peace to my father's house, then 'ה will be God to me, and
this rock that I have set up as a monument shall become a House of
God and of all that You will give me I shall repeatedly tithe to You."
(V. 20–22)

For the moment we will disregard the erection of the monument
and the pouring of the oil upon the rock—certainly acts of symbolic
significance—even as we have disregarded the erection of altars by
Isaac, Abraham and Noah, and other symbolic acts done by men. For
we are now searching solely for data that will document the use of the
symbol as an instrument of communication from God to man. We see
here, once again, side by side with the revealed word, a communica-

tion from God to man through symbols. There is no doubt that we have here a renewal of the covenant between God and the descendant of Abraham who has gone forth to establish a household of his own and to become a forefather in his own right. It is revealed to Jacob that the household he is to establish will be part of the future of the Divinely-promised nation, and that, in fact, the realization of this future will begin in his household.

At the same time we see Jacob so profoundly moved that he anoints the rock, thereby laying the first true foundation for all future "houses of God" on earth. He does so with a newly-acquired dual knowledge. First, that there is on this place the "House of God" and the "gate of Heaven," that God, with His blessed, blissful nearness, will descend into the limited sphere of human affairs. Second, that man, in and through this narrow range of human affairs, can elevate himself to the heights of the Divine. It is here on earth that God comes to us and we are to come to Him. This understanding that came to Jacob has been most aptly epitomized by the statement of our Sages: אברהם קראו הר, יצחק שדה, יעקב בית (פסחים פ״ח). Abraham called the place where God revealed His glory, 'Mountain;' Isaac called it 'Field,' and Jacob called it 'House.'

Jacob expresses his new understanding clearly in the vow which forms the climax of all this Divine revelation and in which Jacob articulates the principle that will motivate the rest of his life. He does not expect to behold God in the vast universe, as did Abraham, nor in the flowering meadows of nature, as did Isaac, but in the protected and blessed foundation and preservation of his own humble, personal life, the life of a man in his own home. And Jacob vows to return to God everything He will bestow upon him, sanctified and uplifted.

The *words* uttered by God at this point are not the source from which to glean the reasons for Jacob's deep emotion, for his new understanding and for his subsequent acts and utterances.

These reasons should be sought, rather, in what was *shown* to Jacob in his dream, and in the *message* that was revealed to him through this vision. Hence, the ladder placed between heaven and earth, with angels ascending and descending on it, is nothing but a communication from God by means of symbols. And that is all we seek to demonstrate regarding this passage for the moment.

Jacob has gone through twenty difficult years of trial. Now, at last, as the head of a family, with wives, children and herds of his own, he sets out on his journey back to his father's house. "Jacob went upon his way, and angels of God met him," (Gen. 32, 2) ויעקב הלך לדרכו ויפגעו בו מלאכי אלקים. When he first left his father's house, he had to find the angels on his way. But now, that God was already near him and with him on his way, it is the angels that come to meet *him* on *their* way. When he saw them and recognized the place as a מחני אלקים, a "camp of God," he named the place מחנים a "Double Camp." For now he understood that his own family contained the Presence of God no less than the camp of the angels.

Jacob-Israel

Nevertheless, as he approaches his homeland, he is afraid. For in answer to the greeting of peace he has dispatched to his brother Esau whom he angered during their youth, he is told that his brother has set out to meet him at the head of a company of four hundred men. Jacob is overwhelmed by fear. He who had received his father's blessing for all his descendants—what had he become? The head of a family, matured under the burden of domestic cares and afflictions.—His angry brother, who had not received that blessing, had meanwhile become a power to reckon with, a warlord setting out at the head of his troops. For the first time, the House of Jacob is confronted by a hostile power. To be sure, God has done great things for Jacob. He had left his father's house and crossed the river Jordan with no other property than the staff in his hand, and now he is a wealthy man and the head of a family. But compared to his mighty brother, had he not remained too small? Had he indeed fulfilled his vow to elevate himself and all that was his to God, in the same measure as God had been near to him in truth and in mercy? These are the doubts that fill his heart with fear, and in this fear Jacob prepares his family for flight, at least for partial flight, on the chance that the tide of battle will turn against him. He then addresses himself to God in prayer, clinging to the promise given him concerning his future nation. While it is still night, he sends a substantial gift of reconciliation to his brother, takes his wives and children across the creek and then returns to the other side, remaining there alone in the dark of night.

Now, as the answer to his prayer, there is one single word that comes to him, and that will not only enable him to take comfort and new courage, to be content in his submission to God and confident in his ultimate victory but will also become a precious heritage to all his descendants. Like no other word, it is identified with their very essence; like no other word, it confronts them, and the rest of the world, in every age and at every moment, with the spiritual image of their vocation. Like a spiritual shield, it would protect them against their enemies and bring them comfort and courage. It would make them happy in their submission to God and confident that in the end they would prevail, whenever, during hours of trial, during the centuries of darkness that lie in store for them, they would find themselves like their ancestor, trembling for the safety of their wives and children in the face of angry brother nations. And that word is *Yisrael,* ישראל. It is the name that proclaims to the world and to all of Jacob's descendants that it is He Who will be strong on their behalf when they are weak and take up the struggle for them when they are helpless; Whose omnipotence has chosen them, precisely because they are weak, as heralds of His rule, and Whose victory will become splendidly evident through their very existence, their survival, their struggle and their ultimate glory.

This one word, the name that proclaims the glory of God's nation in its historic manifestation, is to be bestowed upon Jacob, both for himself and for his descendants. But this bestowal is preceded the night before by a physical struggle, marked by defeat and by perseverance ending in victory. Jacob had remained alone, and someone wrestled "with him until the dawn of the day." When he saw that he could not prevail against Jacob, he gripped the joint of Jacob's thigh, and Jacob's hip joint gave way as he wrestled with him.

"Let go of me, for the day is breaking."

"I shall not let you go unless you bless me."

"What is your name?"

"Jacob."

"Your name shall no more be called Jacob, but Israel, because you have become master with God and with me, since you have prevailed in the struggle."

But when Jacob asked him: "Now tell me also your name," the man replied: "Wherefore do you ask my name?" and he blessed him there. (Gen. 32, 27–30)

We intend to return to this incident in detail later on. But does it not, even when viewed only in superficial terms, present itself as a symbolic experience intended to make Jacob aware, in advance, of the full meaning of the future historic significance of the name "ישראל," of the persevering struggle of both Jacob-Israel and the nation descended from him, through the long, long night of centuries until the coming of that dawn which will banish the night? Does it not proclaim itself as a communication from God by means of a symbolic experience in the fullest, most significant sense of the term? And is not the resulting prohibition against eating the sinew of the thigh, in its very essence, a symbolic institution by which this experience is to be fixed forever in the mind of the Israelite nation?

The giving of the name "ישראל" essentially concluded the Divine revelation to the patriarchs. The budding nation now knew its task and its destiny. The institution of מילה, circumcision, made Israel continually aware of its mission. By recalling Jacob's experience during the night before his meeting with Esau, גיד הנשה, the prohibition against eating the sinew of the thigh, continually reminded the nation of the historic future that would come to it through the name of "ישראל." Thus fortified, the nation goes forth towards an Egyptian inferno with its harsh period of suffering as announced to Abraham.

Messages to Israel's Leaders

The centuries of alienhood, slavery and affliction that had been foretold to the people are now upon them, and the mission of Moses begins—Moses, of whom it is written: "Mouth to mouth do I speak with him, in clear vision and not in riddles" (Numbers 12, 8). His mission required—and therein lay his greatness—that God should *not* communicate with him through symbols. Instead, Moses was to bring to his people the direct Word of God, His Law, without any other medium of communication. Of Moses God said to Aaron and Miriam: "If he were one of your prophets, I would manifest Myself to him in a vision and would speak to him in a dream;" (Numbers 12, 6) I would give him My commands by means of symbolic manifestations, which he then would have to interpret, translate into ideas and clothe them in his own words. But "not so My servant Moses." And indeed, only at the outset of his mission do we note a physical phenomenon: the burning bush, which summoned him to God; and a symbolic act: the command to remove his shoes, an act by which Moses was to demonstrate his awareness that the ground on which he was about to set foot was holy ground. (Exodus 3, 5) From that time forward God speaks to Moses "mouth to mouth." Subsequent communications from God to Moses are introduced by the simple words וידבר, ויאמר ה' אל משה לאמר "God spoke" or "God said to Moses as follows." The word of God to Moses is not supported or supplemented by symbols.

Let us pass over, for the time being, the Giving of the Law. We will shortly concern ourselves with the question as to whether the Divine Law itself calls for symbols, symbolic acts; i.e., acts of commission or of omission, intended to bring to our minds specific ideas, truths and teachings. But first, let us complete our survey of Divine revelations outside the Giving of the Law, noting them in the writings of the post-Mosaic Prophets, to see whether we will not find there, too, instances of messages communicated by God to the Prophets, or through the Prophets to the people, by means of symbols.

Joshua had received from Moses the authority to take over as leader of the people in its march into the Promised Land and in the conquest of that land. He now stood facing the city of Jericho and was about to act as the military commander by making his first conquest. At this point there appears to him a messenger from God armed with a sword. When Joshua asks him, "What does my lord say to his servant?" the reply is a terse command to Joshua to perform a symbolic act: "Remove your shoe from your foot, because the ground upon which you are standing is holy" (Joshua 5, 15). Joshua did so. In all likelihood, this act was intended to make him bear in mind, from the outset, that the ground he was preparing to conquer was holy, that it belonged to God and was subject to a God-ordained destiny. He was to see himself in the service of God even while wielding his sword, and he was to look not to his sword but to God for success in his undertaking.

The land is now occupied, and five-sixths of the nation, particularly the princes and the other leaders who ruled over those five-sixths have long forgotten that they are dwelling on sacred ground. They had discarded the Law attached to the Land and the observance of which was the sole condition for its preservation. They sought to use

Sidonian politics and Sidonian idolatry to preserve that which had been assured to them only as long as they remained "Yisrael."

Eliyahu had appeared in the midst of these outrages, had caused prince and people alike to perceive the wrath of God, and had inspired the people at Mount Carmel to recognize God anew and to destroy the priestlings of Baal. However, it had all been in vain. Jezebel, the Sidonian princess upon the throne of the Kingdom of Israel, wanted to have Eliyahu put to death. Despairing that his mission could ever succeed, he wandered into the wilderness, praying that he may be granted death וישאל את נפשו למות (I Kings 19, 4) and declaring that he is no better than his fathers לא טוב אנכי מאבתי, who also had found peace in death. Commanded to wander far, far into the wilderness, he journeyed for forty days and forty nights until he came to Mount Horeb, the Mountain of God. There he entered a cave to spend the night. And, behold, in this place the word of God came to him:

"What are you doing here, Eliyahu?"

"I have been zealous again and again in behalf of God, צבאו׳, for the sons of Israel have forsaken Your covenant. They have destroyed Your altars and have killed Your prophets. I alone am left, and now they are seeking to take my life also."

"Go outside and stand upon the mountain before God!" (V. 9–11)

And God passes by, preceded by a great and fierce tempest that lifts up mountains and shatters rocks. However, God is not *within* this tempest. The tempest is followed by an earthquake, but God is also not *in* this earthquake. The earthquake is followed by a fire, but God is not *within* this fire. The fire is followed by a still, small voice. When Eliyahu heard that voice, he covered his face with his mantle, stepped outside and stood at the entrance to the cave.

Then the voice addressed itself to him and said:

"What are you doing here, Eliyahu?" (V. 13)

And Eliyahu said: "I have been zealous again and again in behalf of ה׳, God צבאו׳, for the sons of Israel have forsaken Your covenant. They have destroyed Your altars and have killed Your prophets. I alone am left, and now they are seeking to take my life also." (V. 14)

Do not this tempest, this earthquake, and this fire, in which God Himself does not appear, and the still, small voice, which is indeed the messenger of God, constitute a call, an admonition to the prophet who has become tired of his work and of his life? The prophet has despaired of his mission because he does not see its results bursting forth with the might of a tempest, the tremor of an earthquake or the force of a fire. He cannot fathom the work of God, which achieves its purpose even when it is not seen, and Whose voice is the loudest and the most effective when it appears to be silent. Are not the tempest and the earthquake, the fire and the silence, manifestations of symbolic language? Eliyahu failed to influence the Kingdom of Israel and it now lay close to ruin. But even the Kingdom of Judah, which still rallied around the Temple of God, already bore within itself the seeds of its own destruction. The fault lay precisely in the fact that the people of Judah rallied around the Temple. That is, they limited God and His holy Law to the confines of the Temple. They thought they had already discharged the great task of Israel simply by visiting the Temple, by offering sacrifices and by celebrating the festivals there. They forgot that from the Temple God seeks to penetrate into every place where life unfolds, from the festivals into every aspect of daily living. They forgot that the Law was intended to prove its efficacy and to be translated into reality outside the Temple, in everyday life. The Temple was meant to be the heart chamber of the nation, not the prison cell for the Divine. That was the reason why the Kingdom of Judah, too, was threatened with destruction.

Confrontation: Kings and Prophets
The Symbols

Isaiah—But God bestirred the man who was to tear the blindfold from the eyes of Judah and this man was Isaiah. He was to make clear to the people of Judah that the Temple service, the offerings and the festival celebrations were all meaningless if the other aspects of life were not in keeping with the message these observances were meant to convey. Isaiah was to warn Judah that the Temple would not be capable of holding the Glory of God if life outside were such as to drive the Glory of God away. The call to Isaiah came during the year in which the finger of God had touched the defiant brow of a king of Judah,* thus upholding the sanctity of His Temple against the tyranny of princes.

* This was King Uzziah, who, according to tradition, was stricken with leprosy (II Chronicles 26, 20) *Ed.*

Isaiah saw the Glory of God withdrawing from the Temple; only the edges of the throne still filled the chambers of the Temple. He beheld seraphim on high awaiting the Glory of God. He heard them utter the sanctification of God, proclaiming that the whole earth—not just the chambers of the Temple—was filled with His Glory. He saw how the sound of this cry shook the very pillars of the Temple thresh-old and that the building was about to fill with smoke. It was then that Isaiah realized what it really meant to pay homage to God as Master and King, and he lamented that he could not join in the chorus that sanctified God because his own lips and the lips of his people had lost their purity. Then one of the seraphim flew toward him, holding in his hand a live coal that he had plucked from the altar with a pair of tongs. He touched Isaiah's mouth with the coal and said to him: "Behold, once this has touched your lips, your iniquity will depart and your sin will be expiated."

Isaiah then heard the voice of God saying: "Whom shall I send? Who will go for us?"

And Isaiah said: "Here I am, send me" (Chapter 6).

Are not the tremor of the pillars and the filling of the Temple with smoke the language of symbolism? Is this, too, not another most significant combination of symbolic vision and symbolic acts with the spoken word?

One more time does God reveal His wondrous might to Israel. One more time does He reveal before Israel and the rest of the world His holy Zion as the rock against which even the mightiest powers are dashed to oblivion. He allows the power of Assyria to swell like the torrential floods of a river overflowing its banks. He permits the Assyrians, as world conquerors, to trample all the powers of their day beneath their feet. Flushed with victory, Assyria now seeks to conquer tiny Zion. But within sight of the fortress of Zion, Assyria is touched by the finger of God and suddenly goes down in defeat.

All around the Kingdom of Judah they had fallen prey to Assyria. Five-sixths of God's nation have fallen before Assyria's might because they have forgotten their mission to be the nation of God. Political connivance to win the good will of other nations has been of no avail. The Kingdom of Israel has fallen. Wrapped in sackcloth, Isaiah mourns his brethren who have been driven into exile. The forces of Assyria are sweeping on toward Judah. They have already occupied Ashdod, in neighboring Philistia, and now Judah, trembling with terror, awaits the final blow. Judah clings to one last hope: not to God, Whose wondrous power has proven itself so often on Israel's behalf, but to the boldness and courage of two states that still stand up to the Assyrian colossus, apparently defying the would-be conqueror. These states were Ethiopia and Egypt. Judah boasted of the political alliance that it had contracted with Egypt. Then, in the year of the Assyrian capture of Ashdod, God spoke through Isaiah, son of Amoz, saying:

"Go, undo the sackcloth from your loins, and at the same time remove your shoe from your foot." (20, 2)

Isaiah did so and walked about barefoot. Then God said:

"Even as My servant Isaiah has walked naked and barefoot, for three years this shall be a symbol and a sign upon Egypt and upon Ethiopia. For so shall the king of Assyria lead away the captives of Egypt and the exiles of Ethiopia, young and old, naked and barefoot, shamefully bare, to the disgrace of Egypt. Then, dismayed, they shall walk in shame because of Ethiopia, to which they look, and because of Egypt, their glory. And the inhabitants of this land will then say: Thus fare those to whom we have looked, to whom we fled for help, to save ourselves from the king of Assyria. How shall we escape now?" (V. 3–6)

Is this not a symbolic act commanded by God for the prophet to perform in order to stir up, and to keep alive, certain thoughts in the minds of the people? Is this not an act intended to prepare the people, years in advance, for the disaster through which God wished to make His glory known? If we understand this correctly, then Isaiah, by removing the sackcloth he had worn in mourning for the destruction of the Kingdom of Israel, was meant to awaken among the people new hope for the future. However, the fact that, at the same time, he was commanded to walk about naked and barefoot to symbolize the fall of Assyria and Egypt, seems to convey to the people a message as follows: Do not despair. You have good cause for new hope. However, you must not put your hopes in the wrong places. All your many trusted allies will themselves be defeated, so that the only hope left to you is the One Who is Everlasting, after all else is gone.

Jeremiah—The prophet takes off his sackcloth and bares his feet. His hope begins where that of others ends.

God put forth His hand and touched my mouth and said
to me: "Herewith have I put My words into your mouth.

See, I have this day set you above the nations and the kingdoms to crush and destroy, to root out, to pull down, to
rebuild and to plant."

Then the word of God came to me as follows: "What do
you see?"

I said: "I see the rod of an almond tree." "You have seen
well," God said to me. "As swiftly as the almond tree puts
forth blossoms, will I hasten My word, to perform it."

And again the word of God came to me: "What do you
see?" And I said: "I see a seething pot, and its face is from
the north."

Then God said to me: "Out of the north the evil shall
break forth over all the inhabitants of the earth. . . ."

(Jeremiah, Chapter 1)

Here, where the priestly young Jeremiah is called to become a
prophet, we have a symbolic act and its verbal interpretation occurring
together. Jeremiah was to be God's messenger to the Kingdom of
Judah and to the other nations at the time when Babylonia had
emerged from the ruins of the Assyrian empire, enslaved the nations
and destroyed Judah. This simultaneous use of symbolic vision and
symbolic act occurs frequently during the many years of Jeremiah's
mission, in communications from God to Jeremiah and from Jeremiah
to the people.

Thus said God to me: "Go and buy yourself a linen belt
and place it on your loins, but do not put it into water."

I bought the belt according to the word of God and
placed it on my loins. And the word of God came to me
again: "Take the belt that you have brought, which you
wear on your loins, and arise, go to the [river] Euphrates
and hide it there in the cleft of a rock."

I went and hid it in the Euphrates, as God had commanded me. And after many days, God said to me: "Arise,
go to the Euphrates and take from there the belt which I
commanded you to hide there."

I went to the Euphrates and dug, and took the belt from
the place where I had hidden it, and behold, the belt was

spoiled; it was no longer good for anything.

Then the word of God came to me, saying: "Thus has God spoken: In this manner shall I spoil the arrogant pride of Judah and Jerusalem! This evil people, that refuse to hear My words, that walk in the stubbornness of their heart and go after other gods, to serve them and to bow down before them—they have become like this belt that is no longer good for anything. For as the belt clings to the loins of a man, so have I caused the whole House of Israel and the whole House of Judah to cling to Me, to be to Me a nation, for a name, for a praise, and for a glory; but they would not hearken."

(Chapter 13)

Here, again, we see Israel appointed as an instrument of God's sovereignty; it is represented symbolically by the belt, which a man puts on when he prepares for serious action. If we understand the story correctly, Jeremiah's symbolic act conveys the following message: Periodic washing will preserve a linen belt; however, this belt will be spoiled not only if it is never put into water, but even if it is put into the middle of the river Euphrates, yet is buried so deeply in the crack of a rock in the river that the water cannot get into it. In the same manner, ruin will come not only to those who spend their lives away from all the institutions ordained by God to cleanse them and to clear them of sin, but also to those who do dwell in the midst of these God-given commandments but refuse to be influenced by them. Does not the former analogy correspond strikingly to the Kingdom of Israel, and the latter to the Kingdom of Judah.

Let us read on:

"Arise and go down to the house of the potter. There I shall let you hear My word."

I went down to the house of the potter and found him at work at the wheel. The vessel he was making was spoiled, as sometimes happens to the clay in the hand of the potter. So he formed from it another vessel, as seemed good to the potter to make it.

Then the word of God came to me, saying: "Can I not do also to you as does this potter, O house of Israel? . . . At one instant I may ordain concerning a nation and concerning a kingdom to crush and to destroy and to annihilate it, but if that nation concerning which I ordained this turns back from its evil, I will alter the decree of disaster which I had intended to bring upon it. And at one instant I may ordain concerning a people and a kingdom to build and to plant it, but if it does that which is evil in My sight, so that it does not hearken to My voice, I will alter the decree concerning the good that I had intended to bestow upon it . . ."

(Chapter 18)

Or:

"Go, and buy yourself a potter's earthen jug in the presence of the elders of the people and of the elders of the priests, and go to the Valley of Ben Hinnom, which is at the entrance of the Gate of Shards, and say: "Hear the word of God, O kings of Judah and inhabitants of Jerusalem . . ."
and break the jug before the eyes of the men who have gone with you, and say to them: "So shall I break this people and this city, as one breaks a potter's vessel that cannot be made whole again" . . .

(Chapter 19)

Or:

God caused me to see, and behold, there stood two baskets of figs, offered before the Temple of God, after Nebuchadnezzar, king of Babylon, had exiled Jeconiah . . . and the princes of Judah, with the craftsmen and smiths . . . and taken them to Babylon. One of the baskets contained very good figs, like those that are first-ripe; the other basket, very bad figs, so bad that they could not be eaten.
Then God said to me: "What do you see, Jeremiah?"
. . . Then the word of God came to me, saying: "Thus speaks God, the God of Israel: Like these good figs, I shall recognize the exiles of Judah, whom I have sent from

this place to the land of the Chaldeans, for the good. . . . And like these bad figs, which are so bad that they cannot be eaten, . . . so will I make Zedekiah, the king of Judah. . . ."

(Chapter 24)

Or:

"Take this cup of the wine of hot fury from My hand and cause all the nations to whom I shall send you, to drink it . . ." Then I took the cup from the hand of God. . . .

(Chapter 25)

Or:

In the beginning of the reign of Jehoiakim . . . this word came to Jeremiah. . . . "Make yourself bonds and yokes and place them upon your neck. And send them also to the king of Edom, to the king of Moab, to the king . . . of Ammon, and to the king of Tyre, and to the king of Sidon, by the hands of the messengers who come to Jerusalem to Zedekiah, king of Judah, and bid them tell their masters: "Thus speaks 'ה, the God of Israel: Thus shall you say to your masters: I have created the earth and man and the animals on earth with My great power and My out-stretched arm, and I have given them to whom it seemed proper to Me. And now I have given all these lands to Nebuchadnezzar, king of Babylon, My servant. . . . All the nations shall serve him, his son, and his son's son, until the fate of his land, too, will come. . . . The nation and the kingdom that will not serve Nebuchadnezzar, king of Babylon, that will not place their necks beneath the yoke of the king of Babylon, that nation will I visit with the sword, the famine and the pestilence. . . . Do not listen to your prophets, to your magicians, to your dreams . . . that tell you: Do not serve the king of Babylon . . ."

(Chapter 27)

And it came to pass in the beginning of the reign of
Zedekiah, king of Judah, in the fourth year, in the fifth
month (i.e., fifteen years later, see Rashi), that the prophet
Hananiah, son of Azzur, who was of Gibeon, spoke to me,
in the Temple, in the presence of the priests and the whole
people, saying: "Thus speaks . . . the God of Israel: I have
broken the yoke of the king of Babylon . . ."

Then Hananiah took the yoke from the neck of the
prophet Jeremiah, broke it and said: "Thus says God:
'Thus will I break the yoke of Nebuchadnezzar from the
neck of all the nations. . . .'"

And the prophet Jeremiah went on his way. But the word
of God came to Jeremiah, after Hananiah had broken the
yoke. . . . Thus says God: "You have broken wooden
yokes, but you shall make iron yokes in their place . . ."

(Chapter 28)

None of the passages cited above requires additional comment.
They all confirm our thesis that, in order to communicate with the
prophets, and through the prophets with the people, God used not
only the spoken word but also visual symbols and symbolic acts.

Ezekiel—Isaiah had seen the Glory of God lifting itself away from
the Temple. But the edges of its throne still filled the
Temple. When Ezekiel beheld the Glory of God, it was already in exile.
In the midst of the *diaspora,* at the river Kebar, the heavens opened,
and it was there that the hand of God came upon him. The "builders
and master craftsmen" of Judah, among them Ezekiel, son of Buzi, the
priest, had been taken to Babylon along with Jeconiah.

The main components of Ezekiel's mission were: to make the
people aware of the full extent of their guilt, which was to be punished
and *expiated* by the catastrophe that was now in progress; to make the
people understand that the Glory of God would accompany them,
even from the remote heavens, through the centuries of exile, and to
proclaim to the people that, finally, the State and the City of God
would be rebuilt, with God then dwelling there forever—ה' שמה. Here,
again, the words uttered by the prophet were accompanied by symbols
and symbolic actions.

There, at the river Kebar, Ezekiel was told his mission:

"I am sending you to the sons of Israel, to rebellious nations that have rebelled against Me; they and their fathers, until this very day; and the sons to whom I am sending you are impudent and obstinate of heart. You will say to them: "Thus has God spoken!" They may listen or they may leave it, for they are a house of rebellion. Nevertheless, they will know that a prophet has been in their midst. . . . But you, O son of man, hear what I say to you; be not like the house of rebellion; open your mouth and eat that which I give you."

I looked and behold, a hand was stretched out toward me and it held a scroll. He spread it out before me, and behold, it was covered with writing within and without, and its inscription read: קנים והגה והי "Lamentations" "Thought" and "Emerging Existence"(?)

And He said to me: "Son of man! Eat that which you find; eat this scroll and then go and speak to the house of Israel."

I opened my mouth and He caused me to eat the scroll and said to me: "Son of man! Nourish your stomach and fill your bowels with the scroll that I am giving you." I ate it and it was in my mouth sweet as honey.

(Ezekiel, Chapters 2 and 3)

There the hand of God came upon me and He said to me: "Go out into the plain; I will speak with you there."

I arose and went out into the plain, and there stood the Glory of God as I had seen it at the river Kebar, and I fell upon my face. Then the spirit entered into me and put me on my feet and spoke with me, and said to me: "Go home, shut yourself within your house. Behold, son of man, bonds have been put on you and bound you; you are not to step out among them. And I will cause your tongue to cleave to the roof of your mouth. You will become mute; you will not be to them a man who preaches to them, because they are a house of rebellion. Only when I speak with you, will I open your mouth; then you will say to them: Thus God, my Lord, has spoken! He who hears it, let him hear it; he who leaves it, let him leave it; for they are a house of rebellion.

"Also, son of man, take yourself a tile, place it before you and carve upon it a city: Jerusalem. Draw a siege around it, build bastions, cast up a mound, arrange camps around it and set up battering rams against it round about. And take yourself an iron pan and put it up as an iron wall between yourself and the city, and turn your face toward it. It shall be a siege; it shall be a symbol for the house of Israel.

"Moreover, you shall lie down on your left side and let the sin of Israel weigh upon it. As many days as you will lie upon your left side, you shall bear their sin. I give you the years of their sin for the number of the days, three hundred and ninety days. So shall you bear the sin of the house of Israel. And when you have completed them, you shall lie down on your right side and you shall bear the sin of the house of Judah for forty days. One day, each for every year, have I ordained for you. You shall turn your face toward the siege of Jerusalem, with your arm uncovered, and thus shall you proclaim concerning it: Behold, I have put bonds upon you, and you will not be able to turn from one side to the other, until the days of your siege are completed.

"And take yourself wheat and barley, beans and lentils, millet and spelt, and mix them in one vessel, and prepare them for yourself as bread for the number of days that you shall lie on your side. For three hundred and ninety days shall you eat it. . . ."

Then God said: "Thus shall the sons of Israel eat their bread unclean, among the nations where I have exiled them. . . ."

". . . Furthermore, son of man, take for yourself a sharp sword as a razor, and pass it over your head and over your beard, and take the balance for weighing and divide [the hair]. One-third you shall burn in the fire in the midst of the city, toward the end of the days of siege, one-third you shall take and smite with the sword round about it, and

one-third you shall scatter to the wind, and I shall draw the
sword after them. And you shall take from there also a few
numbered ones, and tie them into the corners of your
garments. From these, too, take some and throw them into
the flame and burn them in the fire; for from it fire will
come forth into the entire house of Israel."

Thus has God spoken: "This Jerusalem, I had placed it
in the midst of the nations. . . ."

(Chapters 3, 4 and 5)

The symbolic purpose of all the conditions imposed upon the
prophet and of the acts he was commanded to perform is self-evident.
Moreover, it is expressly stated in the words: אות היא לבני ישראל! Truly,
the context shows that these symbolic acts were to yield results which
could no longer be expected from the spoken word. Ezekiel was to
remain at home, mute and rigid because, for the time being, there was
no reason to expect that preaching to the assembled people would
yield results. Meanwhile, however, he was to continue to carry out his
prophetic mission to Jerusalem (ונבאת עליה) by undergoing all the
symbolic situations and acts described above.

We find a similar motivation for the use of symbolic acts in
Chapter 12 of the Book of Ezekiel, where the prophet is commanded
to enact the departure into exile before the eyes of the people, just as he
had demonstrated to them, in symbolic terms, the siege of Jerusalem
and their own dispersion.

"Son of man! You are in the midst of a rebellious group
that have eyes to see but do not see, ears to hear but do not
hear, because they are rebellious. Therefore, son of man,
prepare for yourself tools for exile, and go forth into exile
during the day, before their eyes. Move from your place to
another place before their eyes. Perhaps they will come to
see; for they are a house of rebellion. Take out your belong-
ings, things for the exile, during the day, before their eyes.
And in the evening you shall go forth before their eyes, in
the manner of one going into exile. Make yourself a breach

in the wall before their eyes and carry out through it.
Before their eyes carry upon your shoulder that which you
will take out in the dark, cover your face, and do not look
upon the ground, for I have set you up as a symbol for the
house of Israel."

I did as I had been commanded. . . . Then, in the morning, the word of God came to me: "Has not the house of
Israel, the house of rebellion, asked you what you were
doing? Now then, tell them: Thus has God, my Lord,
spoken: This prophecy is for the princes in Jerusalem and
for the entire house of Israel in whose midst they dwell.
Say: I am your sign. As I have done, so shall it be done to
them. They will go into exile, into captivity. And the prince
who is in their midst will bear upon his shoulder, in the
dark, and go forth. . . ."

The prophet lying on his left side,* rigid, for three hundred and
ninety days to bear the sins of the Kingdom of Israel was a symbolic
representation of Israel's entire history; i.e., the history of the transgression that is to bring about the nation's final ruin. *Seder Olam,* and
subsequently Rashi, on the basis of the responsa of Rabbi Joseph,
head of the Talmudic academy of Pumbedita, both demonstrate that
these 390 days correspond to the number of years for which the people
had to atone for their transgressions during the period of the Judges,
under pressure from Kushan, Eglon, Sisera, etc. That period, plus the
forty years that passed from Micah until the capture of the Ark of the
Covenant under Eli, totals 151 years. To these is added the 239-year
period of the reign of the kings of the Kingdom of Israel until the year
that the kingdom was destroyed by Sennacherib. This reckoning yields
a total of 390 years. The forty years of the Kingdom of Judah are to
correspond to the period during which that kingdom defected from
God under Menasseh, Amon and Jehoiakim, following the fall of the
Kingdom of Israel.

---

* Rashi points out that Samaria occupied the left (i.e., the north) and Judah the right
(i.e., the south) side of the Jewish Land.

The use of the symbol stands out particularly in Chapter 9 of the Book of Ezekiel. God's call rings out: "The visitations [destined] for the city have come!" and the Divine summons commands every man to come forward with "the tool of destruction in his hand." Six men come forward with hammers used as tools of destruction, and one other man comes with writing implements. This last man is to set a mark upon the foreheads of those who "still sigh and lament because of the abominations that are taking place in Jerusalem." The destruction begins precisely with these, the elders in front of the Temple, because, as our Sages note, (מס' שבת נ"ה,) they sighed and lamented but did nothing to stem the growing defection.

We shall cite only one more passage from the Book of Ezekiel (Chapter 37):

> The hand of God came upon me and led me out in the spirit of God, and set me down in the midst of the plain, and it was full of bones. He led me around these on all sides, and behold, they were exceedingly many on the surface of the plain, and behold, they were exceedingly dry. Then He spoke to me: "Son of man! Will these bones live again?" I said: "God, my Lord, You know it."
>
> He said to me: "Prophesy concerning these bones and say to them: O dry bones, hear the Word of God! Thus has God, my Lord, spoken to these bones. I will cause spirit to enter into you, and you shall live. I will put sinews upon you; I will cause flesh to grow over you, and weave skin over you, and put spirit into you, and you shall live—and then you shall know that I am God!"
>
> I prophesied as I had been commanded. And there came a noise while I prophesied, and behold, there was a storm. And then you, the bones, came near each other, bone to its corresponding bone. And I saw, and behold, sinews came upon them, and flesh grew upon them, and skin was woven over them, but there still was no spirit within them.
>
> Then He said to me: "Son of man, prophesy to the spirit, and say to the spirit: Thus has God, my Lord, spoken: Come, O spirit, from four directions, and breathe into these slain, and they will come alive."

And I spoke as I had been commanded, and spirit came into them, they came alive, they stood up on their feet—an exceedingly great host. Then He said to me: "Son of man, these bones, these are the entire house of Israel. Behold, they say: Our bones are dry, our hope is lost, we have been left to ourselves.

"Therefore prophesy and say to them: Thus has God, my Lord, spoken: Behold, I will open your graves, and will lead you up from your graves as My people and bring you home to the soil of Israel. You will then know that I am God, when I open your graves and lead you up from your graves as My people. I will put My spirit into you, you will live, I will place you upon your [own] soil, and you will realize that I, God, have spoken and accomplished!"

Then the Word of God came to me as follows: "And you, son of man, take yourself a [piece of] wood and write upon it: For Judah and the sons of Israel, his companions. Then take another [piece of] wood and write upon it: For Joseph, the tribe of Ephraim and the whole house of Israel, his companions. And then move them one to the other, so that they become one single [piece of] wood, united in your hand. And when the sons of your people will say to you: Will you not tell us what these mean to you? then say to them: Thus says God, my Lord: Behold, I will take the wood of Joseph, which is in the hand of Ephraim, and his companions, the tribes of Israel, and I will place them, together with him, to the wood of Judah, and I will make them into one tree, and they will become one in My hand. Thus shall you hold before their eyes, in your hand, the [pieces of] wood upon which you have written, and say to them: Thus has God spoken: Behold, I will take the sons of Israel from among the nations where they have gone and I will gather them from everywhere and bring them back to their own soil, and I will make them into one nation on earth upon the hills of Israel, and one king shall be king to them all. They shall not again become two nations and not be divided again into two kingdoms. They will defile themselves no more with their shameful

corruptions, and with their crimes; I will save them from all
their habitations where they have sinned, and I will cleanse
them. They will be a people to Me, and I will be God to
them! And My servant David shall be king over them, and
they shall all have one shepherd. And they shall walk in My
ordinances and observe My laws and practice them, and
they shall dwell in the land that I have given to My servant
Jacob, and where your fathers, too, have dwelt. They shall
dwell there then, they, their children and their children's
children, forever, and My servant David shall be a prince
to them forever. I will establish with them a covenant of
peace. There shall be an everlasting covenant with them. I
will place them there, I will multiply them, I will put My
Sanctuary into their midst forever. . . ."

The remaining books of the Prophets, too, yield instructive
examples of the use of symbolic visions and acts; note particularly
Chapters 1, 2 and 3 of Hosea, Chapters 7 and 8 of Amos, and Chapters
1-6 and 11 of Zechariah.

We believe, however, that for our present purposes we may limit
ourselves to the passages cited above. We believe that we have demonstrated beyond doubt thus far that symbols have been used, both as
signs and as acts, in Divine revelations other than the Law, as God's
instrument for communicating with the prophets or, through the
prophets, with the people. A thoughtful analysis of the instances we
have studied thus far should also convince us that it certainly cannot
be the purpose of symbols to enshroud ideas or to communicate
secrets in the form of complex riddles. In most instances the facts in
the symbol are immediately relevant to those to whom they are
addressed, and in most of these cases the symbol is accompanied by
words that express the meaning of the symbol. Thus the purpose of the
symbol clearly is to provide a more thorough elucidation of the
message to be conveyed by the word, and to achieve an impact that
could not be produced by words alone.

At the present stage of our analysis it is sufficient for us to have
obtained this result and we shall now turn to the next question: Is it
also certain beyond doubt that symbols and symbolic acts occur in
the legislative part of Divine revelation? It is the purpose of the next
chapter to provide an answer to this question.

Symbolism in Jewish Law

We now enter the sphere of the Law, which, in fact, is the essential object of our study. But first we must answer the following preliminary question: Is there really a basis for such a study? Are we at all entitled to assume that God's Law has commanded the creation of objects, or of acts of commission or omission, that could be classed as symbolic? True, our survey thus far has amply demonstrated to us the important uses which Divine revelation has made of symbols and symbolic acts outside the Law, in the course of history, for communicating with the prophets and with the people. However, this alone is no assurance that we might not, nevertheless, turn out to be completely mistaken in our assumption that this holds true also for the Law itself. It is entirely possible that whatever we might say about symbolism in Jewish Law might indeed be a reflection of paganism or Christianity, but not of Jewish truth.

Let us, therefore, now make a survey of God's Law to see whether it contains commandments that entail symbols and symbolic acts. It is understood that, to answer this preliminary question, we can only cite such parts of Divine Law that offer obvious, unambiguous evidence that the object, or the act of commission or omission involved in that particular commandment or prohibition, is indeed symbolic in character. We will omit from our consideration all instances where the question whether an object involved in a law is symbolic or non-symbolic cannot be answered without delving deeply into the total content and context of that particular law. Such an in-depth analysis and an interpretation of the objects of these laws according to their intrinsic, more profound criteria will be reserved for our future actual studies on symbolism in Jewish Law. At the present preliminary stage, where we merely ask whether there really is a basis for assuming the presence of symbols in Jewish Law, we must limit ourselves to the study of laws with very obviously symbolic character.

We will select such laws on the basis of the following criteria:

Category A: Laws containing explicit statements to the effect that the objects or acts entailed in them are symbolic.

Category B: Laws which do not explicitly define the objects or acts entailed in them as symbolic but in which it is clearly stated that these objects or acts are intended to evoke a specific train of thought or to recall specific truths and facts.

Category C: Laws which do not make explicit statements to the effect of (A) or (B), but in which it is obvious, nevertheless, that the objects or acts they entail relate to their causes and effects in a manner that cannot be defined as anything but symbolic.

If the Law of God indeed contains facts included under any of the three categories, then it will be clear that we have a basis for our investigation and that we are justified in speaking of a "symbolism of Jewish Law."

Laws Specifically Designated as Symbols

Category A: מילה (circumcision), the performance of which is called ברית, "covenant," is in itself intended as אות ברית, a *sign* of the covenant. "But as for you, guard My covenant, you and your seed after you, for their generations. And this is My covenant which you shall guard, between Me and you and your seed after you: every male among you shall be circumcised. You are to circumcise the flesh of your foreskin, and this shall be a sign of the covenant between Me and you." (Gen. 17, 9–11). It is clear, therefore, that the commandment of circumcision entails a symbolic act and a symbolic sign instituted as a memorial to the covenant made with Abraham and his descendants. It is a symbolic expression of the observance and maintenance of this covenant by Abraham and his descendants. Failure to observe this covenant, therefore, implies the opposite; namely, an annulment of the covenant. את בריתי הפר, "he has destroyed My covenant."—We note that this commandment is introduced by the requirement which constitutes one of the obligations to be assumed by Abraham under the covenant; i.e., "to conduct himself before God and be perfect." Thus the object of our study can be solely to establish the relationship between this sign and this act, with all the pertinent legal stipulations, on the one hand, and the covenant with its content, its essence and continuity, on the other, that is to be expressed through this sign and this act. The symbolic character of this law as such is no longer subject to question.

Pessach: "The blood shall be to you a sign, לאות, upon the houses in which you are; I will see the blood and will pass over you" (Exodus 12, 13). This pronouncement was made by God concerning the blood of the Pesach offering with which Israel was to mark its emergence as the people of God during the night of its birth as a nation. We will discuss the precise character of this Pessach offering later on, in connection with Category C. At this point, let us note only that the act connected with the offering, which appears to be the purpose of it all, and the performance of which is the condition for God's "passing over," and which gives the offering its meaning, indeed its very name, is called אות, a symbol. This fact alone makes it clear that every aspect of this offering has a symbolic character.

תפלין: "It shall be for you as a *sign* on your hand and as a remembrance between your eyes, לאות ולזכרון, so that the teaching of God shall remain in your mouth, for with a strong hand did God bring you forth from Egypt" (Ex. 13, 9); "It shall be for a *sign* upon your hand and an ornament for the forehead between your eyes, that with strength of hand did God bring us forth from Egypt" (V. 13, 16); "These words shall be . . . and you shall bind them as a *sign* upon your hand and they shall be an ornament for the forehead between your eyes" (Deut. 6, 6–8); "Place these My words upon your heart and upon your soul and bind them as a sign upon your hand and they shall be an ornament for the forehead between your eyes" (Deut. 11, 18). These repetitions make it clear that our *tefillin* are a symbolic sign and a symbolic act.

שבת: The symbolic character of our Sabbath observance is spelled in no less decisive terms. "Only observe My Sabbaths, for it is a *sign* between Me and you for your descendants, that you may know that I, God, sanctify you" (Ex. 31, 13); "And the sons of Israel shall keep the Sabbath, to observe the Sabbath for their descendants as an everlasting covenant. Between Me and the sons of Israel it is a *sign* forever that in six days did God create heaven and earth, and with the seventh day He ceased and withdrew" (V. 16–17).

Here, as with the act of circumcision, we see the Sabbath instituted as a *sign* and the observance of the Sabbath as an ever-renewed *consummation of the covenant*. Note that the Law ordains only שביתת מלאכה, cessation from work, as the proper observance of the Sabbath. The Sabbath becomes manifest only in the cessation from all work, which in fact gives the Sabbath its name. The only violation of the Sabbath that is subject to capital punishment is failure to observe the commandment pertaining to cessation from work. Therefore, only by such cessation from all work can the Sabbath be a "sign" and a "covenant." Not working on the Sabbath cannot merely be a way of gaining time and leisure for some other activities that would presumably be considered the true observance of the Sabbath. Not working on the Sabbath must in itself constitute the proper, real and true Sabbath observance. Cessation from work must constitute in itself the realization of the "sign" and of the "covenant." Hence, cessation from work on the Sabbath must be a symbolic act in its very essence.

The symbolic character of some commands is self-evident. The fire-pans to be used for the altar covering when those who rebelled against Moses were consumed by fire (Numbers 17, 3–5) are expressly described as זכרון לבני ישראל, "a memorial for the sons of Israel." Similarly, the flowering staff of Aaron (V. 25), which was to be placed in front of the Ark of the Covenant for safekeeping, is לאות לבני מרי, "as a sign against men of rebellion."

Laws Evoking Symbolic Meaning

We will now proceed to Category B; that is, commandments whose objects are not explicitly defined as symbols but are nonetheless clearly presented as having the purpose evoking and recalling specific thoughts, so that these commandments are undoubtedly symbolic in character.

גיד הנשה: In this category we note the prohibition against eating the sinew of the thigh. This dietary prohibition is clearly motivated by the symbolic struggle of Jacob during the night preceding his encounter with Esau. It has been instituted expressly as a memorial to this struggle. על כן, "therefore the sons of Israel shall not eat the sinew that is on the joint of the thigh" (Gen. 32, 33). This prohibition is therefore a memorial to this struggle and to the meaning of our role in history, as revealed by this struggle and as reflected in the name "ישראל."

חמץ ומצה: Next, we note the commandment to partake of unleavened bread and the prohibition against eating, or possessing, leavened bread during the Festival of Matzoth, both of which are expressly decreed in Exodus 12, 14–17 and designated to put into practice the remembrance of our deliverance from Egypt. "This day shall be for you as a memorial, לזכרן, and you shall keep it as a festival dedicated to God. . . . Seven days shall you eat matzoth. . . ." See also Exodus 13, 3, where these laws are described as intended to remind us that God liberated us by His direct, miraculous intervention with "strength of hand," and that only by observing these commandments in the hour of our redemption did we make ourselves worthy of the aid with which God intervened on our behalf. "Moses said to the people: Remember this day on which you went forth from Egypt, from the house of slaves, that with overwhelming might did God bring you out from this place; therefore, nothing leavened shall be eaten. . . . Tell it to your son on that day: For the sake of this commandment did God act for me when I went forth from Egypt." (V. 9)

בכור: Category B includes the commandment concerning the sanctification of first-born males of man and animals. All the acts to be performed in this connection, זביחה, עריפה, פדיון, represent the practical implementation of the instruction: קדש לי, "Sanctify them to Me." They thus become an expression of the concept of consecration to God, and so acquire symbolic significance. This particular sanctification clearly refers to the midnight hour of redemption when Pharaoh and Egypt paid for their opposition to God with the death of the noblest among their kin. "When your son will ask you someday: What does this mean? then tell him . . . It came to pass when Pharaoh stubbornly refused to let us go, that God slew all the first-born. . . . Therefore do I offer to God every first-born male from the mother's womb and redeem all the first-born of my sons." (Ex. 13, 14.) Obviously, these are symbolic acts to commemorate a historic truth.

Other examples: God commands Moses (Ex. 19, 10–11): "Go to the people and sanctify them today and tomorrow, and have them wash their clothes, and be ready for the third day; for on the third day God will descend upon Mount Sinai before the eyes of the entire nation."

Further: God's Law (Ex. 20, 22) forbids the construction of an altar from hewn stones, with the added comment: "For you have swung your sword over it and thereby desecrated it."

Moreover: After the giving of the Law, Moses erected "an altar at the foot of the mountain and twelve memorial stones, corresponding to the twelve tribes of Israel" (Ex. 24, 4), "received half the blood of the offering in basins" and "sprinkled half of the blood against the altar" (V. 6). After reading the Book of the Covenant to the people and after the people had vowed: "All that God has spoken we shall do and hear" (V. 7), Moses sprinkled toward the people and said: "Here is the *blood of the covenant* that God has made with you concerning all these words" (V. 8).

All the foregoing are commandments and acts clearly described as symbolic in character.

Aaron is commanded (Ex. 28, 12) to bear the names of the tribes of Israel upon his two shoulders לפני ה' לזכרן, "before God *for a memorial*" and also upon his breast as a constant *memorial* before God (V. 29).

The portion of the מנחה that is offered up to God is called אזכרה, the "memorial part" (Lev. 2, 2).

The salt added to the מנחה is called ברית, "covenant." "You shall not allow salt, the covenant of your God, to be lacking from your offering" (V. 13).

Similarly, the קטורת to be placed with the לחם הפנים is called a "memorial part," and its continual arrangement before God, ברית עולם, an "everlasting renewal of the covenant" (Levit. 24, 7–8).

In each of the above instances the symbolic character of the acts entailed is declared in unambiguous terms.

Moses is commanded (Numbers 10, 2) to make himself two silver trumpets to use for calling the community together, or to signal the breakup of the camp and the continuation of the journey through the wilderness. A long note sounded by both trumpets is to summon all the members of the community to assemble. A long note sounded by only one of the two trumpets is to summon the heads of the community. A combination of long and short notes is to be the signal for breaking up camp and resuming the journey. In case of war, a "broken" note is sounded—as an appeal to God— ונזכרתם, "and you will be *remembered* before God, your God, and you will be helped against your enemies" (V. 9). On days of rejoicing, on festivals and on the New Moon, the trumpets are sounded to accompany the offerings, "and this shall be for you לזכרן, *a memorial* before your God" (V. 10).

Are these signals not symbols expressed by sound?

Note, moreover, that these same notes are sounded on another instrument, the שופר, in the year of יובל, a year that is to be consecrated and which is to summon all the inhabitants of the land to "return home, free." (Levit. 25, 10). These שופר tones are in fact sounded every year on the festival on the first day of the seventh month (Levit. 23, 24), which is therefore called יום תרועה, the "Day of the Broken Tone." The purpose of this festival is summarized by the term זכרון

תרועה, by the remembrance, reflection, and consideration of these tones. How, then, could these tones be anything but symbols expressed by sound?

On the Festival of סוכות we are commanded "to *take* the הדר fruit, and branches of palm trees, myrtles and willows, and to *rejoice* before God" (Levit. 23, 40). Accordingly, it is clear that our "taking up" of these plants is closely associated with that rejoicing, as a cause, an object or the significance of that festive mood. The "taking up" of these plants, then, is as much a symbolic act as these plants in themselves must be symbolic expressions of those objects with which our rejoicing before God is to be demonstrated.

סוכה: Similarly, our dwelling in huts during this festival is expressly commanded as a means for evoking specific memories. Thus, this act obviously has been assigned a symbolic purpose, as it is written: "You shall dwell in huts for seven days, all that are citizens of Israel shall dwell in huts, so that your descendants will *know* that I made the sons of Israel dwell in huts when I brought them forth from the land of Egypt" (Levit. 23, 42–43).

ציצת: "Speak to the sons of Israel and tell them that they should make for themselves ציצת at the corners of their garments for their descendants, and put into the ציצת of the corner a thread of sky-blue wool. This shall be to you for ציצת, so that *you may see them* and *remember* all the commandments of God and do them and not explore after your own hearts and your own eyes, which you follow faithlessly. *So that you may remember* and keep all My commandments and remain holy to your God" (Numbers 15, 38).

What momentous thoughts and truths should the sight of these threads upon our garments evoke and keep awake within our souls! Indeed, the Law has explicitly assigned to these threads a role of profound symbolic significance.

Laws and their Symbolic Context

In this preliminary survey we will not discuss those regulations in God's Law in which symbolic intent is indicated but not stated in such explicit terms. We shall now proceed to Category C to examine such laws which make no mention at all of a symbolic character but which nonetheless must be considered as symbolic in view of the stated circumstances which led to them, and of the effect they are expected to produce.

עגלה ערופה: Let us first consider the עגלה ערופה (Deut. 21), the killing of a female calf to clear the authorities of a city from guilt in a case of an unsolved murder. The body of the victim has been discovered in an open field, and it is not known who killed him. The Supreme Tribunal must send deputies to the site and, by measuring the distance between the corpse and the surrounding cities, must ascertain which city is nearest to the place where the body was discovered. The elders of that city must then declare, in the presence of the priests, that their hands were innocent of this bloodshed and that they had not been aware of the murder. The priests thereupon pray that God may forgive the entire Jewish community and not permit the shedding of innocent blood; i.e., that He Himself might punish the murderer whose identity is still unknown to them.

However, these declarations, especially the declaration made by the elders of the city, must be preceded by certain prescribed *acts*. The elders of the city are commanded to take a female calf with which no work has been performed and which has not yet pulled a yoke. They are to bring the animal down to a barren valley which must not ever have been worked or sown, and there they are to kill the calf with a blow to the neck. Afterwards, they are to wash their hands over the calf that was thus killed in the valley. And only then may they pronounce the words that will clear them of guilt in the murder: "Our hands have not shed this blood and our eyes have not seen it."

Is it conceivable that this calf, with its specified characteristics, the slaughter of this calf in a valley that is also described in terms of specific physical features, and the washing of the hands over the slain animal, should not be closely associated with the event that preceded these acts and with the declaration of atonement that followed? On the other hand, would such an association be conceivable if all these carefully specified actions were *not* symbolic acts; i.e., acts expressing thoughts closely following the significance of the event and the declaration of innocence by the city elders which this event demands? And do these symbolic acts not essentially supplement this declaration, making its impact all the more profound and enduring?

Also in Category C are חליצה (Deut. 25, 9), the removal of the shoe from the foot of a man who refuses to marry his brother's childless widow; השקת סוטה (Num. 5, 12), the drink of bitter waters given to a wife suspected of adultery; the growing and the cutting of the hair of a נזיר (6, 1–21), and the shaving of the Levites (ibid 8, 7), all acts of washing and bathing where the purpose is obviously not the removal of physical dirt, and all acts of anointing where the purpose is obviously not the care of the skin. Can all these be anything other than symbolic acts?

In general, whenever a bodily act of commission or omission whose natural, primary effect would be only physical, is expressly ordered for a purpose that is not physical but spiritual, and, according to the wording of the law, is expected to yield spiritual results, that act must have a symbolic relationship to that purpose and to those results. The commanded act of commission or omission itself must have spiritual significance; it must serve to express an abstract thought, and so we see that we are dealing with acts that are undeniably of symbolic character.

קידוש, sanctification, for instance, implies the imparting of a spiritual character to persons or things. This spiritual character can be acquired only through an appropriate declaration, recited by a person authorized to do so, over the person or object to be sanctified. Sanctification can be performed only through an expression of thought or volition. The Law commands: "Make garments for Aaron to *sanctify* him, so that he may serve Me as a priest! These are the garments . . ." (Ex. 28, 3–4). "Clothe Aaron and his sons in these, anoint them and confer upon them full authority and sanctify them, so that they may perform the priestly service for Me" (V. 41). "But do this in order to sanctify them: Take a bull and two rams . . . and *matzoth* . . . and immerse them . . . and take the vestments and clothe them. . . . Take the bull in front of the Tabernacle, have Aaron and his sons place their hands upon the head of the bull . . . offer up the ram and take of its blood and place some of it on the right earlobe of Aaron and of his sons and on the thumb of their right hand and of their right foot . . . and take of the blood poured out upon the altar and of the anointing oil and sprinkle it upon Aaron and his vestments and on his sons and on the vestments of his sons with him, וקדש הוא ובגדיו ובניו ובגדי בניו אתו, and thus he and his vestments and his sons and their vestments with him become holy" (Ex. Chapter 29).

It is evident that we encounter here a whole series of acts which, taken together, can only express the concept of consecration for the priestly office. The vestments as such, their placement upon the priests, the offering of the bull and the ram, the spreading and sprinkling of the blood and of the anointing oil, cannot be anything but acts and objects of symbolic significance because their result is the sanctification and consecration of the priests.

Let us take, as another case in point, the simple act of the laying on, or more accurately, the "leaning on," of hands: סמיכה. This act is part of the ritual of the offerings. "He shall lean his hand upon the head of the burnt offering, ונרצה לו לכפר עליו "and so it will receive acceptance, to effect attonement for him." (Levit. 1, 4). This association between רצוי, the acceptance of the offering, or even the return of Divine favor, a spiritual act in any event, on the one hand, and the laying on of the hands, on the other, justifies our view that this laying on of hands is a symbolic act. We encounter this act also in connection with other rituals; e.g., when the Levites are turned over to the priests, with the sons of Israel placing their hands upon the heads of the Levites (Numbers 8, 10), and again when Joshua is appointed successor to Moses (Numbers 27, 18–23). Hence, there can no longer be any doubt that this is a symbolic act.

A similar interpretation applies to the acts of תרומה and תנופה, the "uplifting" and the "waving." We note these acts in connection with certain offerings, but also when the Levites are turned over to the priests. והנפת אותם תנופה לפני ה', והניף אהרן את הלוים תנופה לפני ה'. The symbolic character of this act is so certain that the terms תרומה and תנופה are used in Biblical Hebrew to denote a gift of consecration.

On serious reflection, we cannot deny one fact which, in our opinion, is apt to throw considerable weight into the balance in favor of our thesis. The fact is: At moments of supreme significance we might expect not only words, but impassionately eloquent speeches. We might expect proclamations, addresses, sermons, and so forth, to make the nation or the individuals concerned aware of the full meaning and the enormous consequences of that particular moment, so that they might take it to heart and be stirred to a state of enthusiasm commensurate with the significance of the hour. Yet, precisely in such situations, we see that no words are uttered at all! Instead, we see a whole series of acts that must take the place of words, and this with an effect and an eloquence that could not have been attained by the spoken word.

Let us consider the night of redemption and the exodus from Egypt. Certainly this was a moment without parallel in all the history of mankind, a moment toward which all the past history of this people had been directed. This was the moment on which the nation's entire future was to be based, and which required a thorough and immediate transformation of the nation. This is the moment when chains are to be broken, dungeon walls to collapse, slaves to become free husbands and wives, fathers and mothers again. Children are to be restored to their parents, brothers and sisters. Households, families, a community, a nation, a nation of God are to arise from the dust. The pariah is to stand up and become the freest man on earth. Those formerly doomed to the most menial services are now to enter into the highest form of Divine service on behalf of all mankind. What an occasion this could have been for declarations, pronouncements, speeches, sermons, exhortations, presentations and reflections! But what, in fact, is said? Hardly anything! Instead, the people are commanded to perform a series of acts. A lamb is taken four days in advance and kept in reserve for the family, or for the household. Milah, the sign of the covenant of Abraham is performed. The members of each household and of each family are counted. The lamb, one year old, perfect, without blemish, is kept until the critical moment and is then offered up, with the entire community making the offerings at the same time. When the people are girded for the exodus, the blood of this offering is spread, with bundles of hyssop, upon the doorposts and threshold of the houses. The flesh of the animal that has been offered as a sacrifice is roasted in fire and eaten with *matzoth* and bitter herbs. None of the bones of the offering must be broken. When all these acts have been duly performed, the Angel of Death knocks on the gates of Egypt's palaces, while Israel's houses hear the call to rise up again. The pariah people rise and go forth as the free nation of God. The sheep, the blood and the hyssop, doorpost and threshold, the flesh and the bones of the offering, the unleavened bread and bitter herbs, the acts of taking, keeping in reserve, counting and offering, the spreading of the blood and the eating of the offering, the restriction of each offering to one hearth, one closed circle, the stipulation that the offering must be eaten roasted in fire, that its bones must not be broken and that the flesh must not be kept until the next morning—are all these not signs and acts of commission and omission, performed at this sublime moment, with much greater eloquence than any proclamations or appeals, teachings or sermons?

Priests and Levites were to be inducted into office, men whose function it was to preserve "purity and light" among the people, who were to be "dedicated to God," tested against every temptation, steeled for every struggle," men who "were not to know father or mother, brother or son, when it was a matter of guarding the Word of God and preserving His covenant," men who were to "teach God's Justice and Teachings to Israel and to perform the sacrificial service at the altar." What great inaugural addresses could have been delivered on that occasion, what instructions and exhortations could have been addressed to those about to be installed, and to the people! How many prayers of consecration and sanctification could have been recited!

But, instead, what do we see? Vestments are prepared, with materials and colors, cut and execution specified in exact detail. We read about offerings of bulls and rams, unleavened bread kneaded with oil and brushed with oil. The priests to be installed are bathed, clothed in their vestments and anointed, the offerings are presented, hands are laid upon the offerings, the offerings are made according to carefully prescribed ritual. Blood from the offerings is sprinkled upon the altar, more blood upon the ears, hands and feet of the priests. Blood and anointing oil are put on the priests and on their vestments. Next, parts of the sacrificial animal are placed into the hands of the priests so that they may perform the waving, and so on. The animal to be offered is duly offered, and that which is to be consumed is duly consumed by the new priests. And all these acts are repeated over a period of seven days. (Ex. Chapters 28 and 29; Levit. Chapter 8.)

We have here, then, installation festivities going on for seven days taken up completely with acts prescribed in painstaking detail—and without one word being spoken! Could these acts, then, be anything other than silent sermons, sermons of profound significance?

The same holds true for the induction of the Levites for service in the Sanctuary (Numb. Chapter 8).

The Levites are sprinkled with waters to cleanse them of sin, their bodies are shaved, their clothes washed, they undergo purification; there are bulls, meal offerings kneaded with oil, the people lay their hands upon the heads of the Levites, the Levites are presented as a "wave offering" before God, the Levites lay their hands upon the bulls to be offered up as sacrifices, the bulls are sacrificed. . . . We repeat: could these acts be anything other than silent sermons, sermons of profound significance?

The priests have been installed, the Temple has been erected, and the day of glory has arrived, a great day! God wishes to have His glory enter the Temple, to have His glory dwell henceforth in the place where His Law dwells. From there He wishes to penetrate with His Word into the life of the nation, a life He wishes to regulate, to sanctify and uplift, to guide, to clear of sin and to purify, to inspire and to bring to perfection. He wishes to translate into reality the word He has spoken: "They shall make Me a Sanctuary, and I shall dwell in their midst" ועשו לי מקדש ושכנתי בתוכם (Ex. 25, 8). Who can fathom the full depth, the full extent of what should have been called to the minds of the nation and of the priests on that day, and the resolutions and high resolves to which they could have been summoned?

Instead, what do we read? On the eighth day, after the seven days of induction had been completed, Moses called Aaron, his sons, and the elders of Israel, and said to Aaron: "Take for yourself a young calf as an offering of expiation and a ram for a burnt offering, without blemish. Offer them to God and speak to the sons of Israel: Take a male goat as an offering of expiation, a calf and a sheep of the first year without blemish for a burnt offering, and an ox and a ram for a peace offering to God, and take a meal offering mixed with oil, for today God will appear to you." (Levit. 9, 2–4) And when they had come to the Tabernacle with all these things, and all the people had gathered, Moses addressed them, saying: "*Do* this which God has commanded זה הדבר אשר צוה ה' תעשו, then the glory of God will appear to you וירא אליכם כבוד ה'." (V. 6)

And so it was done. All the sacrificial rites that had been commanded were performed, the priests' offering of expiation was slaughtered, some of its blood was sprinkled upon the high corners of the altar, the remainder was poured out at the foot of the altar, the fat, the kidneys, the diaphragm and part of the liver were placed into the fire of the altar. All the rest of the offering was burned outside the camp. The burnt offering of the priests was then slaughtered, its blood was dashed against the altar, it was divided into its parts, and each part individually was placed into the fire of the altar. Then, again in accordance with detailed regulations, the same was done with the offering presented by the people.

Now, after everything had been performed, and Aaron had blessed the people, and also Moses together with Aaron had blessed the people, וירא כבוד ה' אל כל העם, "then did the glory of God appear to the entire people!" (Levit. 9, 23). Let us repeat our question: Could these acts be anything other than silent sermons, sermons of profound significance?

The Jewish Temple was established essentially for the Law of God, because God's Law alone is enthroned in its Holy of Holies. Consecration and a return to this Law following neglect or transgression are the express purpose of the acts to be performed in this Temple. Forgiveness, purity and God's approval are the fruits to be reaped there. The Sanctuary of the Law in particular, and the Law of God in general, strive solely for moral objectives.

If we consider all these things, even only in a superficial manner, there can be no doubt in our minds that all the institutions and acts which are to bring about the realization of these objectives must be such as to have a favorable impact on man's moral impulses. But such an influence from outside can be wielded only by evoking specific concepts and thoughts. Therefore the Temple itself, and all the acts and institutions that are part of it, must act as means for evoking concepts and thoughts that will influence man's moral impulses in the proper manner. The entire Sanctuary, with all the commandments, positive and negative, that apply to it, all that the Sanctuary requires and all that it rejects—these things are set forth by the symbolic character of the Sanctuary.—In סדר קדשים וטהרות we can expect to find a whole range of commandments with symbolic significance.

נזיר: The close connection between the laws of טומאה וטהרה and the sphere of morality is apparent particularly from the laws concerning the *nazir* (Numb. 6). The *nazir* has taken a vow of abstinence. The moral objective of this condition which he has taken upon himself of his own free will is therefore evident. Now three ordinances are prescribed for him: טומאת מת and תגלחת, כל היוצא מן הגפן. He must abstain from every product of the vine, he must let the hair on his head grow, and he must not come near a dead body. The connection between the first rule, the prohibition against the consumption of wine, and the moral purpose of the *nazir* vow, is self-evident. But the relationship between letting the hair grow and the avoidance of contact with a dead body, on the one hand, and moral objective of the *nazir* vow, on the other, can be understood only through a symbolic interpretation of these two regulations. Yet precisely these two prohibitions, especially טומאת מת, stand out as basically important. The growth of hair is called נזר אלקיו, "the crown of his God" upon his head. But טומאת מת, keeping away from a dead body, must have a particularly close link with the moral aim of the *nazir* vow. For if a *nazir* has partaken of wine or cut off his hair, even if he has done so deliberately these acts do not invalidate the part of his vow that he has already fulfilled. But if he has any contact with a dead body, though it happened unintentionally or even against his will, this invalidates all the preceding days he has already fulfilled for his vow (והימים הראשונים יפלו). He must fulfill his vows all over again.

If anyone should, perhaps, doubt the symbolic significance of sacrifices, let him, for the time being, consider merely the offering of the ram that Abraham made "in place of his son" (תחת בנו) (Gen. 22). God had put Abraham to the supreme test. He had commanded him to sacrifice Isaac, who has been destined to carry on the essence of his father's life, which had already passed a span of one hundred years. To sacrifice Isaac meant to sacrifice all of Abraham's past and future. However, God had demanded it, and Abraham was ready to obey, but was prevented from doing so by God Himself. An angel called to him from Heaven: "Do not lay your hand upon the lad, and do not harm him in the slightest! For now I know that you are God-fearing, and have not withheld your son, your only son, from Me!" Then Abraham lifted up his eyes and saw, behold, there was a ram, which was caught by its horns in the thicket. And Abraham went and took the ram and sacrificed it as a burnt offering in place of his son.

If this offering were not a symbolic expression of devotion, equal, or perhaps even superior, in significance to Abraham's willingness to offer his own son as a sacrifice to God; if the sacrifice of that ram had meant nothing more than a pagan offering of one of his precious possessions to his idol—what parallel would then exist between the offering of that ram and the offering of the only son that had been demanded of Abraham? If that were the case the sacrifice of the ram would be a completely senseless gesture, for this ram was not even Abraham's property; it was only an animal which he had happened upon in the wilderness!

Part Two

Analysis of Symbolic Character
of Specific Laws and Institutions

מילה — ציצת
תפלין — מקדש
שמונה עשרה

מילה

It is our intention to choose certain symbolic laws and to attempt the study of their content and significance according to the principles of symbolic interpretation which we have established.

We will begin with an examination of מילה, circumcision, the first of the laws given to Israel, which is proclaimed immediately as אות ברית, a sign of the covenant, and hence a symbol.

Let us first consider the act of circumcision and the pertinent specifications detailed in the Law. Let us examine it within the entire context of the circumstances and pronouncements among which it has been set. From there, let us proceed to search for the range of ideas within which its significance must lie. Then let us establish whether perhaps this act in itself, and the terms used for its designation, has already received a metaphoric explanation in the language of the Holy Scriptures. After that, let us attempt to answer, in the light of our findings, the question as to what idea the act of circumcision is intended to express, and then repeat the same analytic procedure with regard to each of the regulations that go to make up the legal concept of this commandment.

Let us also contemplate the commandment of circumcision in its relation to other commandments. Finally, let us test the understanding

65

we have acquired by posing the following question: Is the concept of the symbol such that all these separate regulations and circumstances can be defined in a simple, uncontrived manner as logical consequences emanating from it? Are all these factors, then, such that our interpretation could possibly be correct? Finally, let us look about for interpretations of this law given by others and, by means of that standard, make a critical evaluation of our own findings.

מילה—פרייעה

The Law commands two distinct acts: מילה and פרייעה. מילה is the cutting off of the ערלה (foreskin); פרייעה is the exposure and freeing of the עטרה (corona) by tearing and folding back the membrane that covers it. Both acts are essential, but they are separate as regards the time at which they were first commanded; לא נתנה פרייעת מילה לאברהם אבינו (יבמות ע"א). In their essence, however, both acts are so closely linked with one another that מל ולא פרע כאלו לא מל (שבת קל"ז).

This act is to be performed on the eighth day after birth, on every male who is a member of the house of Abraham by birth or by virtue of servitude. If it was performed prior to the eighth day, it must be regarded as if it had not been performed at all. (See ש"ך, י"ד רס"ב ב׳; שאגת ארי׳, נ"ב). There are cases in which מילה must be performed on the first day after birth. יש יליד בית ומקנת כסף שנימול לא׳ ויש שנימול לח׳ (קל"ה).

מילה must be performed during the day, not at night. If it was performed at night it must be considered as if it had not been performed at all. (See ש"ך ibid., and שאגת ארי׳, 53).

Let us limit ourselves, for the time being, to these few basic provisions and reflect upon the law: All males belonging to the people of Israel must be circumcised on the eighth day, or on the first day, respectively, after birth, during the day, and the process must include both מילה and פרייעה.

תמים

Let us consider the law of מילה in the context of the circumstances and pronouncements that accompanied its institution.

When Abraham was ninety-nine years of age, ה׳ appeared to him and said: "I am God, ש-די, conduct yourself before Me and be תמים, be whole."

אני הוא שאמרתי לעולמי די (ב"ר). "I am the One Who said to My world: It is enough!" My relationship with the world is not that of an impersonal primeval force acting solely as the impetus to the universe, so that the world would have to relate to Me only as the necessary effect. I have not only created the world and its elements, but even after having created it, I still stand above that world and its elements, and I have ordained the די, the "Enough!" over all these forces and their effects. I set the extent, the duration, and the limitations for everything. שאלמלא שאמרתי לשמים ולארץ די עד עכשיו היו מותחין והולכין (ב"ר). Had I not proclaimed this "Enough!" to My world, heaven and earth would still be in a state of continuous, unlimited evolution. Not only existence alone, but the fact that the existence of the universe, and of every individual in it is limited and complete, i.e., that limits and a state of completion have been set for every individual, proclaims Me as the free being above and beyond the world, not only as its Creator, but as its Lawgiver, Regulator and Ruler. אני הוא שאין העולם ומלואו כדי לאלקותו I am די, the universe finds in Me everything it requires. The fullness of the world does not transcend My Divine Essence, but the fullness of My Divine Essence does not exhaust itself in the earth and the fullness thereof. My Godhood transcends the world. I do not merge with the world. I confront the world as the master confronts one of his works! And therefore דייך שנאי אלוקך דייך שאני פטרונך דיו לעולמי שאני אלוקו שאני פטרונו "it should be enough for you that I am your God, your Protector, and it is enough for the world that I am its God and its Protector."

These statements of the Sages point to but a few of the many profound concepts and meanings of this appellation for God, with which God introduced these first institutions of His Law for Israel. Israel has written this appellation as a constant reminder upon its doorposts for its going out and its coming in. This appellation is taken in the form שקמתי, שגם, the One Who has pronounced the "Enough!" He is the free, omnipotent God Who sets laws, dimensions and limitations, Who alone is "sufficient" in His sovereignty and care for the whole and for its individual components. A related concept views God as משדד מערכת, the One Who rules freely over the order of nature and controls it.

Therefore: I am the free God Who sets bounds and limits for everything, Who alone is sufficient for all with My free almighty sovereignty. התהלך, conduct yourself, do not allow your conduct to be determined by outside influences but only by your own free-willed self-determination. Do not "go," but "conduct yourself," and do so "before My Countenance." Let My Countenance be before you everywhere and at all times; decide and conduct your every move before My Countenance, and be תמים, "whole."

It seems to us a noteworthy peculiarity of the Hebrew language that it uses the same word in one and the same form to express the idea of "ceasing to exist" and that of "completion" ("wholeness" or "perfection"). Thus כלה: כלה הבית לכל דבריו, "the house was completed in all its aspects," (I Kings 6, 38) and כלה ענן וילך "the cloud had vanished and was gone" (Job 7, 9). The same is true for the term תמים. In most of the verbal forms, it designates a complete cessation of existence; תם (תהלים ק"ד, ל"ה), יתמו חטאים (איכה ד' כ"ב), הכסף (בראשית מ"ז, י"ח). At the same time, it denotes the consummate perfection of existence; שה תמים (שמות י"ב ה'), איש תם (בראשית כ"ה כ"ז), גבר תמים (תהלים י"ח כ"ו) and אדומה תמימה (במדבר י"ט ב').

This concept might conceivably be based on a dual truth; namely, that, on the one hand, that which is truly perfect can be only "one" thing, so that anything that is to be truly perfect, truly "one," must have ceased to exist as anything else, and that, on the other hand, any non-existence is only relative; i.e., it is non-existent in relation to anything else but itself, so that it can be complete and "whole" in one respect, namely, in itself.

Upon careful consideration we might interpret the root תמם as indicating a state in which all the parts of an object, or, rather, the object in all its parts, point to one direction only. תם הכסף אל אדוני (Gen. 47, 18), the money has become Joseph's in all its parts. תם כל העם לעבור (Joshua 4, 11), the people, in all its parts, has completed the crossing, no one has remained behind. שה תמים is a lamb that is שה in all its parts; i.e., a creature that corresponds, in all its parts, to the normal character of such an organism. This adjective can, therefore, also express that state of thought and condition in which one's entire capacity for thinking and striving is devoted to only one task, without regard to any other purpose or intention. איש משך בקשת לתמו (I Kings 22, 34), the marksman had no other thought or objective than to let his arrow fly, regardless of the target. קרואים והולכים לתמם (II Samuel 15, 11), those invited accepted the invitation without linking their acceptance to any other purpose, and without any other thought in mind.

The positive concept of perfection and completion is always joined by a negative connotation, the exclusion of all the parts of the subject from any other relationship. This should clarify the interpretation of תמים as the characterization of a person, if it occurs in connection with a relationship in which the quality of תמים is to prove itself; תמים עמו (Ps. 18, 24), ואהיה תמים לו (II Samuel 22, 24), תמים תהיה עם ה' אלקיך (Deut. 18,13). Here, it seems to mean nothing else than belonging to God in and with all of one's relationships, withholding not even a particle of one's essence and no aspect of one's relationships from the covenant with God and from subordination to Him. Thus the admonition תמים תהיה עם ה' is used to introduce the warning against all forms of magic or superstition. Consciously or unconsciously, every superstition is based on the illusion that some aspect of ourselves could be withheld from God's sovereignty and care, and could be subject to the command or influence of another power. But even when the forms תם and תמים are used in absolute connotation to describe a person, as in יעקב איש תם (Gen. 25, 27) and יודע ה' ימי תמימם (Psalm 37, 18), we may assume the existence of a similar relationship. It denotes a man who, in his essence and in all of his relationships, is devoted to his vocation and meets its requirements. There are no contradictions in the character of one described as תם or תמים. Every aspect of his existence, and all of his relationships, are disciplined in one direction only, and are directed by one principle alone and form a perfect harmony of personality. All the facets of his being are in complete accord, with even the smallest component bearing the stamp of the whole. In this respect it is the antithesis of רע and רשע, the "broken one," who has fallen victim to the tempest of his passions.

However, תמים is apt to occur in connection with הלוך and דרך; תמימי דרך (Ps. 119, 1), הולך תמים (Ps. 15, 2), ויתן תמים דרכי (Ps. 18, 33). Thus, it connotes the moral strivings of an individual, of one human being "walking" in the paths of morality, rather than the "social" behavior toward one's fellow men. For דרך and הלוך connote movement toward a goal, a striving after possessions and objectives, and תמים דרך is the individual who, throughout his life and in all his endeavors, has subordinated all his impulses, proclivities and energies to the one principle of purity and goodness. He pursues only those possessions and objectives that meet with the approval of God. In this regard הולך תמים represents one aspect of the task that has been set for man. The other aspect is פועל צדק. Noah was a צדיק in contrast to the חמס, the violence that pervaded the society of his day, and he was תמים in contrast to the השחתת דרך, the moral corruption that caused the destruction of his generation.

If, then, Abraham was commanded: "Conduct yourself before Me and be whole," be תמים, then the second part of this charge can be meant to complement the first part, saying: Be whole in your conduct before Me; conduct yourself before Me with every aspect of your personality. Do not withold any aspect of yourself from this conduct before God. Or it may be a separate admonition to Abraham to subordinate to God, without exception, all the energies and strivings of his being. In either case, it represents a demand for moral integrity and a willing mastery and control over all his energies and endeavors.

We note that two such admonitions are addressed to Abraham. The first occurs when he receives the call from God; the second comes at the beginning of the final stage of his life. The first is לך לך מארצך וגו' והיה ברכה; the second, התהלך לפני והיה תמים. The first causes Abraham to detach himself from his civic and social ties with all his other contemporaries. While all the others of his generation serve only ambitious egotism, which builds a tower as a monument to its own glory נעשה לנו שם, this call states Abraham's task: Become a blessing! Do not live for yourself alone but for others; make it your calling to promote the welfare of others wherever and in whichever way you can. The second call, which goes forth to Abraham after a blessed life of ninety-nine years, cites him as a separate being before God and says to him: "Be whole!" It demands that he complete his moral perfection before God. Thus it seems that even the humanitarian qualities that Abraham had demonstrated throughout his long life in his relations with all his fellow men were not yet sufficient to establish the relationship that was to mark the final stage of his life. Hence there must be a level of moral perfection that represents the final cornerstone of the edifice God wished to erect with Abraham in the midst of mankind. Not even the most altruistic humaneness is sufficient to attain this stage of moral perfection; such moral perfection demands that man work upon his own moral improvement even when he is not among his brethren but stands utterly alone before God.

Indeed, the prerequisite for the covenant which God wished to establish with Abraham was that Abraham must recognize God as the One Who is sufficient for all, Who sets the limits of "Enough!" to all His creations, and that he, Abraham, must conduct himself before God's Countenance with every aspect of his personality, in free-willed, complete dedication.

"Conduct yourself before My Countenance and be whole; thus would I make My covenant between Me and you and to let you grow into a great multitude." Abraham fell upon his face, thereby showing that he had dedicated himself to the task of meeting the requirements of God's call.

Then God continued to speak with him. The text refers to God not as 'ה but as אלקים. With the first words God invites Abraham to enter the covenant of his own free will. Therefore the invitation properly bears the Divine appellation of 'ה (the God of loving-kindness). After Abraham enters the covenant of his own free will, the covenantal relationship between God and himself assumes a legal character, entailing specified obligations, for which God's Name of אלקים (the God of law and justice) is more appropriate.

Now that Abram had accepted the covenant, God said to him: "For My part, behold, My covenant is with you and you will become the father of a multitude of nations. Your name shall no longer be called Abram. Your name shall be Abraham, because I have destined you to become the father of a multitude of nations. I will cause you to flourish exceedingly; I will make nations of you, and kings shall come forth from you. I will uphold My covenant between Me and you and your seed after you, for all their generations, as an everlasting covenant, to be a God to you and to your seed after you. I will give to you and to your seed after you the land of your sojourning, the entire land of Canaan, as an everlasting possession, and I will be a God to them."

"But you, too," God says to Abraham, "must keep My covenant, you and your seed after you, for their generations. This is My covenant that you must keep between Me and you and your seed after you. Every male shall be circumcised unto you. You shall circumcise the flesh of your foreskin, and this shall be a sign of the covenant between Me and you. At the age of eight days every male among your descendants shall be circumcised, he that was born to your house and he that was acquired by purchase from any foreigner, who is not of your seed. Let the one born to your house and the one acquired by purchase be circumcised, circumcised indeed, and thus My covenant upon your flesh will become an everlasting covenant. An uncircumcised male, who does not circumcise the flesh of his foreskin, that soul shall be cut off from its people, for he has destroyed My covenant" (Gen. 17, 1–14).

If we examine this document that establishes the legal institutions of circumcision, we will note that it is a true contract, drawn up between God on the one hand, and Abraham and his descendants on the other. First, this contract specifies the promises which God, on His part, undertakes to fulfill within the framework of the covenant. Next, it states the obligation to be assumed in return by Abraham and his descendants. God's promises are introduced by the words אני הנה בריתי אתך; the obligation of Abraham and his descendants, by the words ואתה את בריתי תשמור. God promised Abraham that He will bless him by having a flourishing nation descend from him (והפרתי), that this nation will possess the land of Canaan forever (ונתתי לך) and that He will bestow upon Abraham and his descendants His constant care and guidance (והייתי להם לאלקים). In return, it is expected that Abraham and his descendants will keep their part of the covenant and will pass this obligation to future generations (ואתה את בריתי תשמור וגו' לדרתם).

The obligation that Abraham and his descendants are expected to keep under the terms of the covenant is then defined in more precise terms by the commandment of circumcision: זאת בריתי אשר תשמרו וגו' המול לכם כל זכר. Thus, the circumcision of every male is mentioned first as an obligation that is a part of the covenant itself. Then, in the following verse, it is described as a sign of the covenant, והיה לאות ברית. The act of performing the circumcision is the obligation; once performed, the circumcision becomes the sign of the covenant. The entire idea of a mutual relationship (between God and Abraham and his descendants), based on the covenant, is stated at the beginning of the covenant, as a preamble of sorts, expressed in two terse sentences, offering the covenant to Abraham so that he may accept it of his own free will. However, the part of the covenant to be fulfilled by Abraham is mentioned first, as the undertaking that Abraham was to declare himself ready to accept. Only thereafter are we told the promise that God will make in return. The obligation to be fulfilled by Abraham is described by the words התהלך לפני והיה תמים; the Divine promise dependent upon Abraham's willingness to carry out his obligations under the covenant reads: ואתנה בריתי ביני ובינך וארבה אותך במאד מאד.

Let us now ascertain the sphere of concepts within which we will establish the symbolic meaning of the act of circumcision. We will note that we must conduct our search within two distinct spheres. The Divine promise, for which circumcision is a condition, extends mainly to the material sphere. God promises to Abraham and his descendants the blessings of abundance and prosperity: they will become a great nation, have a land of their own, and receive Divine assistance—all factors in the richly blessed life of men and nations. By virtue of its function, the body upon which the act of circumcision is performed is also part of the material, physical aspect of man. In fact, the material, physical aspect of human life may be said to be concentrated precisely in that area.

So much for the sphere of the material aspects of the human condition. Seen from the second of the two spheres, circumcision is closely linked to the obligation which Abraham must carry out in return for this Divine blessing. In fact, circumcision is a part, indeed, a sign, a physical expression of this obligation. The obligation assumed by Abraham is spelled out as a preamble to the legal institution of מילה in the sentence התהלך לפני וגו'.

However, as we have already noted, this obligation entails, as a condition for the promised abundant blessing, the discharge of a mission that is strictly moral in nature. Abraham is not told: Be industrious, work hard, till the soil, engage in industry and commerce, and then I will multiply you greatly, but "Conduct yourself before Me and be morally whole." This declaration would direct us to the moral sphere exclusively. True, as we have just pointed out, the object upon which the symbolic act of circumcision is performed belongs entirely to the sphere of the material, corporeal aspects of physical existence, to which the covenant gives a promise of abundant development. However, the act as such is to be a part and a symbol of the contractual obligation that constitutes the precondition for the fulfillment of this promise. This obligation entails a task that is purely moral in character.

In view of the foregoing, the significance of circumcision can be found only in a combination of both spheres, the physical and the moral.

מילה—ערלה

Let us now study the linguistic aspects of the Scriptural text and what metaphoric use may already have been made of this aspect, and see whether our findings in this regard may shed additional light on the significance of the institution of *milah*.

The usual term for the act of circumcision is מול, hence מילה, although some forms of the term seem to be derived from the root נמל. The antithesis of מילה; i.e., the uncircumcised state, is termed ערל, ערלה. Let us consider both these terms in the realm of the Holy Tongue.

מול

The "cutting off" of the foreskin could be described by the term כרת, which is generally used to denote the concept of "cutting off." This term does indeed occur in the Scriptural text; ותכרת את ערלת בנה (Ex. 4, 25). Nevertheless, the specific term employed by Scripture for the circumcision of the foreskin is מול. This term must be particularly appropriate to the act of circumcision because it is hardly ever used in Scripture to denote any other "cutting" or "cutting off." The only other use of the root מול in Scripture is as a particle, מול, in the connotation of "against," or "opposite." We consider it probable that the verbal form אמילם in Psalm 118, is also derived from מול and that המיל means "to oppose." "All the nations had surrounded me, and it was with the Name of God that I *opposed* them" (V. 10–12).

If, then, the term for "cutting" is derived from this basic concept of "opposition" or "counteracting," it can denote only a cutting for a specific purpose, and this purpose must be indicated by מול. כרת denotes any form of cutting, be it for the separation or removal of the object that is cut off, or cut down, or be it for the use or the destruction of that which has been cut; ואת אשריו תכרתון (Ex. 34, 13); נכרתו מימי הירדן (Joshua 4, 7); וכרת הזלזלים (Isaiah 18, 5) and לכרת לו ארזים (Isaiah 44, 14). מול, on the other hand, can denote only a cutting by which opposition is offered to the object from which the cutting was done. The object is not to be destroyed, but to be restrained and limited in its activities.

Before searching for a possible metaphoric use of the term מול in Scripture, we must also examine the linguistic connotations of its antithesis, ערלה.

ערלה

יהיה לכם ערלים לא יאכל (Levit. 19, 23); הנה ערלה אזנם (Jeremiah 6, 10); ערל שפתים (Ex. 6, 12 and 30); או אז יכנע לבבם הערל (Levit. 26, 41); ערל לב (Ezekiel 44, 9) and שתה גם אתה והערל (Habak. 2, 16). We note that in each of these passages ערל denotes a state in which something is withheld from unrestricted use by man; man is prevented from exercising his rightful control over certain objects, especially over his bodily organs and his senses.

Fruit trees during their first three years are termed ערלים because the fruit which they produce during that period is not only forbidden as food for men but must also not be used by man for any other purpose. The fruit produced by a tree during its first three years is termed ערלה. The ears and lips are characterized as ערל if they fail to exercise the controlling functions they were meant to perform, if they are not at the disposal of man, if they do not obey his command, if man cannot properly use his ears for listening and his lips for speaking. Similarly, the term ערל is used to characterize a heart whose tendencies, inclinations and passions elude control. A man who has lost control over his ears, lips or heart is called ערל שפה ערל אזן and ערל לב. הערל, to become ערל, means to be brought into such a state, to become stupefied, insensitive. Perhaps רעל ("stupor," Zechariah 12, 2) is a related word; a narcotic or intoxicating drink is called כוס התרעלה (Isaiah 51, 17) יין תרעלה (Psalms 60, 5) and סף רעל (Zechariah, ibid).

Metaphoric uses of מול

The term מול occurs both by itself, without being followed by ערלה as its explicit object, and with ערלה as its object. One instance of the former use is המלו לה' (Jeremiah 4, 4), meaning: Put up opposition to your own selves for the sake of God; control yourselves for the sake of God, והסירו ערלות לבבכם, remove the rebelliousness, the lack of controllability, from your hearts. One instance of the use of מול in connection with ערלה is ומלתם את ערלת לבבכם (Deut. 10, 16). But when מול is used to express the conquest of ערלה it affords us a more precise approach to the definition of ערלה.

ערלה, the state of recalcitrance, can manifest itself as underactivity or overactivity. A bodily organ that has become dulled, irresponsive or sluggish can fail to perform its intended functions. Such a manifestation of ערלה could not be corrected by מול, by counteracting, limiting or negating the functions of the organ, but only by an awakening and stimulating of that organ. On the other hand, an organ may be over-active, too intense, in the performance of its functions, overstepping its limits and eluding the restraints to which it is properly subject. That would be ערלה manifested by overactivity, and its conquest would be quite properly expressed by מול, opposing it, imposing limits upon it, taming it. Thus, the Biblical command, "circumcise the foreskin of your heart" would demand of us: "Put up opposition to the excessive appetites of your own hearts, in a virile manner, control yourselves!" The opposite aspect, the overcoming of disobedience manifested by underactivity, is expressed in the words וערפכם לא תקשו עוד "and be stiffened no more." In the verse או אז יכנע לבבם הערל (Levit. 26, 41), ערלה connotes disobedience manifested by overactivity, and its control is expressed by the term הכנעה, "bending," or "humbling."

מצות מילה

We have now recognized ערלה as denoting that recalcitrance in which something withholds itself from use, or control, by man. We have noted that ערל characterizes a man who has lost control over one of his organs. We have identified מילת ערלה as a metaphoric reference to the conquest of a type of recalcitrance manifested by overactivity, thus, the "taming" or curbing of excessive appetites. The concept of מילה involves an act of cutting, in the literal sense, performed on one of our bodily organs. As long as this act has not been performed, the organ that is the object of this circumcision is ערלה and the man is an ערל; he is called ערל בשר (Ezekiel 44, 9).

This whole context compels us to view the institution of מילה as a symbolic act. Thus, we would hardly be justified in going any further and looking for the significance of this act anywhere else than in the understanding that is offered to us by the metaphoric use of this term. מילת ערלה literally denotes the conquest of an object that has been recalcitrant in that it has exceeded its proper limitations. Should it, then, have any other meaning than the symbolic one? Hardly so.

Every communication through the medium of speech contains metaphoric expressions. Such is the case, for instance, with the cere-monial acts of lifting and waving which the priest had to perform with certain offerings. There, we have the commonly used figures of speech,

אשר הניף תנופת זהב (Ex. 35, 22), and it ויקחו לי תרומה (Ex. 25, 2) and
makes no difference at all which of the two came first chronologically,
whether the figure of speech originated from the symbolic act, or
whether the act was designated to express this particular idea because
it was already used in colloquial speech as a metaphor for that idea.

What idea, then, would be expressed by מילת בשר ערלתו as a symbolic act, parallel with the common figure of speech מילת ערלה, and what
would be the relation between this idea and the covenant for which it
had been ordained as אות ברית, a covenantal symbol?

From the vantage point of this metaphor the characterization of
ערלה, when applied to the object on which the circumcision is to be
performed, would imply that without circumcision, and outside the
covenantal relationship for which that object is claimed by the act of
circumcision, the object would be lacking the discipline to which man
should subject it. The only question now remaining would be to what
extent the concept of the object of circumcision should be explored.
Should it be interpreted literally, only as an organ, with its own functions, or should it, in the context of this symbol, be interpreted to
include all the physical aspects of the human body? Since the term is
apt to occur in conjunction with בשר; e.g., ערל בשר, בשר ערלה, one might
suggest that it should be interpreted in the latter, broader connotation;
i.e., as representing all the physical aspects of man. Circumcising the
ערלה, or, more accurately, למול בשר ערלה, would then imply our duty not
to permit the physical aspects of our bodies to be ערלה, not to leave
them to their own devices, but to "put up opposition" to them and to
assume control over them for the covenant which circumcision is to
symbolize.

In Jewish thought, the concept of "cutting" has become a
metaphor and symbol for the willpower and determination which
must be applied in the control of the physical aspects of the body.
Furthermore, the concepts of "deciding," "decreeing" and "deter-
mining" are designated in Hebrew primarily by expressions that
denote "cutting" and "separating." For instance, ותגזור אמר, גזר (Job
22, 28); נחתך על עמך, חתך (Daniel 9, 24); ואת אשר נגזר עליה (Esther 2, 1);
כן משפטך אתה חרצת, חרץ (I Kings 20, 40). Also the more recent expression, פסק ("sentence," "judgment") and probably ואשבר עליו חקי, שבר
(Job 38, 10), which therefore could be translated into the Chaldean as:
ופסקית עליו גזרתי.

The basic philosophy here seems to be that before a decision has been made, it is still linked to various, usually mutually opposing factors which keep the decision pending. The act of deciding cuts the decision off from these factors and sets it up as an independent determination, born of inner strength, not dependent upon any other considerations: "Thus shall it be!" This analogy in all probability also offers the most satisfactory explanation for the expression כרות ברית (the agreement, lit., "the decision" of the covenant).

The control over the physical aspects of our bodies is to be the basic condition, set by the sign of the covenant, for that covenant which God has made with Abraham and with all of Abraham's descendants. This sign is such a basic part of this covenant that God considers its performance as an act of upholding the covenant, and its omission as destroying the covenant. Thus our interpretation of this symbol can be correct only if we can prove an immediate and basic connection between this obligation and this covenant; if, indeed, the control over the physical aspects of the body is to be viewed as a basic condition for this covenant. Let us, therefore, examine our own interpretation in this light.

An abundance of progeny (והפרתי אותך), the possession of a fertile land (ונתתי לך את כל ארץ כנען) and visible protection and blessings for both of these (והייתי להם לאלקים); hence, the full measure of one's physical existence—this constitutes the promise given by God in the covenant to Abraham and his descendants. If our interpretation is correct, the sign which is to impress upon Abraham and his progeny for all time the obligation that they, on their part, must carry out in return for God's promise, is to admonish us to control the physical aspects of man, for which God in that same covenant has promised conditions most conducive to a beneficial development. Seen in this light, the connection between the obligation represented by this symbol, on the one hand, and the covenant of which it is to serve as a token and reminder, on the other, becomes readily apparent. God promises us the fullest measure of our physical, earthly existence on the one condition that we do not allow this physical existence to be ערלה; that we do not permit it to luxuriate without limits or restraints. All the physical aspects of our earthly existence, with all its impulses and forces, its riches and pleasures, must be brought under the firm control (מילה) of the holy will of God. This sign poses, as the first and indispensable condition for our covenant with God that we must

circumcise the ערלה of the physical aspect of our body. It is not the
consecration of the spirit but the consecration of the body that marks
the entry into the covenant of Abraham. This covenant categorically
rejects the erroneous concepts of both extremes. It does not condone a
mortification of the flesh on earth for the purpose of gaining life in the
world to come. But it also rejects the worship of physical appetites and
the cult of "beautiful" sensualism.

תמים, תמים, תמים—this word is engraved upon the great seal of the
Divine covenant that lays claim to our total being and says to us: Not
only your spirit, but your body, too, shall be Mine. It requires us to
control our senses even as it promises us the fullest measure of our
physical existence. Or conversely, even as it promises us the fullest
measure of our physical existence, the covenant requires us to control
our senses. It does not comfort its followers with hopes for bliss in the
world to come, but ensures them a Paradise-like abundance for all
their existence on earth. And in return for this—as with the first
inhabitants of a paradise on earth—we need to fulfill only one condition, מילה, the control of the sensual elements of our bodies.

When we first set out to ascertain the symbolic significance of the
act of circumcision, we assumed that, judging from the context into
which this sign has been placed with both aspects of God's covenant
with Abraham, its meaning could not be sought in either the moral or
the material, physical sphere alone. We said that we should rather
assume, from the outset, that the idea expressed by this symbol will
combine both spheres in their significant essence. The Divine promise
ארבה אותך entails physical, material blessings. The condition היה תמים
stipulates a moral requirement. Our findings comprise the physical
and moral alike, in the consummate meaning of both. The object of
the symbol, בשר ערלה, represents sensuality raised to the highest power.
The act entailed in the symbol, מילה, expresses the supreme act of free-
willed morality. Together, these demand of us a most moral conduct in
the midst of the most sensual aspects of our lives.

We have already alluded in passing to the relationship between our
concept of מילה and the תמים-aspect in the preamble to the Scriptural
text instituting מילה. In fact, if we consider everything we have cited
concerning this idea from its use in the Holy Scriptures, especially how
תמים expresses the total devotion of a being in all its parts to one single
destiny, that it touches less on his conduct in public life than on his

personal, human relations; then, truly, it would be difficult to find a more appropriate symbolic act to express the free-willed morality of an enduring self-control as required for the perfection of the חמים-character than the מילת בשר ערלתו.

This requirement to be חמים, so meaningfully demonstrated by מילה, is introduced with the words: אני א' ש'. We are to rise freely above sensuality, to master our sensuality out of our own free will, and to counter it everywhere with measures of moderation, reason and restraint. Hence the appellation for God used in the command of מילה should indeed be א' ש' to demonstrate the close ties between that name of God and the demand God makes of man. What sanction, surety and security does this Name of God impart to His demand! Behold your God! He is not the bound force of nature merging into the physical world that the pagans and the philosophers would have Him be. He is א' ש-די, the free, absolute God Who stands freely above and beyond nature and rules with His all-embracing guiding hand setting limits and dimensions everywhere. He summons you to walk before His Countenance. You, in your own little world, have been called by Him to conduct yourself in His image. He did not intend you to be a blind product of fate, of the interplay of natural forces. He has made you free even as He Himself is free. His freedom is your guarantee that it is indeed possible for you to be free; even His will, which sets limits and restraints, demands this of you. די לערלה עד כאן! If you will be His and if He is to be yours then, like Him, you must never be part of the interplay of physically bound forces and energies. You must learn from Him how to say "די" to the forces of sensuality, making His will your own. You must measure all the endeavors of your sensual being by the standards of His will. With the knife of His "די," His "Enough!", you must apply the מילה, you must set limits to בשר ערלתו, the physical aspects of your body which otherwise you would not control. Only if you impose these restraints upon your physical self can you expect His blessings and His aid.

חוק של מילה

In our preliminary observations we found in the general character of symbols the principle that it cannot be the purpose of a symbol to reveal to us new truths, which, without that symbol, would remain unknown to us. The most proper application of symbols and symbolic acts is to effect the upholding and lasting retention of truths that have been known to us for some time. Now what of the great truth which, according to our interpretation, the symbol of circumcision is to teach us for all times? Is it otherwise unknown in the God-ordained sphere of life? Or do we find it expressed, clearly and precisely, in the Law with which God shaped this sphere, and with such impact as one should expect of a truth chosen by God for His covenant and for the basic condition for His relationship to the Abrahamite nation? Does Divine Law accord a place to the control of the physical aspects of our bodies, and if so, what place do these restraints occupy in the Law?

A mere glance at the Divine legislation given to Israel is sufficient to show that this Law does not in any way limit itself to regulating relations between man and man or to setting standards of justice and kindness for human society. Rather, it exercises the same painstaking care and concern in the shaping and regulating of the little world within which every individual human being moves and where body and soul are at one time opposing and uniting factors in the creation of life. Individuals, differentiated by sex, unite in mutual complementation so that, together, they may form one single entity.

Another glance into this legislation points to a significant group of חוקים, laws that control and moderate particularly the physical and sensual aspects of human life. These laws occupy a position of such prominence that they have been recognized in every age as the shibboleth of Judaism, as the distinguishing trait of the Jewish man and the Jewish woman.

A cursory glance at these laws discloses also that God, Who gave them, did not add them to His Law as an irrelevant dietary or prophylactic appendix, but made them a basic pillar of the Law itself. We see that He linked to these very laws the entire ideal of purity and holiness which He expects His nation to follow. An understanding of His truth, of His justice and of His loving-kindness can come only from individuals who were begotten, nurtured and raised within the framework of these particular laws. God holds out the promise of His protecting, rewarding and blissful nearness only where the physical, sensual aspects of life, too, flourish within the parameter of these hallowing laws. He withdraws, and with Him flee the protection and blessings of

His visible sovereignty, wherever sensuality is permitted to run its course in flagrant immodesty.

We can see that the institution of מילה, has been made the foundation of the entire Covenant of Abraham permeating the entire structure of Jewish Law, Thus, our interpretation of this symbol seems to be fully confirmed. (We refer, in passing, to Ex. 22, 30; Levit. 11, 43—47; 15, 31—32; 17, 10—14; 18, 1—30; 19, 26—29; 20, 18, 22—26; 21, 7, 13—15; Deut. 12, 23; 23, 10—15 also, to the many admonitions, warnings and promises, in almost all of which חוקים are given a paramount place.)

מצות פריעה

Thus far we have considered the symbol of מילה only from the vantage point of the physical act which is its most outstanding feature and from which it has derived its name, מילה; i.e., circumcision. However, the commandment of מילה includes one other act, that of פריעה. This act must be so intrinsically separate that—as mentioned previously—it was decreed only at a later date to Joshua. However, it is such an essential complement to the symbol of מילה that the Law considers מילה without פריעה as not having been performed at all, מל ולא פרע כאלו לא מל.

We must here establish the place of פריעה in the covenantal symbol of מילה, and to find the relationship—or the contrast—between *milah* performed without *periah,* as during the four hundred years between the days of Abraham and the time of Joshua, and *milah* combined with *periah,* beginning with the time of Joshua.

We have already mentioned that *periah* consists of the exposure and freeing of the *atarah* by tearing and folding back the membrane that covers it. If we compare this act with that of *milah,* it appears to be the exact antithesis of the latter. *Milah* is a "cutting back," an act of limiting and restraint, of "opposition," as indicated by its Hebrew term, מול. The act of *periah,* by contrast, is one of exposing and freeing. The very term פריעה, derived from פרע, (to uncover, to bare), implies a complete loosening, a freeing from every bond and compulsion. פרע הוא (Ex. 32, 25); תפריעו את העם (Ex. 5, 4); גדל פרע (Numb. 6, 5), etc.

Thus, while מילה represents restraints on the sensual aspects of life, פריעה would allow these very aspects of life to develop freely, even promoting them within the bounds of the restraints imposed upon them. In context with the entire meaning of the covenant, and the requirement to be תמים, to conduct oneself before God with the whole of one's life and personality, including the sensual aspects of one's life, פריעה would modify this demand as follows: man must belong to God and conduct himself before His countenance, not only by putting restraints upon his sensuality but also by permitting his sensuality to develop freely within these restraints. *Milah* places restraints upon the sensual aspects of life before God. *Periah,* on the other hand, actually demands that these drives be afforded free development and gratification within these limits. *Milah* banishes uncontrolled, lawless sensuality from the sacred parameter of God's covenant. *Periah* elevates the physical side of life, kept pure and holy by the restraints of the Law, to become a *mitzvah,* the fulfillment of a duty, in its own right, an act pleasing to God and sanctified to Him. *Milah* eliminates from physical life that which is displeasing to God. *Periah* channels the physical aspects of life toward purposes that meet with God's approval.

מילת ערלה proclaims, with regard to the sensual aspects of life: סור מרע "keep away from evil." פריעת עטרה proclaims, with regard to those same aspects of life: עשה טוב, "do that which is good" (Psalm 34, 15) We have already noted that the concept of תמים as such includes two distinct aspects, one negative and one positive. While the concept of perfection in itself is a most positive one, the Hebrew term designating it is based on the negative aspect; i.e., "ceasing to be anything else but . . ." and thus demands the renunciation of anything that runs counter to the positive purpose of the object. This is entirely in character with the symbol of *milah,* which is to represent nothing but moral acts, the moral standard demanded for the achievement of the character of תמימות, moral perfection. *Milah,* the elimination of all untoward elements from the physical aspects of life, must come first. But perfection cannot be achieved if the physical aspects of life are supressed, neglected or avoided. Rather, the physical aspects of life, in a state of purity, also serve to attain the purposes for which God has, in fact, created them. מל ולא פרע כאלו לא מל.

The generation of man in whose midst the family of Abraham was to grow into a nation of God rushed headlong to its ruin not because it failed to do good, but because it did evil, particularly in its moral corruption that prevailed around Israel as evident from the Biblical reference (Levit. 18). מילה, renunciation of this evil, was therefore the primary condition for the existence of the nation of God. The laws which God had given to the Noachide generation, the שבע מצות בני נח, were entirely prohibitions against acts displeasing to God.[1] Even דינים, the implementation of justice, which is phrased as a positive commandment, was intended for a prohibition; i.e., to put a stop to acts forbidden by the Law.[2] At that time, prior to the Revelation of the Law on Mount Sinai, God had not yet proclaimed the observance of positive commandments, the active pursuit of purposes pleasing in the sight of God. Abraham and his immediate descendants were directed solely to this Noachide approach. As far as the Law was concerned, they were still Noachides. In the midst of the corruption that prevailed in Asia Minor and ancient Egypt, they still had to go through four hundred trying years in order to achieve and to maintain that level of purity which should have been the goal of the entire Noachide generation, but of which every trace had vanished from their world. During that period of trial, Abraham's descendants lacked the independence and the soil of their own upon which a positive existence, dedicated to God, could have flourished. That was the period of מילה without פריעה; its symbol was purity expressed in negative terms.

The period of trial had come to an end. God had led the Children of Israel out to freedom to take them into the land promised in the *milah* covenant as their reward for the performance of *milah*. For during the period of trial (symbolized by *milah* alone without *periah*), the children of Abraham had proven themselves worthy of God's promise. However, this land so abundantly blessed with the riches of herds and fruits was not to be merely a reward for מילה. The land itself, with all of its abundance, was to become the source for a still higher, positive attainment of earthly existence. It was to serve as a medium for the unfolding of an individual, family and national life in which all resources and energies were to be transformed into things holy to God; all human activity was to be transformed into an act of Divine service. The very fleeting, mundane and sensual aspects of human existence

---

1. שבע מצות בני נח: עבודה זרה, ברכת השם, שפיכת דמים, גילוי עריות, גזל, דינים, אבר מן החי

2. דינים: כיצד מצווין הן על הדינין חייבין להושיב דיינין ושופטים בכל פלך ופלך לדון בשש מצות אלו ולהזהיר את העם (הל׳ מלכים פ״ט הל׳ י״ד עיין בכ״מ)

would also bear the stamp of dedication to God. Every part of life was to be not only pure and free from that which displeases God, but all of life, with all its aspirations and achievements, would culminate in a continuous, everlasting service of God—לריח ניחוח לה'—in homage and glorification of Him.

The Noachide laws were absorbed into the Law of Sinai. The seven prohibitions of the untrue, the false and the unclean were perfected to form a code of 365 מצות לא תעשה, banishing dishonesty, injustice and falsehood, and removing them far from the life of the individual, the family and the nation.

To this was now added a completely new element: 248 מצות עשה commandments which summoned all the forces of man to serve God in positive terms. These commandments assigned both to the individual and the nation, with all their resources and energies, the aims with which to gain God's approval. This was then the time when מילה was to be completed by the act of פריעה.

But above all this was the time when Israel's possession of the Promised Land, which was now to be conquered, would provide the soil for the realization of the task, to dedicate every aspect of life to God. Precisely at the moment when the first step toward the settlement of this land was to be taken, the need of the hour was to impress forever upon Israel's mind the even higher, positive consecration of the sensual and material aspects of life for which the time had come with Israel's settling on the land. The land was to be settled not for subjective pleasures but for objective action on behalf of God. On this land, the material and physical aspects of life were not only to be elevated to a level of freedom from impurity, but even more so to a positive consecration to God. מילת ערלה was to culminate in פריעת עטרה.

Not so much as a pebble of this land was to pass into Israel's possession, not one fruit of this land was to be enjoyed by Israel, until the higher purpose of this physical life with its ownership of the land and the enjoyment of its products, would be impressed upon Israel through both these symbolic acts—*milah* and *periah*.

Joshua stood before the walls of Jericho and the intial step toward the conquest of the land was to be taken. Even as they had passed through the Red Sea, the Children of Israel now marched across the river Jordan and the Amorite kings were gripped by terror. At that moment, בעת ההיא, God said to Joshua (5, 2), the general of the Israelites: "Make yourself sharp swords." For what purpose? To enslave the enemy? To conquer the land? For neither of these. This sword of conquest was to be wielded by another, higher Authority. שוב מל את בני ישראל שנית, go, perform upon Israel, upon your nation of warriors, the circumcision; acccording to Yebamoth 71b this meant the first *and* second parts of the act, the *milah* that is completed by *periah.*

Only then could the offering of liberation be made, only then could the fruit of the land be enjoyed. Only then (עתה באתי) did the "captain of the hosts of God," who was to lead Israel in the conquest of the land (Ex. 23, 20) appear with his sword drawn. And when Joshua, the general of the Israelites, asked him: "What does my Lord have to say to his servant?" the "captain of the hosts of God" had nothing else to say to him but: "Remove your shoe from your foot, for the place on which you are standing is a sanctuary." The ground which you are about to take on Israel's behalf is not simply a land on which there will be erected a "temple for the worship of God" (Joshua 5, 14). The entire land is holy, every foot of ground a sanctuary, and life as a whole—not only in its spiritual heights but also in its earliest, earthly beginnings—all of life in that land is a sacred service of God—פריעה!

ביום ולא בלילה

The act of circumcision must be performed during the day. Is this stipulation to be interpreted only in a literal sense, perhaps as a precautionary measure, considering that such an operation which, after all, is no trifle, should be performed only in bright daylight? Or does this requirement have symbolic significance in its own right, as a complement to the symbolic act?

If we consider that the question is asked (Yebamoth 72a) whether even מילה שלא בזמנה, a delayed circumcision, can also be performed only during the day and that, as the ש"ך explains (י"ד 262, 1), a circumcision performed at night has no legal validity נימול בלילה לא יצא (see שאגת ארי׳ 53), it would seem clear beyond doubt that this requirement has a powerful symbolic significance of its own. We must therefore establish its meaning and its connection with the symbolic act of circumcision itself. The commandment of circumcision has this rule in common with a number of other commandments. Megillah 20 a,b, mentions most of the commandments which, according to the Law, can be performed only during the day. Among these are the following: הזיית טמא מת, מילה, קבלה, מליקה, הקטרה, קמיצה, הגשה, תנופה, שחיטה, סמיכה, וידוי מעשר, וידוי פרים, מוספין, נטילת לולב, תקיעת שופר, טהרת מצורע, עריפת עגלה, השקיית סוטה. To these could have been added the following: דיני ממונות, עיבור שנה, קידוש החדש, מראות נגעים, חליצה, נחלות, ודיני נפשות (Sanhedrin 32a, Yebamoth 104a, Rosh Hashanah 25b), and נשיאת כפים, according to רא"ש מס' יומא פ"ח סי' כ', etc.

With regard to the performance of certain acts, the Law of God stipulates a specific time. In the case of most of the commandments enumerated above, the Law states the time specified in such categorical terms that the legal validity of the act depends on whether it is performed at that particular time. Thus, the entire קרבן was פסול if any of the acts such as שחיטה, סמיכה, etc. was performed at night. A sentence passed by a court of law is legally void if the proceedings were begun at night, or, in the case of criminal proceedings, if any of the court's deliberations took place at night. A New Moon is not considered מקודש under the Law if the act of its sanctification was not completed during the day (Sanhedrin 11b).

If the observance of these time stipulations, or failure to observe them, should basically alter the legal character of the act in question, then that act must have a most significant relationship to human affairs.

What is the significance of day or night with reference to human affairs? What conception in this regard is revealed in the Holy Scriptures?

In the history of Creation, darkness always precedes light. Darkness is the expression of תהו and בהו, the subjective and objective absence of individuality, in which the existence of individual objects cannot be discerned. (תהה and בהה, from which is derived בי, the expression of pain or suffering in the plea for an answer to one's supplications. בי אדני — בראשית מ"ד, י"ח) Light, on the other hand, is the expression of complete existence: כי טוב. However, the creation of light was not intended to eliminate the state of darkness from the terrestrial world. On the contrary, both light and darkness harmoniously alternate in the reign over the earth as ordained by God. With every new day the earth rises from darkness to light. Each new day begins with ערב, the state of being "commingled." לילה (from לול), the state of being "entwined," in which individuality recedes and living things interact only as substances and forces; followed by בקר, the morning, which brings awareness to a "distinguishable," independent form of individual existence.

The life of man, too, moves within the framework of this alternating. Daytime places the terrestrial world at man's feet. During the daylight hours, he stands erect as a free individual, mastering the world around him aggressively and proudly as he sees fit. Night flings man, the "earthly lord of creation," into the bonds of earthly elements. For him, day is the time of independence, of action. Night is the time of yielding, of passivity. It is not only in itself the time when בנפל תרדמה על אנשים, "numbness falls upon men," ובמסרם יחתם "and God places His seal upon their bonds," להסיר אדם מעשה "to separate man from action," וגוה מגבר יכסה "the body is removed from (the will of) man" (Job 33, 15–17).

Night and darkness are also the most universally used metaphors for states of spiritual and physical confinement, for a weakness and helplessness that may come to men and nations. שומר מה מליל, "Watchman, what of the night?" Israel cries out from exile to its God (Isaiah 21, 11). בחנת לבי פקדת לילה "You tested my heart; You visited night upon me," says David as he meditates upon the thorny path of his life (Psalm 17, 3). אתא בקר וגם לילה "Morning comes, even though it is still night" is the answer to the exiled nation that cries out from the darkness (Isaiah 21, 12). וארח צדיקים כאור נגה הולך ואור עד נכון היום "The way of the righteous is as the light of dawn; it becomes brighter until the full daylight," is the comforting word of wisdom from the Book of Proverbs (4, 18).

Human life, then, moves in two basically different semicircles. There is the arc of daytime, whose phenomena are the products of free human creativity, and there is the arc of night, in which man himself acts only as the passive product of telluric and cosmic influences. By day, man is in power and the world is his product. By night, man is himself the product and the universe is the power that restrains and molds him.

Night or day—in which of these two phenomena must man seek his God?

So-called religions which stem from man's feelings of dependence direct man towards the night. Man is called upon to find God at the point where he loses himself. "Religions" equate the end of day, night, with the end of life, death, and seek to liberate man from the fears of night—death. In this perspective, man is seen as helplessly bound to his physical fate unless redeemed by the saving grace of religion. Typically, they erect their temples over the graves of the dead. They celebrate their most sacred mysteries at night, and their most fervent prayers are cries pleading for deliverance from the power of the "evil one" in the world. Such is the passivity, the dark aspect of human existence, which these "religions" employ to "bind" man to the Divine.

Judaism is not a "religion." Judaism summons man into the full, bright light of day and shows him that he is master over the world outside himself as well as over the world within him. It makes him aware of his free-willed, godly power with which he can subdue both the world around him and the world within his own heart. It shows him the One, unique, true, free, almighty God Who, in His free omnipotence, has created the world around and within man. He has created man himself to serve Him, and He guides man and the world for His wise purposes. Both night and day serve Him; death serves Him, and so does life. It is He Who has created the passions in the breast of man so that man control them out of his own free will and employ them for the good in the service of God. Judaism reveals to man the clear, free spirit that dwells within his own heart, and it shows him the One, unique, true God from Whom he has derived that clear, free spirit. It shows him the One Who has imparted to him this light and this freedom as a spark from His own free, almighty Essence. With this spark God has raised man above all else that lies bound by blind necessity and that must operate and behave according to mindless coercion, and has placed man into His immediate proximity. Freely, with every clear impulse, with every lucid thought, with every human act of his, man should pay homage to Him, the One God, and serve Him. By this homage and service, given with his life on earth, man is to elevate all of earthly life, in both its aspects—darkness and light—to the lofty goal of perfection.

Judaism asks man to find God at the point where man finds himself. To Judaism, pleasure and life, strength, freedom and rejoicing are heralds that lead men to God. Judaism builds its sanctuaries upon the shining heights of life. Death and decay are kept far from the halls of its Temple. Grief and mourning must be put aside at its thresholds. The gates of the Temple open when the world awakens and active life begins. When night comes, calling man to rest from his work, the portals of the Temple also close. Only the light and the fire on the altar, feeding on the offerings of the day just past, continue through the night within the closed confines of the Temple, just as in man, too, spiritual and emotional life never ceases but builds a bridge from one day to the next, even while man seems impervious to impressions from without. It is through activity, the daytime aspect of human life, that Judaism summons man to its God. Judaism is not given to sorrowful supplications and litanies of mourning; it calls man to serve God as a vigorous, happy, free and active individual, exercising his dominion over the world.

The "night gods" of the so-called religions are אלילים, "powers that negate," עצבים, powers that make themselves felt in the "pain of renunciation." The God of Judaism is ה׳, He Who "grants ever new, vigorous existence," אלקים חיים ומלך עולם, "the God of life and the King of the Universe." His religion is called "Law" and "the Teaching of Life."

In light of these observations, it should become evident why God's Law specifies daytime, indeed daytime exclusively, for the observance of many of its commandments. We can understand this specification particularly where an observance could be erroneously associated with the "nighttime" aspects of life so that it could easily be misinterpreted, indeed, interpreted to imply the very opposite of the concept it intends to teach; often there is a need to emphasize in clear terms the connection between the law and the active aspect of human life by placing that observance precisely within man's sphere of activity.

If we examine those stipulations in God's Law that must be observed during daytime, we focus particularly on two areas: jurisprudence (משפט) and the Divine service in the Temple (עבודה).

Hearings of witnesses may not take place at night. Civil court proceedings may not begin at night. Criminal suits may not be brought at night. In criminal cases, sentence may neither be passed nor carried out at night. Those sentences derived from or passed as the result of court proceedings that took place at night are legally void. If we are not in error, the purpose of these stipulations is to protect jurisprudence itself against even the faintest semblance of influence from the "nighttime" aspects of human affairs. The implementation of justice places restraints upon the options of the individual, thus making him aware of his impotence. He is forced to yield to a power other than himself. But this power is not outside human society, it is not hostile to human freedom, does not impede human development and does not limit human activity as would a blind, jealous "fate." Instead, it is a power which in itself represents the highest potential of human development. It is completely within the scope of free human activity, and the very individual against whom it may operate has himself helped fashion it and is its active partner. Indeed, this power will be exercised in his own name. The judge acts on behalf of the society to which the litigating parties themselves belong, and which, in some other contingency, may have to wield its authority even against him who now acts as the upholder of its sovereign power.

Thus, the justice administered to the litigating parties is implemented in their own name. The justice that is now to be applied is not the product of some dark, demonic forces of bondage, of passion, hate or fatalism, which would limit and impede man's God-given freedom. It is, rather, the Law of the One, unique, true and living God, Who by this very Law has set the supreme ideals of perfection for the human freedom that derives from Him. He has appointed the community to guard this Law against each one of its individual members, who in turn are represented by the judge. Therefore, the power to which the individual yields in a court of law is a power that bears his own name. The justice that is applied in his case is simply an arrangement of his own free-willed affairs in the realization of which his freedom attains its highest form. God, Whose Law is implemented in court as a limit to man's freedom, is the same God Who has bestowed that freedom upon man. The highest form of this freedom is manifested not in caprice but in self-control within the limits set by God. It manifests itself in its purest form especially when it submits to the Law of God as pronounced by a court acting as the upholder of the power of God's community.

The judges and the parties in court must be mindful at all times of God, of society, and of the God-given dignity inherent in the free personality of every individual as guaranteed by both God and society. The work of the court calls for the daytime, the time when man moves about freely, when man can be seen in terms of his individuality and of his interaction with society. This requirement applies particularly when court proceedings affect the fate of a person—hence especially in criminal trials. On the other hand, proceedings, that involve property, i.e., that deal directly with objects and only indirectly with persons, where persons are involved only in that they are required to make payments in objects or in cash, such proceedings may be conducted at night, the only restriction being תחלת דין, that the proceedings must have been initiated during daytime.

We have already made reference earlier to the close connection between עבודה, the service in the Temple, and the "daytime" aspects of life. Daytime is the true, indeed virtually the only admissible time for the Divine service in the מקדש.

The stipulation that the sacrificial acts must be performed during the day points to the One, true, living God Who makes man free, grants him life, and calls upon man to serve Him with the full force of his self-mastery in vigorous creativity. This requirement categorically refutes any illusion that the service in the Temple is really intended for an overwhelming force of nature manifested in the dark, night-like enslavement of man, and that, in these ceremonies, the gods are worshipped by the sacrifice and the killing of the free human being.

No sacrificial ceremony may be begun at night. Among the offerings particularly restricted to daytime performances are those which symbolize self-control and total dedication to the service of the living God, but which could easily be misinterpreted as a killing and a destructive sacrifice of physical existence. Cases in point are: הקטרה, קמיצה, מליקה, זריקה, קבלה, שחיטה, סמיכה etc. Only הקטרת חלבים ואברים may be performed at night, because they represent the concluding acts of a consecration of life's basic principle acts that had already been performed during the day by means of זריקת הדם.

There are only two acts that, under the Law, must be performed at night: (מנחות עא, עב) קצירת העומר and (ברכות ט׳) אכילת פסחים, partaking of the meal of liberation and the first harvest of the land. But these exceptions only serve to support our interpretation. Both these concepts, freedom and land ownership, are the most outstanding marks of an independent man, standing erect to rule freely over his possessions. The fact that these acts must be performed at night will not make them subject to misinterpretation because, in their very essence, they represent a direct negation of the "nighttime" aspect of human existence. Yet, precisely these acts must be performed at night. Indeed, אכילת פסחים certainly, and קצירת העומר in all probability even בדיעבד can be performed only at night. (See הל׳ תמידים פ״ז הל׳ ו׳, לחם משנה). For Israel

did not attain its freedom and the ownership of its land by its own
power. Israel was still shrouded in night when God first bestirred it to
freedom and independence. Even as the people of Israel are repeatedly
reminded (Deut. 16, 1) הוציאך ה' אלקיך ממצרים לילה, that their God
brought them forth from Egypt during the night, are they constantly
admonished by כי לא בחרבם וירשו ארץ that אכילת פסחים וקצירת העומר בלילה
וזרועם לא הושיעה למו כי ימינך וזרועך ואור פניך כי רציתם that they did not win
the land with their sword, that their own arm had not helped
them, but that they received these blessings only through God's Right
Hand, His arm and the light of His Countenance, because He was
favorably inclined toward them (Psalms 44, 4).

Among the other commandments whose observance is restricted to
daytime, חליצה belongs to the category of jurisprudence (יבמות ק"ד), and
עבודה. תקיעת to the categories of both משפט and עבודה to the categories of both עגלה ערופה and השקת סוטה
שופר ביום—the shofar must be sounded during the day because it calls
on our own free, full power of independent energy to overcome all that
is evil and servile, and bids us to return, of our own free will, to the
service of the living God Who has made us free. This is not a call of
death and night, to frighten and shock us with thoughts of our frailty
and transience.

ישיבת סוכה ביום ובלילה We are to dwell in the סוכה both during the day
and during the night because we are to be reminded, again and again,
that in our entire existence on earth, in both its "daytime" and "nighttime" aspects, we are not protected by our own strength but can find
"security" only in the care of God. On the other hand, לקיחת לולב ביום
the commandment to "take up" the lulav must be observed during the
day, because it invites us to an active, independent life before God,
bidding us to "take for ourselves" the goods of the earth before Him,
to use them before Him and for His pleasure, and thereby to reap the
highest bliss that man can hold within his heart, that of "rejoicing
before his God."

It is most significant that קידוש החדש and עיבור שנה can be done only
during the day. Nothing would be simpler than to link the consecration of the New Moon and attention to the vernal equinox with the life
of nature, which is bound by immutable laws, and interpret these two
observances as being, at best, acts of "worshipping God in nature."
But this is exactly what they are not intended to be. They are not
meant to embody the rejuvenation of nature, but solely the renewal
and rejuvenation of our own selves. Whenever the New Moon and

springtime recur in the cycle of nature, we are to awaken a New Moon and springtime, as it were, within ourselves, as human beings. Again and again, we are to turn all of our human endeavors and creativity toward the light, always looking toward God, Who, even as He brings springtime to nature, addresses Himself to all that has withered in Israel and mankind, and with His call בדמיך חיי! awakens them to a new life. As with משפט, and totally and exclusively as in דיני נפשות, both observances are made applicable to the individual: ואם עיברוה בלילה אינה מעוברת ואם קדשוהו בלילה אינה מקודש (סנהדרין י"א, ראש השנה כ"ה).

We consider it particularly significant that the commandments מראות נגעים, הזיית טמא מת, and טהרת מצורע (the inspection of "leprous" marks, the sprinkling of those defiled by contact with a dead body, and the purification of the "leper") may be observed only during the day. What other laws are so easily relegated to the dark sphere of night as those regarding טומאת מת and טומאת צרעת, the laws concerning defilement by contact with a dead body, and the defilement incurred by "leprosy"? Especially in the case of נגעים one tends to think solely in terms of disease and contagion, although, in fact, these laws have no relationship whatever with the physical health of man.

(It should be remembered that נגעים occuring בקמטים (on parts of the body that have creases) and בית הסתרים (on parts of the body that are covered) are not מטמא. Only "leprous" marks occurring on exposed parts of the body have that effect. The כהן is explicitly directed to take into account only those parts of the body that are readily visible to him when the man whom he examines stands before him in a natural, unconstrained position (נגעים ב'. ולכל מראה עיני הכהן). Whether or not the person is to be regarded as defiled depends entirely on the verdict of the כהן, and whatever was in contact with the "leper" before this verdict was pronounced is in no manner טמא. As a matter of fact, in cases of נגע בית (Levit. 14, 36), it is explicitly required that the house be emptied before the כהן gives his verdict so that whatever may be in the house at that time should not become טמא by virtue of the verdict. Note that, under the law, examinations for נגעים were postponed at times when contagion and a wider spread of disease would be most likely; i.e., when the entire nation assembled in Jerusalem for the pilgrim festivals, or at weddings (נגעים פ"ג משנה ב'). Yet, given all these facts, there are those who would argue that these laws were merely sanitary regulations, with the priest acting as medical examiner!

Let us turn back to the law of *milah,* which must also be carried out during the day. The relevant factors now become obvious. We have recognized that this symbolic act is meant to express the foremost implementation of our moral freedom as a condition of our covenantal relationship with God. What is required of us is not to remain ערל בשר, not to lose control over the physical aspects and drives of our bodies. We are required to perform מילת בשר ערלתו, to oppose, with free-willed energy, the physical forces of nature within ourselves. What is required of us is מילה and פרייעה: to elevate the sensual aspects of our lives so that they become acts in the service of God.

All these factors that summon man to exert his full, free-willed energy would, in themselves, already suggest that this act should be performed during the day. Indeed, in its superficial aspects, the performance of this symbolic act has certain features which, if it were performed at night, would expose it to distortions and misinterpretations even more than we have already noted in the case of such commandments as הזיית טמא מת, etc, and in the case of such sacrificial acts as שחיטה, זריקה, etc. The act as such is intended to render expression to the highest level of moral energy. However, the object of the act is the human body, which with its drives, may reach into the "nighttime" aspects of human bondage.

If we look at מילה superficially, without regard to what Scripture has stated concerning its symbolic character, we could be tempted to consider it purely as prophylactic surgery, without any moral implications. Even a purely symbolic interpretation might see it as a homage offering to the dark powers deified by human delusion, which reach out from the "nighttime" aspect of human existence into the very flesh of man holding him prisoner there with their powerful bonds. Even if we relate *milah* to the moral aspect of man, we might come to think only too easily that it requires the destruction and suppression of the sensual aspects of the body, as if this were yet another bond to fetter man, who is already bound in so many other ways.

But all these conjectures are resolutely refuted by the requirement that circumcision must be performed during the day. This requirement proclaims in no uncertain terms that circumcision is not concerned with the strictly physical functions of human existence. Circumcision is not concerned with the dark powers of an unfree nature. Circumcision firmly directs us to the One, absolute God Whose Law binds the forces of nature, and Whose essence and freedom are reflected in the free-willed creativity of man during his waking hours. It is to such a man that circumcision addresses itself, placing the knife into his hand and demanding that he himself apply the limits of God's Law to the sensual aspects of his body. With his own free will, he must restrict them to these limits within which he is to elevate and consecrate them, so that they will become free-willed, moral acts in the service of God. Circumcision is not intended to repress or enslave the human body. The sole and eternal purpose of circumcision is to have him become part, with all his being, of the absolute sovereignty of God, to have him demonstrate that he is indeed made in the image of the One, absolute God, and that he dedicate all of his being to the service of God. אין מלין עד שתנץ החמה ואפי׳ מילה שלא בזמנה אינה אלא ביום עבר ומל בלילה צריך לחזור ולהטיף ממנו דם ברית (יו״ד רס״ב א׳ עיין בש״ך).

ביום השמיני

Circumcision must be performed on the eighth day. Is this requirement part of the complete picture of the symbol, and thus a basic component of the symbolic act, thereby sharing in the symbolic character of the act as such? Or is it motivated by reasons with no symbolic significance?

It has been argued that an infant less than eight days old is too delicate to be subjected to such painful surgery and that this require-ment was motivated out of mindful consideration for the infant's health.

However, note יש יליד בית שנימול לא׳ ויש שנימול לח׳ ויש מקנת כסף שנימול לא׳ ויש לח׳ (שבת קל״ה). There are cases in which the Law actually requires that the infant be circumcised on the day of his birth. This specification is not concerned with the physical condition of the infant, but only with the social and religious status of his mother, the mode of the infant's birth (natural or by surgical means), and the resultant religious implications for the mother.

This exception itself suggests that circumcision on the eighth day has symbolic significance. An even more compelling argument in favor of the symbolic character of the requirement: בן שמנת ימים ימול לכם כל זכר, an argument that no longer admits of any doubt, as demonstrated in ש״ך on Shulchan Aruch, Yore Deah 262, 1, and even more cogently in שאגת ארי׳ 52, that a circumcision performed prior to the eighth day, (*except* in cases, as indicated above, where the Law actually requires circumcision on the day of birth) is legally null and void.

Before presuming to ascertain the symbolic significance of this regulation, we must first reflect on the object of our research. We have before us the provision that circumcision is to be performed on the eighth day. This provision suggests the possibility of two assumptions:

(1) This regulation can mean merely that circumcision may not be performed prior to the eighth day, but that the eighth day in itself bears no relationship to this act except that it is the earliest date at which circumcision may take place, and that therefore circumcision may not be postponed beyond that date. If this were so, we would have to interpret the regulation as follows: Seven days must pass after the infant's birth before he can be circumcised. We would, then, have to pose the question: What is the significance of the seven-day period that must pass before circumcision can take place?

(2) Or, the emphasis may be on the eighth day, the sole significance of the seven preceding days being that they must be allowed to pass because circumcision is to take place on the eighth day. If this were so, we would have to establish the significance of the eighth day.

It may be difficult for us to decide which of these two assumptions is correct. The Law stipulates that although circumcision may take place belatedly after the eighth day, it must normally be performed on the eighth day, even if this entails a violation of the Sabbath. This would suggest that we should seek the motivation of this provision in the positive significance of the eighth day. However, this assumption may be countered by the fact that הקטרת חלבים ואיברים דוחה שבת even though זמנן כל הלילה, and that the only reason stated for performing these acts on the Sabbath is that שלא להחמיץ את המצות.

In any event, every interpretation of the exceptional cases will have to stand the test of investigation: יוצא דופן, יליד בית ומנקת כסף שנימולים לא׳.

The number seven, as is well known, occurs in many stipulations of God's Law; (a) as the total number of objects to be produced for a specific purpose, (b) as the total number of days to be devoted to a specific purpose, (c) as the total number of times a specific act is to be repeated, (d) as a number of specified periods of days or years, (e) as an ordinal number designating a day, or a year, to be set aside for a specific purpose.

In the case of the seven lamps of the מנורה in the Temple, or the seven lambs of the מוסף offering, the number seven refers to the number of objects by which the light, and the offering, respectively, is to be represented.

On the Day of Atonement the blood of the offering must be sprinkled repeatedly, seven times in all, toward the Ark of the Covenant, toward the curtain and upon the altar of incense. In the act of טהרת מצורע the oil is sprinkled seven times toward the Holy of Holies. In the ritual of the פרה אדומה the blood of the animal is sprinkled seven times toward the entrance of the Temple. In each of these instances, the number seven denotes the total number of times a specific act is to be repeated.

The seven days of the Festival of מצות, the seven days of the Festival of סוכות, and the seven days of מלואים set forth the number seven as the total number of days devoted to a specific purpose.

The Sabbath on the seventh day of the week, שמיטה in the seventh year, the seventh day for הזיית טמא מת and for טהרת זב וזבה (see נדה ס"ז), and the seventh year that brings freedom to Israelite slaves, all utilize the number seven as an ordinal number designating a day or a year to be set aside for a specific purpose.

The seven days to be completed by נדה, מצורע, טמא מת and יולדת in order to become pure on the eighth day, and the seven days that must elapse after the birth of an animal before it may be offered as a sacrifice from the eighth day on, utilize the number seven as the total number of days to be completed before entering into a new state or condition.

By contrast, שבועות, שמיני למלואים, שמיני עצרת and יובל illustrate a positive connotation for the eighth day, the beginning of the eighth week of days, the beginning of the eighth week of years. מילה belongs either into this category or into the preceding one. Only in ציצת do we find the number eight as defining the total number of objects intended for a specific purpose.

We will now attempt to delve into the concept found in God's Law and many of its regulations with the numbers seven and eight, respectively. First, we believe we must cite again the principle that, given the character and the purpose of the symbol, the link between the symbol and the idea which the symbol is to represent must be completely within the conceptual realm of the person for whom this symbol has been chosen and to whom the symbol is to make clear that particular idea.

It has been frequently attempted to present the number seven as a mystery, whose secret lies in certain arithmetic and geometric properties that are not accessible to all. We believe we must disregard all such conjectures and seek the symbolic significance and origin of this number within the realm of the Jewish people and its Holy Scriptures.

In Scripture the number seven also occurs, both in speech and in action, outside the Law as such.

"While the childless woman gives birth to seven children, she who has many children languishes" (I Sam. 2, 5). "Wisdom has hewn out its seven pillars" (Prov. 9, 1). "Seven eyes are directed toward one stone" (Zechariah 3, 9). "Israel will flee upon seven roads" (Deut. 28, 25). "Cain will be avenged twice sevenfold, and Lemech eleven times sevenfold" (Gen. 4, 24). Israel is threatened with "sevenfold chastisement for its sin" (Levit. 26, 18). "The Word of God is refined twice sevenfold" (Ps. 12, 7). Jacob bows down before Esau seven times (Gen. 33, 3). David praises God "seven times each day" (Ps. 119, 164). "Even though the righteous man may fall seven times, he will rise again" (Prov. 24, 16). "The lazy one considers himself wiser than seven councillors" (Prov. 26, 16). The hypocrite hides "seven abominations within his heart" (Prov. 26, 25).

In each of the above Biblical passages the number seven is used to express a full number or a full measure, something "whole" or "complete." What is done seven times in these passages indicates that the action thus performed is to be understood as having been performed in full measure.*

We also encounter a cycle of seven days as a period considered sufficient for a specific purpose. Noah waits for two consecutive seven-day periods (Gen. 8, 10–12). Joseph sets seven days of mourning for his father (Gen. 50, 10). God allows seven days to pass after the plague before He renews His challenge and warning to Pharaoh (Ex. 7, 25). For seven days the daughter is to hide in shame before her father; Miriam remains isolated outside the camp for seven days (Num. 12, 14–15). Samson celebrates his wedding for

---

* Consequently, שבעתים (Prov. 6, 31) may mean that he must pay fully double, the entire כפל, or rather, double the full amount.

seven days (Judges 14). Ezekiel sits dismayed for seven days, among the exiles (3, 15), etc.

In view of all the foregoing, we believe that we are not in error if we interpret the number seven as having the general connotation of "fullness," "wholeness" or "final completion." Now we must answer the question whether the origin of this connotation may be found within the parameter of Jewish thought. Was there any occasion in the realm of the Jewish people to associate the idea of completion with the number seven? In the encompassing universe man recognizes the object of the highest conceivable level of perfection. To the Jew, precisely this object of consummate perfection represents the Creation which the One God completed in seven days. God accomplished His work in seven stages bringing it closer to completion with each day, but finishing it only with the Seventh Day. On the Seventh Day He made His world into a finished entity. Indeed, the Seventh Day itself was the completion of His work. Would this not suggest that from this point on the number seven in general was to become the symbol of completion and conclusion in human activities, in acts performed by man? Would not then a seven-day period constitute a span of time for man during which he could implement an idea fully and adequately, or during which one of his activities or relationships could run its full course to completion?

Now if this work of Creation, completed in seven days, is the concrete example from which the number seven has been taken as a general symbol of completion, we should investigate more closely whether this actual fact of Creation did possibly endow the number seven with a special kind of completeness, thus giving to the "Seventh" a special character as the carrier of completion, making it a very special symbol of that which will make this completion come to pass.

What is the relationship between the seventh day of Creation and the six days that preceded it? What unique contribution did the seventh day bestow upon Creation to make the work of Creation a complete one?

The physically perceptible world was already completed in the first six days. The sixth day had concluded the sequence of physically perceptible works with the creation of man. Thus it became a kind of concluding Sabbath for the physically perceptible world. That is why the Sages refer to it as זו שעה שמוסיפין מחול אל הקדש (ב"ר) הששי. However, real completion came only with the Seventh Day.

The seventh day did this not by adding yet another order of perceptible creations to the physical world, but by granting to man, the
representative of the physically perceptible world, the awareness of the
Invisible Creator and Master, an awareness that became part of the
completed world as the crowning touch of perfection. This awareness
conferred upon each component of Creation, and upon Creation as a
whole, its purpose and completion without which neither the individual component, nor the whole, could exist. Thus, the seventh day
added the Invisible to the perceptible; it established the bond between
the Creator and His creation, between the Master and His work,
between God and His world. While the number seven in general stands
for completion, and the "seventh" for consummate perfection, the
number seven can, actually, also symbolize that which has been
completed in concert with God, so that the "seventh" can indicate the
Invisible Creator and Master, Who is linked with the visible world.

This latter, more specific meaning might find considerable confirmation in the verb הִשָּׁבַע, (to vow) which is obviously derived from
שבע, seven. It is striking that the words אם לא are used to denote a
positive vow (i.e., to do), while the particle אם denotes a negative vow
(i.e., to refrain from doing). If the "seventh" is a reference to the Invisible God, and if the number seven denotes the visible in its connection with the Invisible One, then the verb הִשָּׁבַע, in this reflexive form,
would mean nothing else but to subject oneself to "the seventh," or,
more fully, to subordinate oneself with all of one's material world to
the Invisible Lord and Master, to surrender oneself to Him with all of
one's physical existence—אם if an event should occur or will come to
pass, or אם לא if it does not, or will not come to pass. The former is
negative, the latter positive. Consequently, שבועה would be nothing
other than the subordination of one's physical existence to the authority and to the decree of the God Who is invisible but nonetheless is
present everywhere. It would be literally נשא שם ה' an act of "taking
upon oneself" the Name of God, the placing of one's self beneath the
Name of God. The "seventh" would be nothing else but שם ה', symbolizing God. In that case, total physical submission, under oath, to the
authority of the Lord and Master Who is invisible but nonetheless is
present everywhere would not be an empty hyperbole but a genuine
pledge of one's whole physical being to the veracity of one's word. This
same Invisible-but-Present God has given His promise with the
words: כי לא ינקה ה' וג'. We see, therefore, that perjury committed by one

who swears can bring about the destruction of an entire world (Zechariah 5).

In keeping with this concept of oaths or vows, the oath in court שבועה דאורייתא, is used only to protect property one already owns, not for property one has yet to acquire (נשבע ונפטר but not נשבע ונוטל). For one who takes an oath thereby subordinates all of his material world, all that he possesses, to the authority of God inscribing the Name of God, as it were, on all of his possessions. Only the righteous man will be able to stand up under this Name, while the dishonest one will be destroyed by it.

We would submit for consideration whether the seven sheep which Abraham placed before Abimelech (Gen. 21, 28–30) did not have a dual significance: to symbolize the covenant established between the two men, and to affirm that Abraham had acquired the well by honest means. Along with the term for "oath" or "vow" we find yet another term, אלה, which is most likely also linked to the Name of God, 'א.

If the number seven has the general symbolic connotation of completeness and the particular connotation of the visible in communion with the Invisible God, then the seven lamps of the מנורה in the Temple, for instance, can symbolize the sum total of knowledge, the light of knowledge in its total dimension. Or, they can symbolize a perception of the entire visible world, the "six" in connection with the perception of the "seventh," the Invisible One. The symbolic significance of the מנורה could be expressed in these terms: all knowledge enanates from the "Seventh," the Invisible One, the נר מערבי, and all knowledge, in turn, leads to Him: ממנו מתחיל ובו מסיים (ת"כ פ' אמר).

The number seven of the כבשים in the מוסף offering may be intended to express, in general terms, the fullness and wholeness of the relationship to be symbolized by these כבשים. It could also indicate that this relation is viable only if it is linked to God.—Israel, as its forefather Abraham did with Abimelech, offers anew its seven sheep to its God in each מוסף offering, reaffirming each time that it places its entire existence under the protection of the Invisible One and thus renewing each time its covenant with God.

The seven-time sprinkling of the blood of animals offered up as sacrifices may symbolize the complete dedication of every drop of blood to God, to His holy Law and to the consecration of life as represented by the Ark of His Covenant and by His altar. But such a hallowing dedication of every drop of our physical life to God, to His holy Law, and to the hallowing of our lives may also mean that every beat of our pulse links us with God and His holy covenant. Consequently, the אחת למעלה ושבע למטה of יום הכפורים may teach us, at the most sacred moment of that momentous day, the great truth that our uplifting to the Most High can have meaning only if it causes us to lead a perfect life on earth in concert with Him.

To decide which of these interpretations is likely to be correct, in these and other instances, we will have to consider the whole context in which these symbolic objects and acts occur.

Similarly, there may be the question as to whether the seven days of the Festival of מצות and the seven days of the Festival of סוכות are intended merely to provide an adequate time period for perpetuating the concepts which these festivals are intended to evoke. Or is the number seven also meant to make certain that our celebration will indeed serve to elevate all of our physical being to God, so that, in and through our festival, God will enter into a sacred covenant with us? The fact that in the case of the Festival of מצות, the seventh day is stressed by being marked as a full holiday should speak in favor of the latter interpretation.

The seven days of טומאה for מצורע, נדה, יולדת, and טמא מת most likely signify the completion and conclusion of a period of טומאה which began with the first day. This seven-day period must pass before the state of טהרה can set in again. But wherever the seventh day is singled out, as in הזיית טמא מא, and even in שביעי של זבה and still more so in שבת, שמיטה, and שביעית של עבד עברי, where the full emphasis is on the "seventh" so that the preceding "six" lead up to that "seventh," the number seven occurs in its unique significance as a reference to God. By renouncing the physical world on the seventh day and renouncing the Jewish soil during the seventh year, we pay homage to the Invisible One and so connect our "six" with the "Seven." The whole material foundation of our existence as individuals and as a nation is dedicated to the sacred nearness of God, our Invisible Lord and Master. And the person who has lost his freedom as the result of a transgression for which he has not made atonement can elevate himself, through his six years of servitude, to draw near to the holy covenant of our Invisible Lord and Master and, through this nearness, become free again. The seventh year that brings freedom to the thief who was sold into servitude to make restitution for his theft, thus proclaims: The material world which tempted you, makes you a slave, but God Whom you have scorned, will make you free (שש שנים יעבד ובשביעית יצא לחפשי חנם).

Before returning to the subject of *milah* in order to establish the significance of the seven-day period that must elapse before circumcision can take place, we must first look into God's Law to establish the significance of the eighth day. For it is entirely possible that the significance of the eighth day as the day of circumcision is to be interpreted not only in the negative connotation that it must be preceded by seven years, but that the eighth day has a positive message of its own, such as the eighth day of שמיני עצרת, following the seven days of the Festival of סוכות, the eighth day of the dedication of the Temple following the preceding seven days of מלואים, the Festival of Weeks after counting seven weeks and the יובל year after a period of seven times seven years.

We find the origin of the symbolic significance of the number seven and of the "seventh" as an expression of completion in the unique work of consummate perfection—the Divine work of Creation, which God finished in seven progressive stages and which He completed in its entirety with the seventh creation, the שבת.

When His Creation was completed, God entrusted to the institutions given with and within that Creation the attainment of the goal set with the "Seventh," the שבת, that man should become aware of God and pay Him homage. But is there, perhaps, yet one more work of God, an entirely new institution, that joined the seven previous works of Creation as a new, eighth creation, and from which the symbolic significance of the number eight could be taken?

If we consult the text of the Torah, we will certainly search in vain for an additional work of creation in nature, an additional work of God that could be hailed as His eighth creation. But there is yet another sphere, the sphere of mankind, which emerges already on the sixth day as the visible conclusion of a visible Creation, and for which the seventh day was to provide the Sabbath. This was the day on which man should become aware of the Invisible One, and pay Him homage, and which therefore represents the true completion of the visible world with a covenant that was to come about between man and the One Invisible God. Now within this sphere of mankind the Torah shows us yet another Divine creation, a very special, additional work of God which stands out plainly as the eighth manifestation of God's mighty acts. This creation joins the seven preceding Divine acts of creation as such a significant supplement that it represents, in fact, the true object of the Torah. It presents to us the history of the works of God's seven days of creation as a preamble to this eighth creation, so that we can grasp its significance and purpose. This new Divine creation which the Torah presents to us as the eighth work of God is nothing else but the creation of Israel in the midst of mankind.

Here we face a completely new creation. Israel amidst mankind is not a product of conditions previously given for the development of natural and human history, inherent in the seven preceding works of Creation. On the contrary, Israel was placed into the midst of mankind by an immediate act of God, as direct as His preceding creations.

The creation of the people Israel follows directly the seven earlier works of creation as their continuation and as the instrument for their completion. As the completion of the physical world the Sabbath brought the awareness of and the homage to the One Who is invisible but nonetheless omnipresent. It did so in such a manner that this awareness and homage do not appear as an added flourish, an extraneous supplement, but as a most integral condition for the act of creation, indeed interwoven with creation in its entirety.

Nonetheless, this awareness and this homage might be subjected to many interpretations and misinterpretations, applications and rejections, in the historical development of mankind. Therefore Israel was placed into the midst of mankind as the true herald of the genuine awareness and homage, so that through Israel's historic emergence among the nations, the Sabbath might be safeguarded and ultimately transformed into living reality. While the Sabbath forms the capstone of Creation, of the work of God in nature, Israel represents the beginning of God's work in history, the beginning of God's Kingdom on earth. This relationship of Israel to the Sabbath, and through it to the creation of the world, has been beautifully characterized by Rabbi Shimon ben Yochai. The Sabbath complains to the Creator of the world after the Creation had been completed (Bereshith Rabbah 11):

"You have provided every day of Your Creation with a partner that upholds it, the first with the second, the third with the fourth, and the fifth with the sixth, but I was left without one."

To this, God replies: "Israel shall be your partner (ישראל יהיה בן זוגך).

Later, when the people of Israel stood at Mount Sinai, God addressed them: זכור את יום השבת לקדשו Remember the pledge I gave to the Sabbath to make you its partner. Israel appears as the indispensable complement to the "Seventh," the Sabbath, and its entire historical character is founded on the Sabbath. All the other festivals are rooted in Israel, but Israel itself is an emanation of the Sabbath (hence the sequence מקדש השבת וישראל והזמנים).

We believe, therefore, that, as the number seven is a reference to the Invisible One, Who is linked to His visible creation as its Creator and Master, the number eight represents the visible upholder of this "seven," the perceptible herald of this reverent awareness of God. It represents Israel in terms of its unique mission and status as the chosen people.

The seven-day Festival of מצות celebrates the almighty workings of God, the Invisible One, in Israel's deliverance. The seventh day of this festival marks the full measure of this deliverance, the crossing of the Red Sea. Similarly, the Festival of the Giving of the Law to Israel comes only after the Seventh Sabbath, ממחרת השבת השביעית. For it was not through God's actions in favor of the Jewish nation, but through its commitment, through the pledge of נעשה ונשמע, that Israel became Israel. Only thus can we understand Israel's becoming the Chosen People.

The seven-day Festival of סוכות celebrates the physical survival of Israel and its possessions as a miracle granted by the almighty sovereignty of the One, Invisible God. But the eighth day, שמיני עצרת, represents the culmination of rejoicing, not in Israel's physical survival, but rather, in the spiritual preservation of Israel's calling (אני ואתם). That is why Israel's profound national awareness has expressed this rejoicing so beautifully in שמחת תורה, the rejoicing over the preservation of the Law.

The rest imposed on Israel's arable land and the cancellation of all debts in the seventh year constitute an act of homage paid to the One, Invisible Master and Ruler over all property, within the Jewish state. But only after seven such Sabbatical years does the יובל come, to renew over and again the foundation of the Jewish state, causing Israel in all its components to emerge anew each time from the hands of God. The

יובל calls every son of Israel to the service of his Invisible Master and, starting from this inalienable mission, frees him from every other service. Every one returns to his property and to his own family. ושבתם איש אל אחזתו ואיש אל משפחתו תשבו (Levit. 25, 10).

There is only one *mitzvah* whose observance focuses on the number eight: the commandment of ציצת. Indeed, God has explicitly designated these threads as a symbol to remind Israel of its chosen status and of its calling: וראיתם אותו וזכרתם את כל מצות ה' וגו' והייתם קדושים לאלקיכם אני וגו' אשר הוצאתי אתכם וגו' להיות לכם לאלקים וגו'.

This mission is forever expressed by מילה. The moral perfection required of the family of Abraham is on a higher level than expected of the rest of mankind. The special historic providence that has been assured to them by the covenant of circumcision demands the dedication to the fulfillment of this higher, wider obligation that God expects them to perform throughout history.

The seal of the Divine covenant is applied to the flesh of the infant son of Abraham's family not for ethics in general but as a Jew, for Jewish morality. This covenant specifies categorically that circumcision may not be performed during the first seven days, or even on the seventh day, of the infant's life, but only on the eighth day. A circumcision performed during the first seven days, or even on the seventh day, would remain simply a physical act. Only if it is performed on the eighth day is it elevated to the level of the calling of Judaism because, as we have seen, the number eight refers to Israel and its unique mission.

But what if this connection between circumcision and the unique mission of Judaism, beyond the ordinary human aspect, were presented in another, more significant and factual manner by the circumcision as such? We are referring, for instance, to a circumcision performed on a child whose mother was not Jewish at the time of his birth. Unlike a child of a Jewish mother who is Jewish regardless of whether or not he had been circumcised, a child whose mother was not Jewish at the time of his birth can become a Jew only through circumcision, and thus will cease to be only a part of mankind in general but become a Jew. Is it required, also in such cases, to wait until the eighth day, in order to stress the connection between the act of circumcision and Israel's unique status and mission?

It would seem quite natural if, in such cases, the Law would permit circumcision prior to the eighth day. And indeed, these are precisely the exceptional cases to which we have referred earlier. The rule in such cases is יש ילד בית שנימול לא' וכו'; i.e., that such infants may be circumcised already on the day of their birth. Thus we read (Yerushalmi, Shabbath XIX,5), יש קטן נימול ליומו היך עבידא ילדה ואח"כ נתגיירה נימול גמ' שבת קל"ה ליומו נתגיירה ואח"כ ילדה נימול לח'. There is a discussion in גמ' שבת קל"ה between the תנא קמא and ר' חמא about the practical application of this rule. Whether one must wait until the eighth day to perform the circumcision, depends on whether the mother was already לכם, a member of the House of Israel, prior to the birth of her son. In this respect, תנא קמא and ר' חמא differ only in their interpretation of the legal concept of לכם. According to ת"ק, the eighth-day requirement applies if the mother had become a member of the House of Israel before the birth of her son, even if at the time of the birth she had not yet taken the final step of טבילה to complete her entry into Judaism. According to ר' חמא, on the other hand, the eighth-day requirement is applicable only if the mother had already completed her conversion to Judaism by having undergone טבילה before the birth of her son. (רש"י שם ד"ה יש ילד בית שנימול לא' ותוס' ד"ה כגון).

If our interpretation is correct up to this point, there would be a noteworthy connection between מצות מילה and מצות ציצת. Our garment, which covers the sign of the Covenant upon our body, would then by its eight threads express the same teaching which we believe to have established as the content of that symbol. The message of מילה ופריעה ביום שמיני is best given in those Biblical verses that state the significance of the eight-thread symbol of ציצת?

מילה — ולא תתורו אחרי לבבכם ואחרי עיניכם אשר אתם זנים אחריהם
פריעה — למען תזכרו ועשיתם את כל מצותי והייתם קדשים לאלקיכם
ביום — אני ה' אלקיכם
שמיני — אשר הוצאתי אתכם מארץ מצרים להיות לכם לאלקים

However, the present interpretation of the significance of the eighth day as the day of circumcision will be tenable only as long as the statement of R. Assi in Shabbath 135a that יוצא דופן אינה נימול לשמנה, is not considered as having the binding authority of Halachah. Cases in which circumcision is permitted on the first day come under the concept of לכם only as long as the Jewish status of the mother at the time of the infant's birth can determine whether circumcision must wait until the eighth day or is to be performed on the first day. Only under such circumstances can we explain these exceptions as naturally derived from the significance of the legal provision. Indeed, רמב״ן and רשב״א subscribe to the opinion that R. Assi's statement is not הלכה. (וגם מהא דקטרח הש״ס יבמות ע״א א׳ב׳, למצוא זכריו דאיתנהו בשעת אכילה וליתנהו בשעת עשיה ולא מוקי לה ביוצא דופן ביני וביני משמע קצת דס״ל לסתמא דש״ס דלא כר׳ אסי.) However, as long as there can be some doubt as to the Halachah, and as long as the possibility remains that, under the Law, a child born of a Jewish mother, hence a child born as a full Jew, should not be נימול לשמנה if he was יוצא דופן, we must not dismiss the possibility that our interpretation of the eighth day as the day of מילה, as previously expounded, might be incorrect because it failed to take into account the rule that a יוצא דופן should not be נימול לשמנה. In that eventuality, we would have to look for a concept that takes this legal exception into account. To this end, we would have to use as our point of departure R. Assi's statement.

R. Assi summarizes the pertinent provisions in the following words: כל שאמו טמאה לידה נימול לח׳ וכל שאין אמו טמאה לידה אינה נימול לח׳. The elaboration of this statement contains regulations to the effect that the eighth-day requirement is waived and an infant may be circumcised as early as the first day if (1) the infant was יוצא דופן even for the child of a Jewish mother or (2) the birth was natural but the mother was נכרית; i.e., she had not yet completed her conversion to Judaism at the time the child was born.

Thus, the seven days of the mother's טומאת לידה correspond to the seven days that must elapse before the infant may be circumcised. Since both these concepts are closely connected, they must be based on a common motive. Furthermore, we have a double equation. First, שבעת ימים קודם מילה = יוצא דופן; that, as regards *milah,* יוצא דופן produces an effect that in the case of a normal birth would only be achieved after seven days; or rather, that a delivery by Caesarean section obviates the reason which, in the case of a normal birth, necessitates the passing of seven days before circumcision. We have the same equation with regard to a נכרית even if the birth is normal.

All these considerations lead to the conclusion that the forces of nature to which both mother and child are subject in a normal birth and which, in the case of the mother, result in ז׳ ימי טומאת לידה necessitates for the infant as well a period of seven days that must be allowed to pass before circumcision.

As a consequence, the sole function of the seven days (prior to circumcision) would be that of a period that must be completed and concluded, as in the cases of טמא מת, יולדת, נדה. The only difference would be that, while one who became טמא can return to the previous state of purity and freedom only with the eighth day, the infant, who has entered life as a totally unfree, nature-bound entity, makes his transition with the eighth day, to the higher, independent level of a human being, which in turn qualifies him to be consecrated as a Jew.

However, in cases where the birth was brought about entirely by surgical means, as in the case of יוצא דופן, neither the child nor the mother is required to conclude a specified cycle, because this birth was achieved not by the compelling forces of nature but with human skills exercised by men in their freedom of action. Even in a normal birth, the observance of such a cycle becomes still more irrelevant if the child through his mother was not part of the Jewish people before birth, but joined the Jewish fold only after his birth so that the act of circumcision completes his entry into Judaism. The transition in this case is so vast that no further symbolic designation is required.

The significance of the seven and the eight is forcefully conveyed to us by the description of the Creation, the celebration of our weeklong holidays, the laws of purity and last, but by far not least, the fundamental institution of the מילה. In all these cycles of seven, the "eight" is not only the upper limit of the "seven" but also the starting point of a new phase, solidly established on the foundation of the seven. Thus, the "eight" becomes a new refined "first"—as the first note of the musical scale finds its renewal in the octave on a higher level.

Seven signifies completion and conclusion. The "eighth" represents a new beginning, but on a higher, clearer plane. The state of טומאה is concluded with the seventh day, and the eighth day then is a new beginning, but on a more refined level. The state of evolving טהרה reaches its completion with the seventh day, and the eighth day provides another beginning, but here, again, on a higher plane, even לקודש.* The work of Creation that was begun on the First Day was

---

* The state of טהרה for מקדש קדושיו (except טבול יום כשר למעשר שני) requires הערב שמש—the onset of the eighth day.

completed on the Seventh. The eighth is the beginning of a new process
of creation, on a higher plane than what has gone before moving
toward completion within the realm of the unbounded, spiritual
development of mankind.

The work of the physical creation of the people of Israel attains its
completion with the seventh day of the Festival of מצות, but on the
seventh octave, the fiftieth day, introduces the higher spiritual creation
of Israel, the תורה. The Festival of סוכות, which lasts for seven days,
comprises the celebration of Israel's physical survival. The eighth day
resumes the celebration of survival, but this is a higher, spiritual form
of survival, the survival of Israel for its God and for its mission.

Therefore, the physical birth of the child is completed on the
seventh day. The eighth day, the octave of birth, as it were, repeats the
day of birth, but as a day of higher, spiritual birth for his Jewish
mission and his Jewish destiny.

ציצת

מצות ציצת

 וראיתם אתו—וזכרתם—ולא תתורו

Of all the Divine commandments which we will attempt to examine
in the present study, none has a more obviously symbolic character
than does the commandment of *tsitsith*. The Divine Law itself has set
down the meaning and content of this commandment in unambiguous
terms. There can be no doubt about the message to be conveyed by the
fringes we are to attach to our garments and this would not require an
intensive study. The law that commands us to attach these fringes to
the corners of our garments also explicitly states the purpose of this
directive: וראיתם אתו וזכרתם את כל מצות ה' ועשיתם אתם (Num. 15, 39). The
sight of the fringes is to remind us of the entire scope of the Divine
commandments and to inspire us to obey them all.

If, then, the symbolic character of these fringes on our garments is
so obvious, and the ideas to be conveyed to us by this symbol are clear
beyond any doubt, our study can have only this purpose: to establish
the relationship of the symbol itself to the ideas it is to express, and to

attempt to ascertain the meaning of the symbol in terms of its separate components.

To be sure, the Word of God has essentially achieved its purpose by having us attach fringes to our garments and thereby proclaiming: Whenever you look at these fringes, remember Me. This would be true even if there were no other connection between the physical reminder as such and the subject of which it ought to remind us. Yet, it is difficult to conceive that the Divine Law should have chosen such a reminder at random without a deeper rationale. We are certainly justified in the assumption that here, too, there must be an intimate link between the symbol and the idea that constitutes its object.

We must first recall the details of this commandment as specified in the Written Law and single out, as precisely as possible, the concepts which this symbol is meant to express. Next, we must bring to mind the symbol as such in terms of its actual performance according to the Law and for this purpose, ascertain from the *halacha* the Biblical (דאורייתא) precepts pertaining to *tsitsith*.

Only thereafter can we address ourselves to the question: What is the relationship of the individual components of this symbol, and the symbol as a whole to the idea for which the Divine Law has chosen and ordained it as a reminder.

> "God spoke to Moses as follows: Speak to the sons of Israel and say to them that they make for themselves *tsitsith* on the corners of their garments for all their descendants, and that they put on the *tsitsith* of the corner a thread of sky-blue wool. This shall be to you for *tsitsith* that you may look upon it and remember all the commandments of God, and fulfill them, and not seek after your own heart and your own eyes, which you follow, unfaithful to Me; so that you may remember and fulfill all My commandments and remain holy to your God. I am 'ה, your God, Who has brought you out from the land of Egypt to be God to you; I, 'ה, shall be your God" (Num. 15, 37–41).

Thus, the *tsitsith* on the corners of our garments, and the sky-blue threads within the *tsitsith,* together shall become *tsitsith* for us.

The *purpose* of our looking upon the *tsitsith* should be:

a. That we remember all the commandments of God;

b. That we fulfill them in their entirety;

c. That consequently, when we "seek after," i.e., explore the meaning of God's Law, we should not follow the lead of our hearts and our eyes, which could cause us to become unfaithful to God.

d. That we remain holy to our God.

The foundation for this commandment is our redemption from the land of Egypt, which was accomplished only so that 'ה might be our God.

However, 'ה will be our God only if we fulfill His commandments and remain holy to Him.

The *tsitsith* commandment is reiterated in Deut. 22, 12, immediately following another commandment regarding our clothing; שעטנז. It is stated in one terse sentence: "You shall make yourself *twisted threads* on the four corners of your garment with which you cover yourself."

Let us now turn to the Oral Law (Menachoth 39) for a general description of these threads and twisted cords according to Biblical law. We find that they consist essentially of גדיל (twisted cord) and פתיל (thread). פתיל, usually referred to as ענף (lit. "hanging loose"), is the basic component of the ציצת: אין ציצת אלא ענף. Each *tsitsith* consists of a specified number of threads folded over double. One of these threads is taken and wound around the others to form a cord, from which they then hang down freely. עשה גדיל ופותלייהו מתוכו, חוט של כרך עולה מן המנין, וצריך לפרודה כצוציתא דארמאי. The *tsitsith* should be prepared in such a manner that ענף should be longer than גדיל; i.e., the length of thread left to hang down freely should be double the length of thread formed into a cord: ונויי תכלת שליש גדיל ושני שלישי ענף. These threads, partly formed into a cord, must be firmly attached to the corner of the garment by means of a knot; קשר עליון דאורייתא. However, it is uncertain whether this basic knot must be positioned precisely midway between the corner of the garment and the beginning of the cord, or whether it should be placed at the point where the cord ends and the free-hanging length of thread begins (תוספ' שם ד"ה קשר עליון).

According to רמב"ם and רשב"א, the number of threads for each corner is restricted to eight (i.e., four threads folded over double), including the original thread of תכלת.

The תכלת thread constitutes a מצוה in its own right; however, התכלת אינה מעכבת את הלבן. When, as is the case at present, we cannot obtain the genuine sky-blue violet dye, the threads partly twisted into a cord must be made without that dye. According to the tradition recorded in רמב״ם, only one of the eight threads was violet-blue. The threads were bound together first by one of the white threads, then by the blue thread, and finally again by the white thread; מתחיל בלבן ומסיים בלבן. Moreover, the reference to "white" does not mean that the threads must be white; it merely denotes those threads that are not violet-blue.

Let us now pause at these essential details which present to us the *tsitsith* in terms of their main components as specified by the Law, and search for their relationship to the broad concepts which they are to symbolize under Divine Law.

If we ponder these concepts with this purpose in mind, we will note immediately that they are grouped into prohibiting and positive aspects.

The prohibiting function of *tsitsith* is: לא תתורו אחרי לבבכם ואחרי עיניכם וגו׳.

But the positive function of *tsitsith* is: וזכרתם את כל מצות ה׳ ועשיתם אתם. This is the positive aspect of the commandment, to which the Scriptural text imparts double emphasis. First, it occurs in the verse just quoted. However, even this verse stresses the prohibiting more than the positive function, because a negative element follows from it. That statement is followed by an independent clause which concludes the whole passage on a positive note: למען תזכרו ועשיתם את כל מצותי והייתם קדשים לאלקיכם.

In the Scriptural text we come upon the term תור. The use of that term in this particular context is all the more significant because—except for several instances in Koheleth—Scripture does not use it anywhere else in an ethical and philosophical connotation, but in its literal meaning.

It connotes generally the testing or investigation of the qualities or the character of objects in relation to ourselves. It is never used to describe the nature of an object. Note particularly תור הארץ, to explore a land in order to form a judgment with regard to what that land is capable of giving us, and to determine whether and how we can obtain that land; in general, how the land relates to our wishes and abilities, and whether it is desirable and attainable as far as we are concerned. Similarly, יתור הרים מרעהו ("the range of the mountains is its pasture") (Job 39, 8), referring to an animal that freely roams the woods. The animal grazes on anything that it discovers in the hills, on anything it considers desirable and attainable. Thus, too, in I Kings 10, 15, peddlers, itinerant traders who go from place to place in search of merchandise which they expect to sell at a profit, are called אנשי התרים. Even in Koheleth, the term rarely occurs in an abstract connotation. Koheleth is not seeking to obtain a metaphysical knowledge of things, and even less a knowledge of things as such. He is investigating only the practical value which specific things may have for us. מה יתרון לאדם בכל עמלו וגו׳ ("What profit has man from all his toil . . .") (1, 3); תרתי בלבי וגו׳ עד אשר אראה אי זה טוב לבני האדם אשר יעשו וגו׳ ("I searched in my heart . . . till I might see which it was best for the sons of men that they should do . . .") (2, 3). Koheleth is searching for the practical value of things and actions for man (initially, even irrespective of their moral value).

And here we have arrived at the main point of our discourse. For the general connotation in which the term תור is used in our passage can only mean an assessment of objects and behavior patterns in terms of their practical value for us. The connotation of תור is to ascertain what is, or is not, desirable or attainable for us, to judge what is good or evil for us, to differentiate between good and evil. However, we must add one qualification: תור does not connote merely absolute knowledge but an evaluation that will facilitate the task of deciding what should be pursued and what should be avoided by us.

Wherever אחרי occurs in Scripture, it denotes dependence on, submission to, or "following after," a person or an object; it implies subordination to the leadership of another. מלאו אחרי (Num. 32, 11) היה לב (Prov. 28, 32); מוכיח אדם אחרי לא סרו מאחרי ה׳ (II Chronicles 34, 33); לא תהיה אחרי רבים לרעת, אחרי איש ישראל אחרי אבשלום (II Samuel 15, 13); רבים להטת (Ex. 23, 2).

In view of all the foregoing, לא תתורו אחרי לבבכם ואחרי עיניכם would mean: Do not form judgments by following the impulses of your hearts and eyes! Do not rely on your hearts and eyes in deciding what to accept or what to reject! Do not call anything "good" merely because your hearts are drawn to it and your eyes yearn for it! Do not call anything "evil" merely because it is distasteful to your hearts and to your eyes!

אשר אתם זנים אחריהם: If you subordinate yourselves to the direction and domination of your hearts and eyes, you come to break with God!

Tsitsith are meant to counteract a trend in which man is led solely by his instincts, in which he is held by the bonds of "his heart and his eyes" and knows no higher code of ethics to guide his choice of values and actions than his own wishes and urges.

The knotted threads on our garments are meant to protect us from forming judgments based solely on the dictates of our hearts and our eyes. By looking at them, וראיתם אותו, we are to be reminded of all the commandments of God, וזכרתם את כל מצות ה', and to remember that we are in the service of God with all our faculties and with all the strength of our willpower. He alone tells us what is good and what is evil.

Let us consider the function of the *tsitsith* on this fundamental level. They are to lead us from being the slaves of our physical desires to a state of moral freedom through self-restraint, from a condition of carnal bondage to the level of a free human being. This is what makes us human beings—but not yet Jews. When we have reached this level, we confront God only in general terms as all other human beings do. At this stage we do not yet perceive Him directly as אלקיכם and His commandments as מצותי but still heed His commandments only in indirect terms, as מצות ה'!

For us, as Jews, this elementary requirement, valid for all human beings, assumes a higher, more comprehensive significance. For this invisible God, invisible though He is, has addressed Himself to us directly and revealed to us His Law. He has entered into a particular covenant with us; He has become *our* God, has hallowed us for His service, and has created us for His service not merely as individuals, but as a nation in the midst of the nations.

Every man faces God and thus is expected to control his senses, for he is God's creation. But this obligation rests upon the Jew with double importance, because he is a party to the Divine covenant and the bearer of the revealed Law of God. The Jew must subordinate to God, in an even higher measure, all the sensual aspects of his nature, all his desires and aspirations. He must never lose his awareness of God, mindful at all times that God is *his* God; he must fulfill all of His commandments, ready to do so at all times, at any hour, without hesitation or wavering, without doubts or mental reservations.

The *tsitsith* will not permit us to remain at that elementary level which all human beings are required to attain. They elevate us to that level, but only to say to us: למען תזכרו ועשיתם את כל מצותי והייתם קדשים לאלקיכם אני ה' אלקיכם אשר הוצאתי אתכם מארץ מצרים להיות לכם לאלקים אני ה' אלקיכם!

Follow the calling of Man so that you may then become Jews!

We have interpreted the concept of קדושים as the highest level of Jewish characteristics. It implies an unhesitating, unwavering readiness to serve God. The profound concept of קדושה is best defined by Man's unconditional preparedness to do the Will of God.

קדש always occurs in Scripture as a concept that implies complete dedication or surrender, be it to the absolute good (קדוש) or to evil and immorality (קָדֵש Deut. 23, 18). God also characterizes Himself as קדוש, so that, with reference to God, the adjective קדוש is identical with the idea of the "absolute." It implies an eternal, complete, maximum readiness of will and energy. In this state, doubt and hesitation are completely absent because the moral element in the Supreme Being presents itself in such absolute purity that there can be no conflict.

We can and therefore we ought to raise ourselves to that level of absolute morality, to that state of moral resolve in which we will be receptive, at all times and at any moment, without inner struggle and hesitation, to all that is good and true. This level of morality represents the highest stage of perfection within our reach and, by detaching man's God-given self from dependence on, and enslavement to, our physical nature, assures us of our portion in immortality here on earth. והיה הנשאר בציון והנותר בירושלם קדוש יאמר לו, כל הכתוב לחיים בירושלם, מה קדוש (סנהדרין צ"ב א') לעולם קיים אף הם לעולם קיימים ("*And it shall come to pass that he who is left in Zion and he who remains in Jerusalem shall be called holy, indeed, everyone that is written among the living in Jerusalem (Isaiah 4, 3): As the Holy One endures forever, so shall they endure forever*").

The absolutes of morality and of existence coincide because they derive from one and the same source.

The Garment

מלבוש—בושה

In light of what we have said in the preceding section, it follows that the express purpose of the symbolic threads on our garments is to remind us of our calling as human beings and as Jews, and to admonish us to subordinate the sensual elements in our thoughts and emotions to the entire Law of God.

God chose threads—materials used in the making of clothing, to

remind us of His Law, and He ordered us to attach this symbol to our
garments. Some relation might already exist between clothing, as such,
and the Divine Law in general and its moral calling, so that clothing,
and materials from which clothing is made, might be suited to serve as
a symbol of God's Law and its moral requirements.

God's Law contains numerous references to clothing. In the case of
garments designated for a certain purpose, the Law gives detailed
specifications as to fabrics and colors. Certain garments are considered closely identified with the wearer's calling; that a כהן may offi-
ciate only if he is clothed in the vestments specified for this purpose.

Similarly, the terms בגד, "garment," and, even more so, לבוש "to be
clothed," are commonly used in Scripture to denote the assumption of
specified characteristics. Thus, God has clothed Himself with sovereignty, power and majesty; גאות לבש, לבש ה' עוז, הוד והדר לבשת "He is
clothed in majesty; God is clothed with strength; You are clothed
with glory and majesty" (Ps. 93, 1 and 104,1). וילבש צדקה כשרין וילבש
בגדי נקם תלבשת, "He clothes Himself with benevolence as with an armor
and puts on the garment of vengeance for clothing" (Isaiah 59, 17).
כהניך ילבשו צדק, וכהניה אלביש ישע, "He clothes priests with salvation, and
priests clothe themselves with righteousness" (Ps. 132, 9 and 16).

Job clothes himself with righteousness, and righteousness clothes
itself with him, צדק לבשתי וילבשני (29, 14); Job was תוכו כברו; righteousness was alive within him, his character and actions were of the
same mold.

Scripture also uses clothing as a figure of speech in a negative
connotation. Thus, one can "clothe oneself" with a curse as if it were a
garment suited to him, וילבש קללה כמדו (Ps. 109, 18); and the enemies
of the righteous clothe themselves with shame, שונאיך ילבשו בשת (Job
8, 22).

In all the passages cited above, forms of "garment" and "clothing
oneself" are used as figures of speech to denote the intensification of a
given character trait. Consequently, God's command to attach the
symbol of His Law to our garments may signify that we are to "clothe
ourselves" in lawful conduct, that we should let the Law be the chief
characteristic of our personality and the identifying mark of all our
actions.

In each of these instances, the figure of speech refers to the assumption of any character trait, virtuous or not. But in the context of our
present study our objective is to prove that there is a direct relation-

ship between clothing and fabrics used for clothing, and the Law of God and the morality deriving from it, a relationship so significant that the mere contemplation of these objects becomes an eloquent reminder of God's Law and of our sanctification. If, indeed, there is such a relationship, we must find it in a sphere other than that of mere language.

If we look into the history of clothing, we note one fact on which we must elaborate: Clothing is traced back to the time when man disobeyed a command from God, and it served as the initial means in man's return to his Divine calling.

When the enticements of sensuality won their initial victory over man, shame first addressed itself to him and taught him to cover the sensual manifestations of his body. Only if it is subordinated to the forces of the free-willed, godly element in man is even the most physical aspect of his body pure and holy, serving purposes no less pure, sacred and Divine than the spiritual aspect of human nature. Once he has thus subordinated himself entirely to God, man need not feel ashamed of his body as a physical object, because he then serves God with his body as well as with his spirit. For this reason man could walk about unclothed in the Garden of Eden. All of nature in its own harmony delighted then in man's inner peace and tranquility.

But when sensuality exceeded the limits assigned to it and assumed direction over man, shame draped a loincloth around the sensual part of his body. Thus man is reminded of his human dignity and his Divine calling by virtue of which the sensual aspect of his body, concealed by a covering must retreat, permitting only the godly, free-willed element to come to the fore.

Shame is the awareness of our own inadequacy, the feeling that we have fallen short of the requirements and standards of our calling, that we have not performed according to what is expected of us. The word בוש is actually used in Scripture to express disappointment in one's hopes or expectations. לא יבשו קוי "For they shall not be ashamed that wait for Me" (Isaiah 49, 23) and also ויחילו עד בוש "They waited until they were ashamed" (Judges 3, 25). And we read: וירא העם כי בשש משה (Ex. 32, 1). בושש means to cause disappointment, to stay away longer than expected. "Shame" is the realization of one's shortcomings. The sense of shame derives from a twofold awareness: the awareness of one's true purpose, and the awareness of not having fulfilled it. It is the awareness of one's calling coupled with a sense of guilt. The garment with which shame covers our nakedness reminds us of both: our calling as human beings and our failure to live up to it.

Shame, that messenger of our own conscience, the voice of God within ourselves, also functions as the hand of God that raises up the fallen and does not let him rest until he is on his way back to God and to the high level of his calling. For this reason God excluded man from Paradise and set nature in opposition to him. Henceforth the terrestrial world would be harsh to him, offering him only עצבון, "renunciation," instead of pleasures. Through physical deprivation man might learn to become spiritually free. Through struggle and toil he is to become aware of this great truth: Only if the body subordinates itself to the spirit, and the spirit, in turn, subordinates both the body and itself to God, will God subordinate the terrestrial world to both. Then man will stand upon his earth as the true representative of God, and nature will gladly present its ruler with the tranquility of Paradise. But if the body rebels against the spirit and the spirit rebels against God, then nature, too, will confront them both as an enemy, and instead of the blossoms and fruits of Paradise, only "thorns and thistles" will grow upon the field of mankind. Yet, before the gates of Paradise fell shut behind man, until the time he would be permitted to return there, and when God pushed His children out into harsh reality, He "made them garments to cover their bare skins," thus protecting them from the bitter world that awaited them.

It was shame that concealed their nakedness with leaves, חגורות; it was God's benevolence that covered their naked bodies with clothes, כתנות עור. Hence, every garment, with its dual function of concealment and protection, continues to this day as the most eloquent memorial to that harmony within and without for which we were created, and which at the same time reminds us of the conflict that confronts us when we go astray. We can resolve this conflict only by covering up our nakedness; by subordinating the sensual aspect of our nature to the spiritual, free-willed element within us, and subordinating both of these to God.

In light of the foregoing, clothing and any material from which clothing can be made functions as a powerful reminder of our human calling, and warns us not to forfeit that calling, and with it, our peace with ourselves and the world.

One might even say that, in view of its historical origin as the result of a transgression, clothing should have an even closer, more direct link to that concept of which we are to be constantly reminded by *tsitsith,* that symbol of human clothing.

The commandment of *tsitsith* was not one that could have been regarded as inherent in the human intellect. It was a positive commandment revealed by God, מצות ה', the first test of man's obedience to God's Law.—

It was a "dietary Law"—one of the חוקים—whose purpose was questioned by the ordinary human mind and inclination, as the Sages teach us: יצר הרע ואומות העולם משיבין עליהם. The עץ הדעת טוב ורע is a specified tree which is to serve as a criterion for distinguishing between good and evil. To abide by God's order is "good"; to disobey is "evil."

The tree seemed good to eat, it was a delight for the eyes, it seemed desirable also by any standard of common sense. טוב העץ למאכל, תאוה הוא לעינים, and ונחמד העץ להשכיל (Gen. 3, 6). The tree appealed to the taste, to imagination and to human reason; every human consideration spoke in favor of partaking of the fruit of this tree. Why, then, should God have forbidden it?

A glance at the animal made it clear to man that all other living creatures need never have doubts about what is good or evil for them. They walk unconcerned upon the Eden of earth. Whatever stimulates their senses, whatever promises pleasure is there for them to enjoy and is good for them: conversely, whatever they are not meant to enjoy has no appeal for them, and they pass by it with utter indifference. They do not need a voice from God to tell them what is good or evil. Their eyes and their hearts, their instincts suffice. They do not have to deny themselves anything, for it is, in fact, the voice of God that speaks to them through their eyes and their hearts. Why, then, should man be different? Is it possible that his palate, his eyes and even his reason should tell him, "This is good for you," and that, nevertheless, in deference to an even higher Authority, he should have to avoid it as evil? No, no, the serpent hissed near the tree, והייתם כאלקים ידע טוב ורע, be like God in the knowledge of good and evil! Just try it, ונפקחו עיניכם, and your eyes will be opened. You will see how good that which God has forbidden can be, and henceforth you yourselves will know, like God, what is good and what is evil.

That was the story and its outcome was the garment, the only object that mankind was able to salvage from Paradise. If the garment could speak, could the message to be conveyed by the garment, indeed by every thread that goes into its making, be expressed in better, more appropriate words than these: וראיתם אתו וזכרתם את כל מצות ה׳ ועשיתם אתם ולא תתורו אחרי לבבכם ואחרי עיניכם אשר אתם זנים אחריהם "Look at it, and remember every one of God's commandments and fulfill them, and do not form judgments according to your hearts and your eyes, and, following them, break faith with God."

ציץ, ציצת

Clothing, even in its negative function—that of veiling our shame and covering our body—becomes the most eloquent preacher of the concept to be taught by *tsitsith*. It is a symbol reminding us of man's moral calling, of God's Law, and of our duty to control our sensuality. It warns us against going astray. The symbol of *tsitsith* is the most visibly compelling emblem of these ideas, even if it only directs our attention to our clothing and says to us: Consider your garment, its origin and its purpose.

However, the garment alone does not contain all the lessons to be conveyed by *tsitsith*. Indeed, when contemplating a garment with *tsitsith* our attention is directed not so much to the garment in general but to the knotted fringes that hang from its corners. וראיתם אותו: the sight of this fringe is to serve as a reminder, a warning and an admonition. We must therefore now turn to the fringes and ascertain their relationship to the concept expressed by the symbol of *tsitsith*.

Let us first consider the term ציצת, which obviously describes the symbol in terms of its appearance as well as its purpose. For the commandment clearly states: והיה לכם לציצת, ועשו להם ציצת "Make yourselves *tsitsith,* and they shall be *tsitsith* for you."

אין ציצת אלא ענף. אין ציצת אלא דבר היוצא: ציץ (Menachot 41, 42). The basic connotation of ציץ and צוץ is a movement characterized by "breaking through," a forward push to emerge; it is the most intensive form of the idea conveyed by זיז (projection), סוס (horse, in terms of its forward movements) and שיש (rejoice); also the phonetic affinity between שמח (rejoice) and צמח (growing plant). Hence, ציץ, the parts of a plant—twig, leaf, blossom—that have sprouted, that have "broken through." Similarly, ציצת on the body of an animal denote wings (Targum, Ps. 139, 9), and ציצת on the human head is a "lock of hair" (זבחים כ"ו). Metaphorically, הציץ means to look through a lattice, and ציץ (the Rabbinic term, זיזין הבולטין, "projections") is the engraved plate that "stands out" upon the forehead of the כהן גדול.

Thus, "make yourselves *tsitsith* on your garments" means: Place branches and blossoming sprouts, as it were, upon your garments; cause "sprouts" to emerge from your garments. And what else would these "sprouts" say to us than: Do not wear a garment without reflecting on it; let your garment bear "blossoms" and "sprouts," let it bear the fruit, let it yield the result that is expected from it? והיה לכם לציצת, they shall not be mere symbolic "sprouts" upon your garments. They shall be real, genuine "sprouts" and "blossoms" *for you*. They are to help you yourself "sprout" and "blossom forth;" they are to assist you in your personal development and completion. וזכרתם ועשיתם, וראיתם אותו: the sight of them should guide your spirit to an understanding and your will to the fulfillment of your purpose, whose essence is evidenced by your garment.

And now, examine these "sprouts" upon your garment. Although God's Law bids you knot them, and knot them firmly to your garment, קשר עליון דאורייתא, they are, nevertheless, merely threads of the same kind of material as that from which your garment has been woven. הכנף מין כנף (שם ל"ח). The sole purpose of this commandment is to act as ציצת, to develop your human nature to the highest level of perfection. It does not seek to accomplish anything else than what is already part of your original vocation as a human being. Its observance does not make you into anything else but a human being, a human being at its best, achieving your highest potential as man.

ענף—גדיל *Restraint and Freedom*

Now these "sprouts" to be attached to your garment are both "entwined" (restrained) and "loose." They are bound together at the base but then allowed to hang down freely beyond that point. First, there is a bundle formed by threads wound tightly over them. Emanating from this bundle are "sprouts" that are allowed to hang loose. It is from the "restraint" that the free threads flow: צריך לפרודה כצוציתא דארמא, (מנחות מ"ב) עשה גדיל ופותלייהו מתוכו, (ל"ט).

The simple description of this arrangement conveys the message of these symbolic threads.

All the "sprouts" and forces that lie dormant within the human being should indeed develop and attain full bloom, but not without controls. That which is to become ציצת must first have been גדיל. That which is to develop freely must first make itself fit into the מוסר, into the מסרת הברית (Ezek. 20, 37). It must submit to that bond which encircles and restrains all the energies that strive for expression. This very submission makes the highest form of freedom attainable.

Let us examine our symbolic bundle of "sprouts." The idea conveyed by its threads is not restraint from the outside, but *self-restraint*. It is not an alien, extraneous bond that binds these threads which emanate from man's garment. חוט של כרך עולה מן המנין; the thread that is wound over the others to "restrain" them is itself one of the threads that "sprouted forth" from man's garment. The restraining force is innate in man himself; it is that force of free self-determination which makes man into a human being. Man is to restrain himself of his own free will and to adapt himself with all his own energies to a higher order. הִוָּסְרוּ (Ps. 2, 10), "If you wish to become free, restrain yourselves of your own free will." That is the great sermon of the fringes.

Now let us look again at our symbolic bundle of "sprouts." גדיל and ציצת (ענף), restraint and freedom, limitation and unfolding, negation and positive expression, prohibition and commandment: this is the message of the fringes, so that they are completely in character with the thought they are meant to implant in our hearts. גדיל (the twisted cord) tells us לא תתורו and ענף (the bundle of threads hanging loose and free) adds למען תזכרו ועשיתם, thus teaching us truly to understand the significance of the word למען. No thread, no "sprout," no human energy is to be "tied off" or suppressed. Each human potential is given the chance to develop freely; it is only restrained by the bond of the bundle in order that, within this bundle and sustained by it, it may be realized in all the more freedom and equality. The prohibitions—לא תתורו—help bring out the Divine in man; the positive commandments—ועשיתם—teach us the goals whose realization is the end that truly justifies all our forces. Only by obeying God's prohibitions does man truly become master over himself. By fulfilling God's commandments he learns to rejoice in himself, and also in his talents and energies because he gladly employs them in His service. Only in His service does man become happily aware of himself and of his life's purpose. If the fruit of the prohibition is not limitation but mastery, so, too, the fruit of the commandment is not coercion but joy: פקודי ה׳ ישרים משמחי לב (Ps. 19, 9).

Also, there is more freedom than restraint, more unfolding than restriction. נויי תכלת שליש גדיל ושני שלישי ענף "The length of the twisted cord is one-third; that of the free-hanging threads, two-thirds." In every sphere of life, more will be permitted by the Law than forbidden. Of course, to one who is overcome by his senses, a single prohibition which forbids him to partake of just one fruit looms so large that he considers all of Paradise lost. But to the pure human spirit serving God, the forbidden is negligible compared with the abundance of the fruits of Paradise granted him by God.

The Colors—The Numbers

תכלת

Thus far we have studied the *tsitsith* symbol without regard to the תכלת thread and to the number of threads that belong in it, because the former is not מעכב (indispensable) and tradition is not quite clear with regard to the latter.

We have seen that, even without these two components, *tsitsith* admonishes us strongly to observe the commandments of God and to subordinate our physical nature to His will. Even without these two components, *tsitsith* teaches us, in self-restraint and through our free development derived from self-control, the paths we must take in order to fulfill this task. Hence, essentially, the *tsitsith* symbol, even without the two components named above, already conveys the ideas implicit in the Biblical verses למען תזכרו וגו׳, and וזכרתם וגו׳.

However, one thought still remains to be discussed. Thus far we have dealt only with the general human aspects of the commandment. We have not yet addressed ourselves to the specifically Jewish aspect, the selection and sanctification of the people of Israel for the Divine Law that was revealed to them as a consequence of their redemption from Egypt. This particular aspect is set forth clearly in the second part of the commandment.

True, by reminding the Jew of the obedience he owes to God's commandments, the garment is especially suited to remind him of the Law that was revealed expressly to him. The garment can perform this function particularly because it owes its origin to man's transgression of a positive commandment which, let it be noted, was known to Chava through a communication from Adam, conveying to her the commandment of God (תורה שבעל פה).

פתיל תכלת

ונתנו על ציצת הכנף פתיל תכלת. The תכלת color, which tradition describes as blue-violet, is mentioned in God's Law only in connection with the Sanctuary.

The high priest wore a מעיל כליל תכלת, a mantle all of תכלת color. When the Ark of the Covenant traveled before the Children of Israel in their wanderings through the wilderness, it was covered with בגד כליל תכלת מלמעלה, an outer covering all of תכלת color. The other accessories of the Sanctuary—the table, the menorah, the altar of incense and all the utensils used within the Sanctuary—were covered directly with an inner cover of תכלת. Thus, the High Priest and the Ark appeared draped in תכלת. Similarly, we note פתיל תכלת, threads and loops of תכלת wherever separate objects had to be connected or bound together for the purpose of the Sanctuary. The יריעות were joined into one piece by לולאות תכלת, loops of תכלת. The High Priest's breastplate was joined to his אפוד with פתיל תכלת, threads of תכלת, to form one inseparable unit. Also the ציץ, the frontal plate worn by the High Priest, was held by a פתיל תכלת.

We may insert here a conjecture regarding the significance of the Hebrew names for the colors. We find only three terms to encompass the colors of the spectrum: אדום for red, ירק for yellow and green, and תכלת for blue and violet.

The only other form in which the root אדם occurs in Scripture is as אדם, "man." אדמה is undoubtedly derived from אדם, thus characterizing the earth as the soil for human dominion, the earthly world wed to man (as אשה is to איש) but not in the reverse. We recognize the root אדם again in הדם, the root of הדום, "footstool," and also in אדן, the root of אדן, "the base of a column." Accordingly, we believe that אדם designates man as הדום רגלי שכינה ("the footstool for the foot of the Divine

Presence"), the bearer and agent for the Divine and for God's dominion on earth. הדום is nothing other than an object that meets the foot as it moves toward the ground, offering the foot a place of rest and thus sparing it the trouble of having to step squarely on the ground. Thus the position of a human being in between earth and God could hardly be expressed in more significant terms than הדום = אדם.

The only other form of ירק we find is ירוק, "to cast away from oneself." (Num. 12, 14)

תכלת, being derived from כלה, would mean literally, "the end."

Within the spectrum which is shown by the rainbow through the refraction of light and which is present wherever a prism breaks up a ray of light, the Hebrew language combines the colors into three groups, in the following order: red, yellow-green and blue-violet.

Red is the least refracted ray; it is the closest to the unbroken ray of light that is directly absorbed by matter. Red is light in its first fusion with the terrestrial element: הדום = אדום. (Is this not again man, the image of God as reflected in physical, earthly matter: ותחסרהו מעט מאלקים (Ps. 8, 6).

The next part of the spectrum is yellow-green: ירק.

Blue-violet is at the end of the spectrum: תכלת.

The spectrum visible to our eye ends with the violet ray, תכלת, but additional magnitudes of light radiate unseen beyond the visible spectrum. Likewise, the blue expanse of the sky forms the end only of the earth that is visible to us. And so תכלת is simply the bridge that leads thinking man from the visible, physical sphere of the terrestrial world into the unseen sphere of heaven beyond.

The basic color of the Sanctuary was blue-violet. For the Law of God originated neither from the light that is contained in earthly matter, nor from the Divine spark that is innate in man. It was handed to us from beyond the limits of physically visible matter; מן השמים השמיעך את קלו (Deut. 4, 36). It was handed to us by God Himself. If we obey it, the heavens will incline toward us. The color reflecting the splendor of heaven will then enrich man and all things human, ועשו לי מקדש ושכנתי בתוכם (Ex. 25, 8), and the glory of God will dwell in our midst.

תכלת is the basic color of the Sanctuary and of the High Priest's vestments; the color blue-violet representing heaven and the things of heaven that were revealed to Israel; תכלת דומה לים וים דומה לרקיע ורקיע

לכסא הכבוד שנאמר ותחת רגליו כמעשה לבנת הספיר וכעצם השמים לטוהר (מנחות מ״ג).
Therefore no other color was as appropriate as תכלת to signify God's
special relationship with Israel. A thread of תכלת color on our garments conferred upon all of us the insignia of our high-priestly calling,
proclaiming to all of us: אנשי קדש תהיון לי ("And you shall be holy men
to Me"—Ex. 22, 30), and symbolically expressing our calling: ואתם
תהיו לי ממלכת כהנים וגוי קדוש ("and you shall be to Me a kingdom of
priests and a holy nation" Ex. 19, 6).

If we now turn our attention to the פתיל תכלת on our *tsitsith,* we will
note that it was precisely this thread of תכלת color that formed the
כריכות, the גדיל, the thread wound around the other threads to make a
cord. In other words, the vocation of the Jew, the Jewish awareness
awakened by the Sanctuary, that power which is to prevail within us,
must act to unite all our kindred forces within the bond of the Sanctuary of God's Law.

Our calling as Jews, our Jewish awareness, cannot be separated
from our calling as members of humanity. It is certainly not alien to
our human vocation. The Jew cannot dispense with the requirements
of his calling as a man, or expect to realize his purpose without the
latter. The fulfillment of our calling as Jews is linked to our calling as
members of humanity and serves to perfect us in the fulfillment of our
human vocation. The Jew can accomplish his purpose as a Jew only
within the context of his purpose as a human being. The highest degree
of Jewish perfection is nothing else but the highest level of accomplishment in human destiny. Thus, too, the winding of the threads in *tsitsith*
begins and ends with the ordinary thread (לבן) used in the making of
man's garments, taking the תכלת threads into the center. תנא כשהוא
מתחיל מתחיל בלבן הכנף מין כנף, וכשהוא מסיים בלבן מעלין בקדש ולא מורידין.
(מנחות ל״ט)

רש״י comments as follows:
מין כנף תחלה ואח״כ פתיל תכלת וכיון דאקדמה קרא למין כנף ש״מ חשוב הוא לפיכך אי
מסיים בתכלת הוה ליה מוריד סוף הציצת מתחילתה.

נימוקי יוסף explains:
לא משום שהלבן חשוב מן התכלת שהתכלת דומה לכסא הכבוד אלא דכיון דהעלתו ללבן
תחילה מטעם הכנף מין כנף אין מורידין אותו ויעשו ממנו קשר האחרון שהוא קיום הבנין
כן פרש״י ז״ל.

רמב״ם interprets it as follows:
וכריכה אחרונה של לבן מפני שהתחיל בו לבן מסיים שמעלין בקדש ולא מורידין.

Since one ends with the same type of thread as one began, the concept of מעלין ולא מורידין in *this* context requires further comment. וצ"ע

שמנה חוטין

We have already noted that tradition is not quite clear with regard to the Biblical commandment concerning the number of threads in the *tsitsith*. Likewise, there are varied views regarding the proportion of the number of תכלת threads to the others. However, if we accept the proposition followed by general practice and also established halachically by רמב"ם (הל' ציצת פ"א הלכה ו' עיין בכ"מ) that the total number of threads is eight, and if we link this assumption with that of the relation of the תכלת threads to the others, which was also stated by רמב"ם and is supported by the wording of the Scriptural text and by ספרי, we will see that this numerical ratio serves only to enhance the significance of our symbol.

For according to רמב"ם, the fourth of the threads to be folded over double was תכלת-colored in only half of its length, so that the *tsitsith* consisted of seven threads that were white (or the color of the garment to which they were attached) and the eighth thread that was תכלת-colored. Thus, in each fringe, six threads were surrounded by a seventh thread of white and an eighth thread of תכלת.

We believe that we have already established in our essay on *milah* the symbolic significance of the numbers seven and eight. There we noted how the scale of tones progress to a harmonious conclusion with the number seven, only to begin again with the number eight but on a higher level. We also noted that certain phases and developments reached the goal of their progress with the number seven, only to enter into a new, higher phase with the number eight. We have observed this numerical series particularly in God's work of Creation in the history of mankind. The visible world, created in six days was given the seventh day as a day of remembrance and as a covenant with the invisible Lord and Creator. This seventh day marks the completion of Creation. The eighth work of God, the creation of the people of Israel, laid the foundation for a world and mankind reborn and raised to a higher level. It is the cornerstone for those שמים חדשים and that ארץ חדשה for which Israel and its vocation is to serve as His agent in bringing about a renewal of the world (Isaiah 65, 17).

Accordingly, we noted the number seven in both language and Law as a symbol of God, the invisible One Who rules over the visible world and Who has made a covenant with it as its Lord and Master. The number eight symbolizes the people of Israel, the agent appointed by God to effect the rebirth of the world.

Now the "sprout" and "blossom" symbol upon our garment shows us the numbers six, seven and eight in its threads, thus placing before our eyes all the elements from which our character is formed and which, through us, will attain the flowering and development ordained for them by the will of God.

The physical aspects of the human body, like all the rest of the physical, visible world of Creation are symbolized by the number six.

The emanation of God, unseen and originating from the invisible One, is symbolized by. the number seven.

The vocation of Israel, rooted in the historic selection of Israel, is symbolized by the number eight.

These are the elements from which we are woven; these are the threads that God has placed into our hands so that we may unite them into one harmonious whole, to develop them in accordance with His will and thereby fulfill our calling, both as men and as Jews, in the midst of our world and by means of all powers placed at our disposal.

As human beings, and even more so as Jews, we are to subordinate, with free-willed, godlike energy, our "six" to the "seventh" and the "eighth." We must control our physical, sensual element by means of the human and Jewish element within us; we are to restrain the former by means of the latter, and bind up the former with the latter into inextricable knots. But then we must permit all our faculties, held together by this bond, to unfold freely in equal importance and in complete harmony.

That is the message of the six threads which are surrounded and held together tightly by the seventh and eighth threads, and kept firmly in place by tight knots, from which they flow forth freely from our garment, together with the seventh and eighth threads, each equal and parallel to the other, as *tsitsith* threads.

In view of the foregoing, there is no need for further explanation to show that the interpretation of the רמב״ם, according to which only the eighth thread was of תכלת color, accords fully with the symbolic significance of both the number eight and the תכלת color.

ארבע כנפות

גדלים תעשה לך על ארבע כנפות כסותך אשר תכסה בה, "Make yourself twisted cords upon the four corners of your garment with which you cover yourself." These are the words of the second Scriptural passage (Deut. 22, 12) setting forth the law of *tsitsith*. ארבע כנפות, "upon the four corners of your garment" is an additional specification to which we have not yet addressed ourselves but which plays such a basic and significant role in the language of the symbol that tradition explicitly states: על ארבע כנפות כסותך ארבע ולא שלש; the law of *tsitsith* cannot be carried out with a garment that has only three corners. ארבע ציציות מעכבות זו את זו שארבעתן מצוה אחת "the four *tsitsith* are interdependent, for together, they form one *mitzvah*." (מנחות כ"ח)

The specification that *tsitsith* must be attached to the four corners of the garment occurs only in the second Scriptural passage relating to *tsitsith*. The first passage (Num. 15, 37) merely states, in general terms, that the *tsitsith* must be placed "on the corners of their garments." However, as we have already noted, these two passages are complementary. The first passage is the commandment relating to the ענף (פתיל, ציצת), the parts of the threads that are not restrained but allowed to hang down freely. The second passage deals with the גדיל, the parts of the threads around which the two other threads are wound to form a cord.

If we look more closely at these two Biblical passages, we will note that the first one names בגדים "garments," or "clothes," as the object of the commandment, while the second refers to כסות, "covering," which it further defines as אשר תכסה בה, "with which you cover yourself."

We note yet another peculiarity worth remembering. In the first passage, the corners of the garment are called כנפי; in the second, כנפות (both stat. construc.).

The origin of clothing shows us that, from the very beginning, clothes have a two-fold function: concealing (moral) and protection (physical). It was man's sense of shame, which is innate in him, a constant reminder of his higher moral purpose, that taught him to use clothing to cover his nakedness. But it was God's mercy that provided man with clothes to protect his naked body against the assaults of a world of nature turned hostile and unpleasant.

Our two Biblical passages appear to parallel these two functions of clothing.

Although בגד is the term most generally used for "garment," the literal meaning of the root בגוד, "to be unfaithful," "to deceive," already hints that בגד essentially denotes clothing as a means of "covering over" (or "concealing") for the sake of outer appearance. It thus seems to accord with the moral requirement of shame.

כסות, on the other hand, as a noun form, like מכסה and כסוי, seems to denote primarily a protective covering, although, indeed, כסה can denote a covering for any purpose, including concealment from the view of others. Thus: כי הוא כסותה לבדה (Ex. 22, 26), מכסה התבה (Gen. 8, 13), and מכסה האהל (Ex. 40, 19). As regards the covering of the sacred utensils during Israel's wanderings, the בגד תכלת (Num. 4, 7), and the בגד תולעת שני (Num. 4, 8) that were intended as concealing covers, are distinguished clearly in the Biblical text from the כסוי עור תחש and the מכסה עור תחש (Num. 4, 6;14 and Num. 4, 8;11 and 12, respectively), which served as a protective covering.

The terms כנפי and כנפות are also not synonymous. They relate to each other in the same manner as קרני and קרנות, ידי and ידות, עיני and עינות, etc.

קרני, קרנים, denote primarily horns in the literal sense of the term. Even when used as a metaphor, it denotes those functions of force, defense or attack which are performed by an animal with its horns. By contrast, קרנות is never used to denote horns in the literal sense. It may denote man-made instruments of destruction, but in most cases Scripture employs it in the metaphoric meaning of "corners," as in קרנות המזבח ("the high corners of the altar"). Similarly, ידות, as distinct from ידים, denotes "cones" or "parts," and עינות, as distinct from עינים, is used in Scripture only for "wellsprings," never for "eyes." The same is true of כנפי as distinct from כנפות.

כנפים, is the masculine plural of כנף (related to גנב, to withdraw or take something from another). ולא יכנף עוד מוריך, "your teachers will no longer be hidden from you," והיה עיניך ראות את מוריך but "your eyes shall see your teachers" (Isaiah 30, 20). כנפים always denotes literally wings or the covering parts of wings, or metaphorically what it is that wings do for birds. כנפות is never used in Scripture to denote wings in the literal sense. Apart from the passage under study (Deut. 22, 12), כנפות occurs only as כנפות הארץ, where, much like קרנות, it connotes only ends, directions, the regions of the world. Thus, while כנפי בגד denote the "wings" of the garment that complete the "covering over" of the body, the expressions כנפות בגד and כנפות כסות would not connote the effect of the כנף as such, but, as in כנפות הארץ, would denote only "ends" or "directions."

על כנפי בגדיהם, literally, "on the wing-corners of their garments"— this is the wording of the *tsitsith* commandment in the Biblical passage where the garment is referred to as בגד, in its function of "covering over" the nakedness of the human body. ופרשת כנפך על אמתך (Ruth 3, 9). The significance of כנף in *tsitsith* as that part in which the concealing function of the garment seems to be concentrated, is so basic that *tsitsith* attached too close to the hem, or too far away from it, are considered פסול. They are כשר only if their position is already, and still, תוך שלש, רחוק מלא קשר גודל (מנחות מ"ב) i.e. כנף;.

But in the passage which refers to the garment as כסות, in its function of warming and protecting the human body, and which specifies that *tsitsith* must be attached to the "four corners" of the garment, the wording is not על ארבעת כנפי כסותך, but על ארבע כנפות כסותך. We will therefore have to seek the significance of this commandment in terms of the garment's function as a means of protection against outside elements, not in terms of its function to conceal what it envelops.

But note that there is one word, לדרתם, in the first passage which we have not yet considered and to which על ארבע כנפות in the second passage may perhaps serve as a contrasting complement.

לדרתם: The passage referring to תכלת = ציצת = בגד directs us to the voice of God within us, which, in the form of shame, makes us aware of our higher moral calling as human beings. This passage demands of us not to ignore that Voice and show us that we can satisfy the demands of that Voice only by subordinating all the physical aspects of our nature to the Law of God, which brings our human vocation to its most complete development within Judaism. Only by seemingly limiting ourselves can we truly bring about the fullest development of our human abilities and powers. We Jews can fulfill our vocation as human beings only through our Judaism; only as Jews can we become truly perfect as human beings. על כנפי בגדיהם לדרתם for all their generations, לדרתם for all their ages! Even if one day they should become דור חם, having entered an era of apparent consummate moral perfection (as תנא דבי אלי׳ puts it with such profound insight), there will never be a generation of Jews that could waive this symbol of warning or that should seek to attain moral perfection as human beings upon a foundation other than the foundation of Judaism and of an unabridged Divine Law.

על כנפי בגדיהם לדרתם, God says, על כנפי בגדיהם לדרתם. For this Law of God represents not a beginning, but a final accomplishment. It is not a preliminary stage which will become outdated in time and upon which some future generation might look down with cynical disdain. It is, rather, the supreme goal toward which all our generations, לדרתם, from century to century, should strive. As long as man is aware of his humanity, God will attach the "blossoming" symbol of His Law to our human garment, saying, אני ה' אלקיכם אשר הוצאתי אתכם מארץ מצרים להיות לכם לאלקים אני ה' אלקיכם "I, ה', your God, Who brought you forth from the land of Egypt to be God to you, I, ה', am still your God." There never will be an era that can emancipate you from My service. (See ספרי ibid.)

The word לדרתם documents that the Divine Law, symbolized by the *tsitsith,* is binding for all time to come. This concept is complemented by the specification על ארבע כנפות כסותך, with the same meaning as ד' כנפות הארץ, indicating that the Law is independent of space; it is applicable no matter where Jews may dwell, enduring through all time, everywhere and forever, in ever-youthful vigor.

על ארבע כנפות כסותך! The concept documented in the symbols of גדילים = כסות points to the contrast between man and his environment. It teaches man self-restraint by recalling the Paradise he lost when he surrendered to the impulse of a fleeting moment. But man, and the Jew in particular, requires something more than only a warning not to forfeit the tranquility of Paradise by succumbing to sensuality. He needs more than a warning to regain that peace by exercising self-control. He must be on guard lest this external dichotomy—in which he has found himself ever since, armed only with his clothing, he left the gentle Paradise to face the vicissitudes of a harsher world—cause him to disintegrate within. It is particularly the Jew who must be made aware that, torn by many conflicts, he must exercise his own unique self-discipline, and, steadfastly and single-mindedly, pursue his own path back to the Tree of Life.

Having forfeited Paradise, with only his clothing to protect him, man has had to wrest his existence from a natural environment that is antagonistic to his survival. He must eat his bread as לחם, a prize won in a battle he has had to fight by the sweat of his brow, with a spirit created to look toward God. Ever since man's loss of Paradise, the ability to survive has become an objective so highly prized that our yearning for Paradise has made us embellish our own sterile existence with the artificial blossoms of ever-growing self-deception. As a result, man is in danger of losing sight of the real purpose of his existence and its material blessings, and to sacrifice his human dignity, his human calling, and his human morality, all for one wretched moment and for one miserable fling of transient ecstasy.

Judaism ennobles man's working clothes by adorning them with the symbol of the freedom inherent in high-priestly self-control, and by teaching him to knot the גדילים to the כסות. Judaism, despite thorns and thistles, sweat and toil—or perhaps precisely because of these—understands how to preserve for man his human vocation, his human dignity, his morality and his holiness.

However, this struggle of man against nature has set off also a struggle of man against man. Man who has mastered nature and must make and keep it subservient to himself over and over again by the sweat of his brow, becomes an egotist. He will view every other man only as a rival, as one more obstacle on his path to survival and contentment. If he is to view his fellow man at his side with peaceable tolerance, indeed, with feelings of friendship and brotherhood, he must first be convinced in his egotism that such a friendly co-existence will be of advantage to him, that sociability and a division of labor with his fellow man will enrich his own existence and make it easier. Men join—and split apart—into groups. Self-interest promotes unity within the group and hostility toward those outside the other group. For the goal of the group now is a concerted effort to wrest from its neighboring group the largest area of territory possible in order to rule over it and to exploit its natural resources.

And into the midst of these self-interest groups that populate the globe God now sends the sons of His people with the גדילים בכסותם, the Divine symbol of high-priestly dedication to God's Law upon their "working clothes." This is in every respect a most eloquent protest against all the dictates with which egotism and self-interest, covertly and overtly, seek to shape the lives of men and nations all over the world.

גדילים תעשה לך על ארבע כנפות כסותך אשר תכסה בה! The priestly insignia of the Divine Law on our garments are not meant to be worn in only one part of the world. Conforming to the ארבע כנפות הארץ, we wear them in every land, in any part of the world where we may dwell. True, God has destined Eretz Yisrael for us; we were to translate the Divine Law into reality in a land of our own, a soil free from all alien influences, and to demonstrate to an awe-struck world how the blessings and the prosperity will result from the fulfillment of the Law, and how, by dedicating personal, family and national life totally to the fulfillment of the Law of the One God, man can regain Paradise. This was our mission in the past, and this is our vision of the future.

When God chose us for His Law, He prepared us for a two-fold mission. Even before we set foot on that soil, He foresaw that this land, one nation's renewed Paradise could be lost through failure to obey His command. It would be regained only by a repentant return באחרית הימים, after long centuries of trials and tribulations. He foresaw and proclaimed that, instead of being ישראל in our land, we would be יזרעאל, a seed of God scattered among all the lands and nations of the world. Dispersed among the nations, in the realms of "idols of wood and stone," we would not only have to hold our ground in the struggle against nature and man, but we would also emerge victorious in our all-out battle for survival against the fierce hatred we would incur among the nations because of our adherence to the Law of God. And in this very struggle it will be our task to make all the world aware of the power of His Law and of its almighty protective strength.

That is why He said to us: Make yourself symbols of your free-willed priestly dedication to the Law of God, and bind them firmly to your garment אשר תכסה בה, with which you gird yourself to wage the struggle for your survival, על ארבע כנפות כסותך, in all four directions, toward the east and the west, south and north. Wherever you may set foot in your wanderings in search of survival, be it in the torrid South, the frozen North, the unchanging East or the ever-changing West, wherever you may go, you are to carry with you the symbol of the Ark of your God's covenant. Wherever you go, you will have the same duty to fulfill. Our law is not dictated by the conditions encountered on our wanderings. The Law that we will take with us will be the unchanging norm for our life wherever we may be. The scene may change, but our task remains. Be steadfast and true! For in this steadfastness lies our vocation and also our happiness. If we endure and persevere, the time will come when the nations will strive to join with us, as it is written:

כה אמר ה׳ צבאו׳ בימים ההמה אשר יחזיקו עשרה אנשים מכל לשנות הגוים, והחזיקו בכנף איש יהודי לאמר נלכה עמכם כי שמענו אלקים עמכם.

Thus צבאו׳ ה׳ has promised: In those days it shall come to
pass that when ten men out of all the languages of the
nations will seek a support, they will take hold of the
corner of the garment of a Jewish man, and they will say:
We will go with you, for we have heard that God is with
you.

—Zechariah 8, 23

A Parallelism:

מילה—ציצת

Many ordinances related to ציצת—none of them דאורייתא—should
be examined in the light of our exhaustive study of the main aspects of
מצות ציצת and its symbolic content. We did not examine the significance of the number of כריכות, חוליות and קשרים, the number of
windings, divisions and knots in the *tsitsith,* the total of which,
combined with the numerical value of the word ציצת, is customarily
interpreted as an allusion to God and His holy Law. We made this
omission purposely because all these specifications are not דאורייתא.

Nevertheless, an exhaustive study of the subject would have to
consider several more specifications whose origin is דאורייתא. Among
these is, for instance, the specification stating that, at least to a given
extent, the material of the garment and of the thread must be צמר
ופשתים, either wool or flax. This restriction certainly has a relationship
to the character of the symbol. However, we will reserve the in-depth
consideration of this particular subject for our commentary on שעטנז, a
law related to clothing, which in fact has a basic relationship to the
tsitsith commandment.

[Editor's note: צמר ופשתים are regarded everywhere as the only
natural clothing materials (ד׳ יבמות). ציצת, as the symbolic ideal result
of the concept of clothes, are therefore preferably made from these
materials. (The ramifications of this דין are discussed in או״ח סימן ט׳.)

צמר-wool represents animal-derived material in clothing and
פשתים-flax represents plant-derived material. At Creation the world
was founded on the principle of למינו—each to its own kind. Hence the
laws which prohibit admixture (כלאי זרע בהמה ובגד, בשר בחלב, עריות) are
intended to preserve for man his למינו—his own calling. Man is
composed of both "higher" animal (perception, feeling, will and
motion) and "lower" vegetative (urges for food and reproduction)

forces. In the non-human world the "higher" forces serve and find their purpose in the "lower" vegetative ones; man submits both to the supremacy of his will, but assigns each to its distinctive function. Clothes, by their historical significance for man to carry out his moral vocation, are therefore not to contain a mixture (שעטנז) of the animal and plant (vegetative) worlds (צמר ופשתים יחדו). Hence the law of שעטנז enhances the moral meaning of clothes.

שעטנז teaches us in a negative sense not to be an animal. ציצת in a positive sense is the sanctification and subordination of the *whole* human being, with all his diverse forces, by and for the Torah. In *this* case the difference between the animal and vegetative forces of man's nature is eliminated and therefore the שעטנז law can be suspended in order to fulfill מצות ציצת. However, we do not practice this tolerance of שעטנז in the case of ציצת as we are not nowadays able to complete the מצות ציצת by the תכלת thread. Hence the specific juxtaposition (סמוכים) of the laws of שעטנז and ציצת from which the general rule עשה דוחה לא תעשה is derived.

See commentary to Levit. 19, 19 and Deut. 22, 11–12 and *Horeb,* Chapters 39 and 57.]

The requirement that *tsitsith* can be manufactured only by a ישראל and only לשמה is clear in view of the fact that this symbol aims to document the vocation of the Jew in a comprehensive manner. Similarly, the specification that טלית שאולה פטור, one need attach *tsitsith* only to garments that belong to the wearer personally, becomes readily understandable if one considers that, as we have already seen, this symbol is basically linked to the relationship between the garment and the human personality, and to man's need for clothing both as a covering for his nakedness and as a protection against the elements.

The reference of *tsitsith* to daytime; i.e., that the *tsitsith* commandment, as מצות עשה שהזמן גרמה, is applicable to a daytime garment or during daytime, may already have been clarified in our essay on *milah.* What *milah* means for our bodies, *tsitsith* expresses for our clothing which cover our bodies.

We have outlined the parallels between the commandments and the ideas they represent, as follows:

מילה = לא תתורו
פריעה = למען תזכרו
ביום = אני ה' אלקיכם
שמיני = אשר הוצאתי אתכם

In light of our evaluation, it appears that מילה = גדיל and פריעה = ענף. With regard to the specification restricting the wearing of *tsitsith* to daytime, we recall to the reader the pertinent references in the discussion of *milah*.

It is indeed peculiar that the *tsitsith* commandment does not require us to wear a suitable garment to which the *tsitsith* symbol has to be attached. The Law requires of us only that, should we wear a garment to which the *tsitsith* commandment is applicable, we must attach *tsitsith* to its corners. Thus, the commandment only teaches us its symbol; it does not state positively that we are duty bound to get ourselves a garment requiring *tsitsith*.

We do not know of any other comparable commandment with this peculiarity, except to a certain extent in the case of a *mezuzah,* where the commandment to attach *mezuzoth* is applicable only to certain specified types of doorposts, but we are not commanded to use doorposts that meet these specifications.

The following may elucidate this problem: The text reads: ויאמר ה' אל משה לאמר, דבר אל בני ישראל ואמרת אליהם ועשו להם ציצת וגו'. We believe that this preamble is without a parallel in the legislative portion of Torah, with the exception of Levit. 21, 1, ויאמר ה' אל משה אמר וגו'. The text, as a general rule, uses the word ויאמר only to introduce discursive or narrative statements, or directives called for by the immediate needs of the moment. The word commonly used to introduce purely legislative regulations is וידבר. Furthermore, no other commandment opens with the past tense and ו' ההיפוך (*vav conversivum*) as ועשו להם in our text. In a direct form of address, the text uses the imperative: ואמרת אלהם קדשים תהיו, or, more commonly, in indirect discourse, it employs the future tense; דברו אל כל עדת ישראל וגו' ויקחו להם איש שה — דבר אל בני ישראל ויקחו, ויסעו. The past tense with *vav conversivum* occurs only in the concluding clause of a conditional statement; ואם עז קרבנו וגו' והקריבו; כי תשא את ראש וגו' ונתנו, et al., or with reference to the purpose and fulfillment of a preceding general instruction; דבר אל בני ישראל ויקחו לי תרומה, ועשו לי מקדש, ועשו ארון.

The *tsitsith* commandment should have declared in categorical terms: דבר אל בני ישראל ויעשו להם ציצת; say to the sons of Israel "that they make for themselves *tsitsith* on their garments." However, the text reads: דבר אל בני ישראל ואמרת אלהם ועשו להם. This means: say to them and urge them in such a manner that, as a consequence of your address, they will attach *tsitsith* to their garments. Let the making of the *tsitsith* be a *consequence,* not the categorically commanding content, of your words.

However, if we now search for the connection between the peculiarity described above and the basic character of the *tsitsith* symbol, we would know of no better source to find it than in the basic character of the object with which that symbol is most closely linked as a complement and extension. The human garment was not draped around man's physical nakedness in fulfillment of a positive commandment but as a result of shame; i.e., the awareness of moral imperfection and weakness. Such a realization of one's own moral imperfection and of one's need for protection against the temptations of sensuality is the most important factor in working towards man's moral uplifting and perfection.

In Jewish law, man's awareness of his own moral imperfection and need for protection is to be intensified by *tsitsith* only in relation to the function of Jewish morality representing a mission of the highest level. Accordingly, this awareness should be properly cultivated and demonstrated in that the Jewish individual, impelled by his own sense of imperfection and weakness, as well as by his awareness of the moral goal set for him should, of his own free will, reach for the means that God has offered to him: ועשו להם ציצת.

תפלין

מצות תפלין

The two symbolic commandments which we have examined more closely up to this point, namely, those of *milah* and *tsitsith,* address themselves primarily to the physical impulses intrinsic to human nature. We have stated that the control and sanctification of these impulses and forces constitute the essence of these symbolic requirements.

We will now pursue the study of a commandment that is a symbol of both the spiritual and practical aspects of life: the commandment of *tefillin.* Scripture explicitly describes *tefillin* as לאות על ידך ולזכרון בין עיניך, a sign and a reminder to be worn upon the arm and the head, as a symbol addressed to the centers of action and thought.

According to the requirements of this commandment, as taught by tradition, four passages from the Torah: קדש (Ex. 13, 1–10), והיה כי יבאך (Ex. 13, 11–16), שמע (Deut. 6, 4–9) and והיה אם שמע (Deut. 11, 13–21), written on parchment and inserted into cubed parchment casings, are to be bound by leather straps around the upper part of the left arm toward the heart, and above the forehead perpendicularly upon the space between the eyes. The four passages essentially form one unit. Even the slightest imperfection in their writing on the parchment renders them unfit for use in the observance of the *tefillin* commandment. ארבע פרשיות שבתפלין מעכבות זו את זו ואפילו כתב אחד מעכבן (מנחות כ"ח).

All the components of the *tefillin*—the hides used in producing the parchment for the writing and for the compartments, the hides from which the leather straps are made, the sinews with which the casings are sewn, and the animal hair with which the parchment scrolls are tied around inside the casings—must be the products of טהור animals. לא הוכשרו למלאכת שמים אלא עור בהמה טהורה בלבד (שבת ק"ח). For the תפלין של ראש the four passages are inscribed on four separate pieces of parchment which are placed into four compartments inside a casing that is divided into four sections. This division of the casing into four sections must be visible from the outside. For the תפלין של יד all four passages are inscribed on a single piece of parchment which is placed into a casing containing only one compartment. כותבן על ארבע עורות ומניחן בארבע בתים בעור אחד ואם אין חריצן ניכר פסולות, תפלה של יד כותבה על עור אחד בבית אחד (מנחות ל"ד). The sequence of the Biblical passages, the square form of the casings, the leather bases of the casings and the loops provided upon them (through which the leather straps are passed), the letter ש' on the casing of the head *tefillin,* and the black color of the leather straps on the outside are all essential components of the *tefillin.* החליף פרשיותיה פסולין. מרובעות, תיתורא, מעברתא שין של תפלין, רצועות שחורות הלכה למשה מסיני. (מנחות ל"ד, ל"ה). Essential, too, are the knots of the straps. קשר של תפלין הלכה למשה מסיני (שם).

The commandment requires that the *tefillin* for the arm be put on first and the head *tefillin* next; the *tefillin* are removed in reverse order, first the head *tefillin* and then the *tefillin* for the arm. כשהוא מניח מניח של יד ואח"כ מניח של ראש ושכשהוא חולץ חולץ של ראש ואח"כ של יד (שם ל"ו). Originally, the requirement was that the *tefillin* be worn both day and night, with the exception of שבת and יו"ט. הלכה ואין מורין כן (שם), על ידך זו קבורת בין. עיניך זו קדקד מקום שמוחו של תינוק רופס (מנחות ל"ז).

ד' פרשיות

It is essential that the four passages in the *tefillin* must be inscribed upon the parchment pieces in full and in the proper sequence. Let us therefore first analyze the contents of the four Scriptural passages contained in the *tefillin* to find the connection between them.

The opening verse of the portion beginning with קדש (Ex. 13, 1–10) is a command from God to Moses; the remaining verses consist of words spoken by Moses elaborating on God's command to consecrate to God all the first-born in Israel. However, the part of Moses' address to the people which immediately follows the opening verse contains no reference to the command to sanctify the first-born. This command is discussed only in the second passage, which opens with the words והיה כי יבאך (Ex. 13, 11–16). Since this passage is a continuation of Moses' address to the people, the first part is thus an introduction to the second part. Before the Jewish people receive the second commandment that is to perpetuate the memory of their redemption from Egypt,—namely, the commandment to sanctify the first-born to God—they are reminded once again of the first commandment—the observance of the Festival of Matzoth which they were still celebrating when they received this message from Moses (Pesachim 96b). This reminder is then amplified by the *tefillin* commandment. Only thereafter are we given additional details relating to the consecration of the first-born. The passage then concludes with the *tefillin* commandment.

קדש לי "Sanctify to Me all first-born, whatever opens the womb in Israel among men and animals; it is Mine," God said to Moses. Then Moses turned to the people and said to them: "Remember this day on which you came out from Egypt, the house of slaves; remember that by almighty power God led you out from here; therefore no leavened bread may be eaten! Today you are going forth, in the month of springtime! And when God will have brought you into the land of the Canaanite ... which He swore to your fathers to give to you, to the land that overflows with milk and honey, then you shall carry out in that month this Divine service. You shall eat matzoth for seven days ... and no leavened bread and no leaven shall be seen in all your domain, and you shall tell it to your son on that day: For this purpose has God acted for me, when I went forth from Egypt, and it shall be for a sign to you upon your hand, and for a memorial between your eyes, so that the Teaching of God may be in your mouth, that by almighty force God brought you out from Egypt; and you shall observe this commandment at the appointed time from year to year." (Exodus 13, 1–10).

והיה כי יבאך "But when God has brought you into the land of the Canaanite that He has sworn to you and to your fathers, and He will have given it to you, you shall dedicate all that opens the womb to God; of the animals that you will have, the males of the first-born shall belong to God. Every firstling of a donkey you shall redeem with a lamb; if you do not redeem it, you must kill it by a blow on the neck, and all the first-born of men among your sons you shall redeem. If your son will then ask you: What is this? you shall say to him: By almighty power God brought us out from Egypt, from the home of slaves. And it came to pass when Pharaoh stubbornly opposed our release, God slew all the first-born in the land of Egypt, from the first-born of man to the first-born of beast; therefore I offer up to God all male firstlings, and all the first-born of my sons I redeem. And it shall be for a sign upon your hand and as a frontlet between your eyes that with almighty power God brought us out from Egypt."

A careful examination of these two passages, which clearly belong together, will show that both refer to symbolic acts to be performed at recurring intervals, or on specified occasions, or every day. The stated purpose of each of these acts is to recall Israel's redemption from Egypt, which came about solely through God's almighty power and therefore serves solely to proclaim His omnipotence. The first of the two passages deals with an act to be performed at recurring intervals, namely, the observance of the Festival of Matzoth, and also with one that must be performed daily, namely, the putting on of *tefillin*. The second passage discusses the act that must be performed on specified occasions; namely, the consecration of the first-born, and then, once again, it turns to the daily putting on of *tefillin*. Note also that these passages draw attention to Israel's redemption from Egypt in both its aspects, joyful and solemn. Israel's deliverance from Egyptian slavery shows God both as Redeemer and as Judge. To us, He is the Redeemer Who rescued us from bondage so that we might arise to a new life. To the Egyptians, He was the Judge Who struck them down in His almighty power. The former aspect of God is noted in the first passage; the latter, in the second. And since both passages conclude with the *tefillin* commandment, it is clear that both these truths are basic components of the thoughts which the *tefillin* are meant to arouse within us.

The consecration of the first-born was communicated to Moses as a command and, as the second passage teaches us, it is closely linked with the solemn aspect of God's omnipotence in Egypt, showing us God as the almighty Judge.

Before transmitting to the people of Israel the commandment that perpetuates the solemn lesson to be drawn from the miracle of redemption, Moses first speaks of the wondrous fact of their deliverance, and their vocation which derived therefrom. He directs their eye to the blossoms of spring around them, and he says to them: Behold, today, in the month of spring, you are going forth into a spring of your own! As the green blades of grass around you, so you, too, are about to awaken to a new life and that same God now awakens you to a new life. And each year when this day recurs and finds you free and strong and blessed with abundance, think of your plight at the time of your redemption. Remember that you went forth to freedom with the bread of slavery in your hands. Remember that it was God Who fought for you, and that you owe your freedom and your new life solely to His all-embracing might. And on that day of remembrance, when you recall the Divine origin of your freedom and independence, tell your sons that the very homage which you now render to God was the sole purpose of your redemption.

However, this open reverence to the One Who saved you should not take place but once a year; it should be more than a mere commemoration of past history; it should become a permanent sign upon your hand and a continuous reminder between your eyes so that every word you utter be rooted in the Teaching of your God. These symbolic reminders are to bring to your mind at all times that God led you forth from Egypt with an almighty hand. Let all your life revolve and unfold around this remembrance, the memory of which you are to refresh through the festival and its celebration each year at springtime.

But remember also this: when you will become strong and independent, a nation upon its own soil, when you delight in the blossoming of your families and in your increasing wealth, do not forget that you, a nation of slaves redeemed by God, arose to life and freedom, while Egypt, proud of its dynasties, its soil and its power, was drained of its lifeblood through God's punishment. It was God's hand that saved you and smote Egypt. Why? Because Egypt claimed as "mine"—as its own—all that truly belongs to God and which He only bestows upon men so that men might use it in His service. Drunk with power, Egypt dared to take up the struggle against God, and became defiant when God demanded obedience.

For that reason God commands you: "Sanctify to Me every first-born in your midst; it is Mine!" And once God will have brought you into your land and will have given that land to you, you shall bring all your first-born before God. The firstlings of your herds shall remain dedicated to God while the firstlings of your beasts of burden must be redeemed. "If you do not redeem it, you yourself must kill it by a blow on the neck." The first-born of your sons, too, must be redeemed.

When your son asks you about this, you shall say to him: "God, in His almighty power, has delivered us from Egypt, our home as slaves. But Pharaoh, who was stubbornly opposed to seeing us go free, He crushed by destroying all of his first-born. Therefore I offer and dedicate to God all the first-born of my family and of what is mine."

But this solemn remembrance must not be relegated only to a time when you behold and enjoy the benefits of your prosperity. Rather, it is to accompany you throughout your life as a solemn admonition. In your relationship to God you must always consider your own hand as "weak" (the unusual feminine form, ידכה). You must not only realize that God alone upholds you in your life as an individual part of a larger entity, you must wear the symbol of this remembrance לאות על "ידכה", as a sign upon your hand and as a frontlet between your eyes, to remind you that God, in His almighty power, "הוציאנו" brought us, all of us, forth from Egypt.

Thus the words קדש לי which open the first of the four passages are the summary of all the preceding thought. These words are elaborated upon in the second passage, the remainder of the first passage serving as a preamble to that elaboration. The central thought to be conveyed is clear: *By virtue of its redemption from Egypt, which revealed the sovereignty of God, Israel becomes totally subordinate and must surrender itself entirely to God as the Redeemer Who bestowed new life upon it and as the Master Who judged its oppressors.*

May we be permitted a parenthetical comment regarding the Oral Law, the תורה שבעל פה. A careful study of the first commandments that

the Jewish people received through Moses will provide us with a striking confirmation of the processes of the Oral Law. Both of these
commandments, one relating to the Passover offering and one concerning the sanctification of the first-born, include details that were
not contained in God's pronouncements to Moses.

Let us compare Exodus 12, 7 with Verse 22 of the same chapter.
God's command to Moses that the people should place the blood of
the Passover offering on the side-posts and on the thresholds of the
houses where the offerings were consumed does not specify how to
fulfill this order. The manner in which the blood was to be placed on
these parts of the homes of the Children of Israel was left to תורה שבעל
פה, communicated by Moses orally to the people.

The same is true in the passage we are referring to. God's command to Moses concerning the sanctification of the first-born is
phrased very briefly: קדש לי כל בכור וגו' (Exodus 13, 2). Its detailed
explanation, תורה שבעל פה, comes only in Moses' communication to the
people: והעברת וגו', וכל פטר חמר וג' וכל בכור אדם וגו' (Exodus 13, 12–14).

Thus we can say with certainty: זה בנה אב לכל התורה כולה. The wording of these two first commandments affords us a model for the whole
Law, written and oral. In general, too little thought has been given to
the fact that actually תורה שבעל פה antedates תורה שבכתב. The entire
Law had been given verbally to the Jewish people over a period of
forty years before anything was handed to them in writing. Thus, the
Written Law was set down with the assumption that the Law was
already known to the Jewish people. It was then given to the people in
such a form that it should help them retain the more complete oral
version.

So much for our parenthetical note. Let us now examine the two
remaining passages inserted in the *tefillin*: שמע (Deut. 6, 4–9) and והיה
אם שמע (11, 13–21).

שמע intensifies the people's knowledge of God and clarifies their
obligations toward Him; that their God is ה', that He is the one God of
the universe which He has created and the Master of all developments
of history. He is the only true God to Whom all things are subordinate
as His creatures and His servants, and the Jewish people must render
homage to this One God as their God, dedicating themselves completely to Him, and with all their possessions: ואהבת וגו' בכל לבבך ובכל
נפשך ובכל מאדך. Indeed, they must be ready to sacrifice all these if need

be, in order to acquire the one true worthwhile possession, God's near-ness. This is the literal meaning of loving God with all of one's heart, all of one's soul, and all of one's possessions. Furthermore, this passage teaches us that the people of Israel can put this love into prac-tice only by holding the Divine laws, which they are under obligation to observe, close to their hearts and by handing them down to their children by earnest, constant teaching and personal example: ושננתם לבניך וגו' בשבתך בביתך וגו'. Finally, this passage tells them that, for this purpose, they ought to bind these laws as a sign around their hands, wear them as a fróntlet between their eyes and inscribe them upon the doorposts of their homes, representing their private, domestic lives, and upon their gates, symbol of the nation's public and communal life.

The passage opening with והיה אם שמע proclaims to the Jewish people that their fate depends on the fulfillment of their obligation toward God. If they will hearken to the commandments which God gave them only once but for all time, to love Him and to demonstrate this love by serving Him, by accomplishing His will with all their hearts and souls, with body and spirit, then God will lavish upon them prosperity and abundance in their own land. However, as they are repeatedly warned, there is danger in this abundance! If, in the midst of this prosperity, their hearts should "become open" (this is the literal meaning of פתה—in פן יפתה לבבכם, Verse 16) to other resolves, if they turn aside from God's laws and serve "other gods," they will not only lose the wondrous abundance that blossoms under God's special providence, but God will deny them even the bare necessities of life upon their own soil, and they will have to leave the splendid land that God had given them. Therefore, they are to take the words of God to their hearts and keep them in mind at all times, bind them as a sign upon their hands, let them be an ornament on their foreheads between their eyes, teach them to their sons by constant personal example, and inscribe them upon their doorposts and upon their gates, so that their days and the days of their children might endure upon the soil pro-mised them by God, for as long as the days of the heaven above the earth.

It is worth noting that in the above passage Israel is addressed predominantly in the second person plural. The plural form is evident also in the commandment of *tefillin,* וקשרתם . . . ידכם, וגו', in contrast to the singular וקשרתם . . . ידך, וגו' in the first passage. Indeed, the Sifri explains this difference, as follows: כאן ביחיד כאן בצבור. While the passage opening with שמע is addressed primarily to the individual, the passage beginning with והיה אם שמע is addressed primarily to the community as a whole. For והיה אם שמע discusses not the fate of the individual members of the nation but the fate of the nation as a whole in terms of its dependence on whether or not the nation fulfills the Law of God.

It is most significant that in this address to the entire community, which formulates the well-being and the role of the nation, there are two verses in which the address shifts abruptly from the second person plural to the second person singular; i.e. ונתתי מטר ארצכם וגו' ואספת וגו' and ולמדתם אתם את בניכם וגו' בשבתך וגו'. Does not this peculiarity in the text imply that the Word of God cannot conceive of a nation that prospers and flourishes while the individual is wanting? The state can prosper only if the soil and the fields of its citizens also flourish, so that the individual can eat and be satisfied.

The word of God appears indeed as totally unconventional; it dares to contradict the classical wisdom of statistics, present, past and future. In the Biblical passage addressed to the individual, the individual is shown as consisting of "heart, soul and possessions;" he is described as having a mind, a body, and property. In the passage addressed to the nation as a whole there is no reference to what is usually regarded as the vital nerve and soul of the modern state, with no mention of מאדיכם, of wealth and of financial resources. The Jewish state as such has no capital. Its treasure consists of the throbbing hearts and the breathing souls of its citizens, and it attains perfection when the bodies and souls of its sons unite all their thoughts and endeavors to serve the One God. The Divine Ruler of this state needs no state treasury. He has control over the rays of the sun in the heavens and over the clouds in the air, and He grants prosperity, abundance, growth and bloom to field and meadow, to man and beast, as long as minds and hearts surge toward Him and all of physical and spiritual life aspires to perfection within the sphere of His Word. In the Jewish state, material wealth is not the basis but only the reward and the fruit of the nation's vibrant development.

The connection and the relationship between the four passages contained in the *tefillin* should be clear. Together, the passages beginning with קדש and והיה כי יבאך show the constitution of the Jewish people on the basis of their redemption from Egypt. The passage beginning with שמע and והיה אם שמע designates the Jewish people for the fulfillment of God's Law. The first two passages explain Israel's coming into existence; the latter two, its purpose. The former two recall יציאת מצרים; the latter two, קבלת התורה והמצות; יציאת מצרים and מתן תורה are the two facts which together form the concept of Israel and Judaism. Furthermore, קדש substantiates Israel's subordination to God, its Redeemer; שמע cites the purpose and content of this subordination. והיה כי יבאך presents God to Israel as the Master and Judge; והיה אם שמע teaches the Jewish people about their own destiny under the rule of this Master and Judge.

The parallels between the passage in the *tefillin* can be seen in the fact that while קדש and שמע refer primarily to the life of the individual, והיה אם שמע and והיה כי יבאך address themselves to the life of the community and the state. In והיה כי יבאך the Egyptian state goes to ruin because it defied God. In והיה אם שמע the Jewish state is promised prosperity provided it obeys God; if it defies God, the state will be destroyed.

There is hardly need for further documentation to establish the symbolic significance of the commandment enjoining us to bind these passages from the Torah upon hand and head. These Divinely-ordained acts are meant to symbolize the subordination of hand and head to the ideas expressed in the *tefillin* passages. They bid us place the imprint of יציאת מצרים and of תורה upon all our actions and thoughts. All our thoughts and actions are to be founded on יציאת מצרים and to see their purpose in the תורה.

Our next task is to examine the תפלין themselves and to study the detailed specifications regarding the manner in which they must be tied and placed upon the body. We will then try to ascertain their symbolic relationships.

בתים

In their basic outer shape, the תפלין are two cubical boxes, each provided with a base and a loop through which its straps are passed. The cubic shape, the base and the loops are essential components of the *tefillin*: מרובעות, (the cubic shape), תיתורא, (the thick leather of the base), and מעברתא (the loop) are הלכה למשה מסיני.

Thus the בתים as such, including their shape and structure, are more than a necessary means for binding the pertinent passages from the Torah upon head and hand. These "houses," together with their bases and loops, are an essential complement to the message conveyed by the פרשיות. Clearly, the purpose of the "houses" is to teach us how to perpetuate the contents of the Torah given us by God and to translate them into reality. Only in combination with one another can the requirement symbolized by the "houses" and the contents of the פרשיות spell out the purpose to which we are to devote all the energies of hand and head. It may be assumed that the "houses of the *tefillin*" have the same relationship to their contents as does the ארון of the מקדש to the Torah, the purpose of the ארון being to receive and to guard the Law. As the פרשיות symbolize the Law of God in its briefest form, so, too, every בית might be regarded as an Ark of the Covenant in miniature.

To make or to build a house for a person or an object means, in idiomatic Hebrew, to prepare for him a lasting place on earth. For example: בית יעשה (II Samuel 7, 11); בית יבנה לך ה׳ (I Chronicles 17, 10), or as the question is raised in the Book of Zechariah: Whither were they carrying the woman that was sitting in the midst of the bushel measure and eating a round weight of lead (a graphic simile for the passionate nature that feels at ease only amidst material wealth and when feeding on material things)? The answer we are given is לבנות לה בית בארץ שנער והוכן והניחה שם על מכונתה "To build her a house in the land of Shinar; it is prepared, and she will be placed there upon the ground prepared for her" (5, 11).

"Establishing a house" for תורה and מצות on earth, then, should be the task designated for each one of us since our redemption from Egypt. The mere fact that the Torah is enshrined in the Temple does not make Judaism a reality on earth. The truth and reality of Judaism can emerge only if every Jew, in his own small circle, establishes a temple for it, if the תורה finds a "house" in the everyday endeavors and actions of each and every one of us.

Nor may the place that we prepare for תורה on earth, the house we create for it, be something accidental or transitory. It must be firmly established on earth and in earthly affairs. Judaism does not regard the earth as an accursed vale of tears that has fallen to "the Evil One," where things heavenly and Divine can exist only as aliens in exile. But, it is the purpose of Judaism, set by the תורה, and so significantly expressed in the words of the Prophet: לנטע שמים וליסד ארץ ולאמר לציון עמי אתה "to plant the divine on earth, to provide a foundation for the things of earth, and to say to Zion: You are My people" (Isaiah 51, 16). The task of Judaism is to provide a permanent foundation for earthly, transient things by wedding them to the immutable eternal. Judaism teaches us that if the truth of תורה is realized on earth, then the earth will be more Divine than heaven itself, עיקר שכינה בתחתונים (בראשית רבה י"ט); the glory of God has its primary place on earth.

However, this foundation has a מעברתא. It must, in essence, be upheld by man himself. We must not say היכל ה' היכל ה' (Jeremiah 7, 4), we have built a temple for the Torah, its very own temple, and forget that היכל ה' המה, that we *ourselves* must become the temple of God. The Temple can have its foundations and be completed only within ourselves, if we dedicate ourselves body and soul to the תורה. The שכינה of God will take up its abode not in wood and stone, but in the myriads of hearts and bodies that flow toward it.

When the Ark of the Covenant came to rest, Moses prayed: שובה ה' רבבות אלפי ישראל (Numbers 10, 36): Take your place, O God, in the midst of the myriads of the thousands of Israel. Moses did *not* say: Take Your place, O God, in the temple adorned with gold and purple, which we have built for You.

In the same vein we read: the carrying poles must never be removed from the Ark of the Covenant; לא יסרו ממנו (Ex. 25, 15), indeed, the poles had to protrude visibly through the sacred curtain, offering themselves to Israel, as it were, to bear the Law aloft at all times—ויראו ראשי הבדים מן הקדש ("the ends of the poles were seen from the Holy Place"—I Kings 8, 8). So, too, the loop must never be removed from the base of the *tefillin,* saying to each and every one of us: Uphold me, if you wish me to uphold you. Thus, the בית of the *tefillin* and its components express the thought of the prophet Isaiah (51, 16), as follows:

בית = לנטע שמים

תיתורא = וליסד ארץ

מעברתא = ולאמר לציון עמי אתה

The "houses" and their base must be square; מרובעות הלכה למשה מסיני. Tradition specifically emphasizes that they must not be circular or spherical in shape; העושה תפלתו עגולה סכנה ואין בו מצוה (Menachot 35a;

Megillah 24b). We note that the square was the predominant shape in the construction of the Temple and its accessories.

If we consider the shapes created by the vital forces of nature; i.e., all the physical forms produced by organic energies operating without a free will of their own, we will note that most of these formations have a round shape. If we imagine an organic force that operates without a will of its own, it will operate from one starting point, equally in every direction to the full extent of its creative and formative capacity and will not of its own volition restrict itself to any one direction. Therefore, unless conflicting forces or obstacles intervene from the outside, the creative and formative processes of the organism will produce a rounded shape; a perfect square is not found in organic nature.

Of all the creative organic forces it is only the energy of man, who thinks and acts freely, that constructs linear or angular forms. We therefore maintain that the circle characterizes the structures produced by organic forces not endowed with a free will, while angles and squares are hallmarks of man, who can use his intelligence and free will in building his creations and structures.

We may thus understand why the circular form was not used in the makeup of any sacred structure or object in Judaism. We will then understand, too, why the same rule was applied to the shape of *tefillin*: the *tefillin* represent, in miniature, the abode we must prepare on earth for the Law of God. This type of construction is expected from man because he is a human being endowed with the Divine freedom, not a creature restricted in its development by the forces of nature. The circle is associated with constraint and lack of freedom; the square is the mark of human freedom which masters the material world.

תפלין, like any other symbol serving to advance מלאכת שמים, the elevation of man toward God, may be made only from substances permitted as food; לא הוכשרו למלאכת שמים אלא עור בהמה טהורה בלבד. In the case of *tefillin*, tradition links this general principle to the Biblical dictum למען תהיה תורת ה' בפיך (Ex. 13, 9). The purpose of *tefillin* is that "the Teaching of God may be in your mouth." For this reason they must be made מן המותר בפיך, from substances "permitted to your mouth." Symbols may be misinterpreted as external forms so that the symbol is considered to have performed its function as soon as it has been produced. We might then come to regard the *tefillin* as amulets and the *mezuzah* as a charm to protect us against bad luck, and think that we have satisfied the requirements of the Law if we have commissioned the writing of a beautiful Torah scroll and have prepared a fitting cover and a fine Ark prepared for it.

Instead, the very material from which a Sefer Torah, *tefillin* and *mezuzah* is prepared and upon which its passages are written should comply with the order that God addressed to Ezekiel (3, 1,3): אכול את בטנך תאכל ומעיך תמלא את המגלה הזאת המגלה הזאת "Eat this scroll!" "Nourish your body with this scroll and fill your inner parts with it." In other words, תורת ה׳ תהיה בפיך! Let the Teaching of God enter your mouth! The Torah in its entirety and in its individual parts is not intended for you as a means of external, physical protection but as spiritual nourishment to be absorbed within you. The Torah has achieved its purpose only if its contents and the ideas to be conveyed by its symbols have been absorbed into our flesh and blood, giving strength and nourishment to our minds and emotions. This—so we believe—is the reason why, as with the Tabernacle and all its appurtenances, no part of a בהמה טמאה may be used in making *tefillin* and their accessories.

In view of the foregoing, it is interesting that, nevertheless, it is permissible to use in making *tefillin*, עור נבלות וטרפות of בהמה טהורה. This peculiarity was already the subject of a question put to R. Joshua HaGarsi by a disciple of the heretic Boethus (שבת ק״ח). It appears that since the "eating" of the parchment is not meant literally but only symbolically, it is sufficient that (in order to stress that this ingestion is merely meant as a metaphor) the material used should be derived from an animal which belongs to a species permitted as food, even if this particular animal by reason of an individual defect (טרפה) or death other than by proper שחיטה (נבלה) cannot be consumed. We believe that this is also the intent of the reply which R. Joshua gave to the Boethu-sian: אמר לו אמשול לך משל למה הדבר דומה לשני בני אדם שנתחייבו הריגה למלכות אחד הרגו מלך ואחד הרגו איספקליטור איזה מהן משובח הוי אומר זה שהרגו מלך אלא מעתה יאכלו אמר ליה התורה אמרה לא תאכלו כל נבילה ואת אמרת יאכלו אמר ליה קאלוס.

R. Joshua compared בהמה טמאה to the man who was put to death by the executioner, and נבלת בהמה טהורה to the man who was put to death by the king. By this analogy he seems to have meant that בהמה טמאה is "dead;" i.e., alien to man, forbidden for man to acquire, because of its natural properties, while נבלת בהמה טהורה did not acquire forbidden status because of its natural properties but solely due to circumstance. In any event, the only meaningful features in this symbol are those that can be physically perceived and are essential, not circumstantial features of the material concerned.

של יד—של ראש

The "house" of the *tefillin* to be worn on the arm is quite simple, containing only one compartment. By contrast, that of the *tefillin* to be worn on the head contains four compartments, each of which is intended to hold a piece of parchment with one of the four Biblical passages. Consequently, the four passages inserted in the hand *tefillin* are inscribed on only one single strip of parchment which is then rolled up and tied around with animal hair and placed into the one compartment provided for it, while the four passages for the head *tefillin* are each written on a separate strip of parchment, each separately rolled up and tied around with animal hair. Thus, four separate scrolls of parchment are inserted into four separate compartments of the head *tefillin*.

This arrangement is to teach us: whatever memory and contemplative intelligence [the head] perceive as four distinct factors must become one single motive directing our will and our actions [the arm], and place one and the same imprint upon everything we do. Our loving surrender to God as our Redeemer and Liberator (קדש); our subordination to God as our Master and Judge (והיה כי יבאך); our demonstration of this love by dedicating all the aspects of our essence to the fulfillment of the Word of God (שמע); and the dependence of our future on whether or not we fulfill these requirements; (והיה אם שמע); each of these concepts calls for separate comprehension, reflection, realization and recognition (לזכרון בין עיניך). Each concept must be understood and recognized in terms of its own significance and profundity. Each represents a unique jewel in טוטפות, the diadem of Judaism. However, they all merge into one, לאות על ידך, as the single motive for all our actions. At every moment of our lives, God appears to us in both His qualities; our Liberator and Redeemer with all His loving-kindness, and our Master and Judge applying His stern justice.

The "house" that contains the head *tefillin* has the letter "ש" on both of its side walls. This letter is not superimposed on the wall from the outside but is formed from the material of the walls themselves, pressed into the proper shape. The "ש" on one of the sides has four vertical strokes. According to custom this four-stroke ש' is on the left

side, the outer wall of the first compartment. Tradition does not cite
any specifications in this respect (see תוס׳ ד״ה שין של תפלין הל״מ
Menachoth 35a).

It is difficult to establish the significance of this "ש" with any
degree of certainty. According to Rashi (שם ל״ה: ד״ה שין של תפלין הל״מ),
this "ש", together with the knot of the head straps which forms the
letter ד, and the knot of the hand straps which forms the letter י, spells
out the Divine Name ש־ד־י. However, תוס׳ refutes this interpretation. In
our halachic literature, these knots are never describes in terms of the
letters they might form, but only as קשר, "knot," while the "ש" on the
walls of the casings is described simply as a letter; שין של תפלין הלכה למשה
מסיני.

In view of the foregoing, we must study the "ש" on the *tefillin* as a
letter in its own right. Many letters of the Hebrew alphabet have
symbolic significance (שבת ק״ד מנחות כ״ט). We therefore cannot regard a
single letter, placed in a position of significance, as a mere abbreviation or initial, even though such abbreviations are commonly used in
the Hebrew language. We must, instead, analyze this letter itself to
determine its linguistic significance and do so in the context of the
passage in which the letter occurs. If the letter should then yield, in an
intelligible, unforced manner, an idea that would harmonize with the
context in which it occurs, there would be little justification for us to
go further and interpret the letter as an abbreviation for a word, unless
that word is so obvious in this context that it only requires its initial to
call to our minds the word and the idea that the letter is intended to
convey.

Let us look at the שין של תפלין from this point of view, as a letter by
itself. Let us ask ourselves whether its linguistic significance as such
might perhaps imply an idea which would be symbolized by the walls
of the "*tefillin* houses" where this letter is visible, and we would be
justified in seizing upon that idea as the one meant to be expressed in
this context.

The letter "ש" has a definite, explicit linguistic connotation in the
Hebrew language. It represents the relative pronoun "who," "which"
or "that," frequently with an added demonstrative שהוא, שהיא, שהם,
such as in שהם ד׳ שבועות לעומר: ספירת העומר. The function of the
relative pronoun is to introduce to the subject of a sentence an attribute for which the subject has not been known before. The relative
pronoun directs the thought to the subject in order to describe it in

terms of the attribute. In the declarative sentence, "the man is good," the subject is known to us even without the adjective "good"; the adjective serves only to supplement and broaden our knowledge of the subject. In "the man *who is* good," on the other hand, the subject is introduced to us initially as an unknown, to be made known only in terms of its attribute. This is precisely the function of the Hebrew אשר and 'ש.

Thus, "ש" in general indicates a subject that will become known to us only through its attributes. Our awareness of the subject is the result of our perception of its attributes. This relationship of a subject to our power of comprehension, not merely as an accidental, transitory or abstract concept, but in terms of real attributes basic to, and typical of, the subject, would present the letter 'ש in the following connotation: ש would refer to a subject that is not merely accidental and transitory and unknown to us, but one whose relationship to us is basic and permanent, and of such a kind that we can perceive our subject only in terms of its attributes. At the same time, however, the subject itself remains inaccessible to our cognitive faculty. Therefore, the most complete characterization of a subject such as God can only be one that dispenses with attributes altogether, because any assignment of attributes, no matter how comprehensive, would only restrict the inexhaustible attributes of perfection relevant to that particular subject.

Thus the ש of the *tefillin* is a demonstrative pronoun pointing to God as the invisible One, Who reveals Himself only in the manifestations that can be perceived in nature and in history, and to Whom all attributes of being and creating can be ascribed in boundless abundance and therefore awesome perfection.

The significance of the "ש" of the *tefillin* would then be the same as if the word "He" were to stand in place of the letter. We would then say that there is only one "He," and we would perceive this as the expression defining God in terms of the absolute character and the authenticity of His being.

If we interpret the "ש" of the *tefillin* as an abbreviation or an initial, the likely words appropriate to this context would be either שם or the Divine Name to be formed by adding to the ש the letters ד and י. Either of these interpretations thus encompass both the concepts that we have found in our study of the "ש" not as an abbreviation but as a letter.

Indeed, שם is simply an attribute. But שם has become a designation
par excellence for God in exactly the meaning implied above: as the
One Who is revealed to us only in terms of His attributes, of Whom we
can be aware only in terms of His Name. This designation for God,
which eventually came to be so widely used, seems to be at the root of
the passage in II Samuel 6, 2, אשר נקרא שם, שם ה׳ צבאו׳ ישב הכרבים עליו
("whereupon is called the Name, the Name of the God of Hosts Who
thrones above the cherubim"), where it is said of the Ark of the
Covenant that נקרא שם עליו (the Name of God is called upon it) and the
שם is further defined only in parenthetical terms.

According to our Sages, the other designation for God, formed by
the addition of די, corresponds precisely to the second concept which
we noted above as being expressed by ־ש. The former conceives of
God in the infinite and therefore ineffable abundance of His Being and
creating. In the same manner, according to our Sages, that name
characterizes God as the One Who is די; i.e., sufficient for all things
and in all things, but for Whom no description is exhaustive. Not even
the whole universe is sufficient to encompass the infinite abundance of
His being and His might and Whose essence exceeds by far even that
which has been revealed concerning Him in the universe. שאין העולם כדי
לאלקותו: this is precisely ־ש.

Consider the designation by which the Sanctuary to be established
for the Law of God, the place chosen by God for this purpose, was to
be known: לשכן שמו שם (Deut. 12, 11), to have His Name rest *there*. Let
us consider, too, the promise that has been made to Israel if it will
observe the commandments of God and walk in God's ways: וראו כל
עמי הארץ כי שם ה׳ נקרא עליך ויראו ממך, "all the nations of the world will see
that the Name of God has been pronounced over you, and they
will be afraid of you" (Deut. 28, 10). Furthermore, the Ark of the
Covenant in which the Law of God is kept is described as אשר נקרא שם
עליו . . ., "over which the *Name* is revealed" (II Sam. 6, 2). All the foregoing should be sufficient for us to understand the thought expressed
by the ש upon the *tefillin* "house" which we are bidden to make for the
תורה, and by the fact that the Jew, to whom the task [of proclaiming the
Name of God] has been assigned, must wear this *tefillin* "house" upon
his forehead: The thought, throughout the range of Jewish Scripture,
is the realization of that unique and rewarding nearness of God which
has been promised to us as the fruit of our complete and loyal dedication to God and to His Law.

If, now, this Name of God becomes visible on the *walls* of the *tefillin,* if, in fact, it is formed from the walls themselves, this should convey to us in graphic terms a most significant idea as follows: If we build a בית for the פרשיות של תפלין; i.e., if, through our own presence and life on earth, we establish on earth a place for the fulfillment of our mission and purpose as Jews, then not only the Law which reveals our mission and purpose will bear the Name of God. But earthly matter, shaped and utilized in accordance with the Law of God, will then be elevated by virtue of our conduct into the sphere of the Divine.

This house which we build for the תורה, our entire life on earth which we will imbue with the fulfillment of the Divine Law and with the accomplishment of our mission and purpose as Jews, will become a bearer of the Name of God. The realization of the ideas expressed in the פרשיות will apply the seal of the Divine Name upon this house. By contemplating the mere walls of the house we obtain a glimpse of what is inside.

The talmudic specification קדש והיה כי יבאך מימין, שמע והיה אם שמע משמאל concerning the order and arrangement of the four פרשיות has its importance. The four Biblical passages in the *tefillin* are divided into two distinct groupings. Indeed, the passages introduced by the words קדש, והיה כי יבאך, and those that begin with שמע, והיה אם שמע, form two "sides" which, together, encompass the structure and substance of Judaism. The first two relate to the last two, as יציאת מצרים does to מתן תורה, as does our history to our mission. The "ש" upon the walls of the right-hand and left-hand compartments place the imprint of the Name of God upon our ultimate destinies as well as upon our day by day actions. It assigns both "sides" of our existence to the sublime task of becoming the bearers of His revelation. It expresses in full the earlier promise: "God will raise you for Himself as a holy nation, as He has sworn to you, if you will keep the commandments of God, your God, and walk in His ways. And all the nations of the world will see that the Name of God has been pronounced over you, and they will be afraid of you" (Deut. 28, 9–10).

It is more difficult to explain the meaning for the "ש" with four strokes visible on the left wall of the head *tefillin.* This unusual shape is not mentioned in the Talmud, but it has been established by time-honored practice. We already noted the number four in connection with the *tefillin,* particularly with the head *tefillin.* The four פרשיות are inserted into the head *tefillin* into four separate compartments, with the four divisions visible also on the outside of the casing. The four-stroke "ש" might intend to convey the idea that if the thoughts expressed in the four passages are implemented, they merge to form the שמו של הקב״ה; i.e., translating these פרשיות into reality will become the proclamation of His Name on earth, placing the imprint of God's Name upon the earthly "house." After all, the four compartments constructed inside the "house" for the head *tefillin* to accommodate the four Biblical passages in themselves form a "ש" with four strokes. Thus our whole life, devoted to the fulfillment of the teachings contained inside the *tefillin,* will become the most obvious manifestation of God on earth. ומי כעמך כישראל גוי אחד בארץ אשר הלכו אלקים לפדות לו לעם ולשום לו שם, "And who is like Your people, Israel, a nation one in the earth, whom God went to redeem for Himself as a people and to make Him a name?" (II Samuel 7, 23).

קשר של תפלין והנחתן

קשר תפלין הלכה למשה מסיני. The knots tied in the straps of the head *tefillin* and in the *tefillin* worn on the arm are not identical. The knot of the *tefillin* worn on the head is a union of the two parts of the strap into one knot at the back of the head, opposite the "house" worn on the forehead. This knot serves to hold the *tefillin* casing in the proper place on the wearer's head. The two straps are allowed to fall over either shoulder, the left strap extending over the chest and the right strap reaching down to the abdomen. The knot of the *tefillin* worn on the arm is tied on one side only, very close to the loop, apparently to make the casing fit as tightly as possible to the upper arm.

The knot of the *tefillin* worn on the head which is tied from both sides, right and left, seems to symbolize the idea of Israel's fulfillment of its life and its mission, as expressed by the two "sides" of the head *tefillin.* Israel's complete dedication to the accomplishment of this task constitutes the "knot of the Covenant," which consecrates the people of Israel and its individual members in every generation, as bearers of the "*tefillin* house." Israel's historic identification with the Law is Israel's true link with God. From this point of view, one can readily understand the statement in Menachoth 35b: קשר של תפלין צריך שיהא למעלה כדי שיהו ישראל למעלה ולא למטה וצריך שיהא כלפי פנים כדי שיהו ישראל

לפנים ולא לאחור ("The knot of the *tefillin* should be placed high up so that Israel may be high up and not low down. Also, it should face the front, so that Israel should be ahead and never trail behind").

The symbolic meaning of the specified order in which the *tefillin* must be put on is clear.

The *tefillin* for the arm are put on first, those for the head next. The *tefillin* are removed in reverse order, the *tefillin* for the head being taken off first, followed by the *tefillin* of the arm. Thus, as tradition puts it, כל זמן שבין עיניך יהיו שנים, the *tefillin* for the head must never be worn without those for the upper arm. This specification accords completely with the first great basic principle of Jewish Law, נעשה ונשמע. In Judaism, practical observance always takes precedence over theoretical understanding. For Judaism, the search for intellectual understanding of the Law presupposes the unqualified obedience to that same Law. The dedication of the hand takes precedence over the dedication of the eyes; the former is both the starting point and the goal for the latter.

The place for the arm *tefillin* is at the biceps of the left upper arm, opposite the heart. That for the head *tefillin,* on the front part of the head, above the space between the eyes, at the beginning of the hair-line. Thus, the *tefillin* for the arm are bound to that muscle which accomplishes the principal movement of the arm, namely, seizing an object, holding it, and placing it under one's control. Since this position is also next to the heart, the "house" of the *tefillin* for the arm is close to the source of all human initiative and action, the heart.

A left-handed man must put the *tefillin* on his right arm, which in his case becomes his "left" arm. The binding of the *tefillin* to the arm must always be done with the strong "right" hand, implying the dedication of all our energies to the "bond" of obedience to God's Law.

The casing and knot of the head *tefillin* are placed upon the center of intellect and memory. The contents of the *tefillin* must be comprehended by the mind and guarded by the memory. From and through the mind—as implied by the straps that are allowed to hang down over the shoulders—the ideas contained in the *tefillin* are to penetrate into the heart. The ideas which the mind has identified are to be adopted by the will, and thus to be translated into life and action, a symbol already noted in the proximity of the arm *tefillin* to the heart.

Originally *tefillin* were to be worn during all of one's waking hours, be it day or night, with the exception of שבת and יו"ט. (Nowadays מצות תפלין is restricted to תפלת שחרית in order to avoid desecration of the *tefillin* during extended wear.) The Sabbath and the festivals are themselves called אות, symbols in their own right. They are, from beginning to end, towering monuments of God and of His unique relationship to the Jewish nation. They therefore neither require other symbols, nor, in fact, could there be a meaningful role for them during these very days.

The Sanctuary

Basic Concepts

The Sanctuary on Earth — לא בשמים היא

God and man, heaven and earth, are the two powers between which the Tabernacle was intended to serve as the connecting link. There is hardly a phase of the cosmic, physical, moral or metaphysical relationships between heaven and earth, between God and man, real or hypothetical, that cannot be evoked as the basis of the structure.

Let us consider, in its broad outlines, the sphere of ideas within which the teachings and revelations of Divine Law operate. A superficial view will be sufficient to eliminate many of the areas in which the symbolic significance of the Tabernacle and its accessories has been sought. In this connection it can indeed be said of the Divine Law that לא בשמים ולא מעבר לים היא. Nowhere in the Law do we find statements intended to teach us about matters beyond our own immediate perspective.

This confirms what our sages have asked us to remember: the Torah begins with the letter ב, סתום מכל צדדיו ופתוח מלפניו, "a letter closed on all sides and open only to the front," not to teach you מה למטה מה למעלה מה לפנים מה לאחור, "that which is beyond our horizon and below it, and that which dates back to the beginning of time, but rather, אלא מיום שנברא העולם ולהבא you may turn to the Torah only for knowledge about things that fall within the span of time begun with Creation" (R. Levi in בראשית רבה א'). Or, as Bar Kappara put it: כי שאל נא לימים ראשונים אשר היו לפניך למן היום אשר ברא אלקים אדם על הארץ ולמקצה השמים ועד קצה השמים

(דברים ד' ל"ב) למן היום שנבראו אתה דורש ואי אתה דורש לפנים מכאן ולמקצה השמים
ועד קצה השמים אתה דורש וחוקר ואי אתה חוקר לפנים מכאן. You may seek to
comprehend that which falls within the time span following the creation of man on earth, but not that which came before. Likewise, whatever is within the earthly realm, enclosed by the physical universe, may
be the legitimate object of your investigations and research, but not
anything beyond that sphere (see Haggigah 11b).

Let us consider the most sublime revelation that was communicated to Moses, the greatest of all human spirits, when he asked for the
ultimate—to behold God. His request was denied him because, given
man's earthly limitations, the knowledge of God was beyond the grasp
of human comprehension. לא יראני האדם וחי "man shall not see Me and
live" (Ex. 33, 20). But what was the revelation which, in fact, was
granted to Moses and which therefore denotes the ultimate of what the
human intellect can grasp? Did it convey transcendental disclosures
about the essence of God, about metaphysical, cosmic laws, or about
truths whose understanding could only satisfy a purely theoretical
curiosity?

ה' ה' א' רחום וחנון (Ex. 34, 6). This was the wording of the supreme
revelation; characterizing God in comparatively limited terms in
which He is described only in terms of His sovereignty in relation to
man. Apparently God acceded only to the first request with which
Moses prefaced his prayer for the ultimate revelation. This request,
which God granted to Moses in full, was הודעני נא את דרכך, "Pray let me
recognize Your ways." The object of this request seems so far removed
from mere theoretical, transcendental speculation that Moses immediately added to it a most practical consideration: ואדעך למען אמצא חן
בעיניך "so that I may recognize You, in order that I may find favor in
Your eyes."

Thus, the entire realm of Divine Laws does not contain one single
statement that would be only of theoretical interest; to the contrary it
enhances our knowledge and influences our moral conduct. If no such
theoretical statements are found in the Torah, we also must not expect
to find them in the symbolism of the Torah. Having established the
essential character of symbols, we found that symbols cannot represent truths that were entirely unknown to us before. Rather, the
objects and ideas that the symbol is meant to express must already be
part of the perspective of the one to whom a symbol is addressed.

Forceful perceptual recollection of previously known truths is the purpose of the symbol.

To comprehend the symbols and their interpretation, we will do well to refer to God's pronouncement with regard to the provisions for the Tabernacle:

> God said to Moses: Speak to the sons of Israel that they may accept for Me an uplifted offering. Of every man whose heart moves him accordingly, you shall accept My uplifted offering. And this is the uplifted offering that you shall accept from them: gold, silver and copper. Sky-blue, purple and crimson red wool, fine linen and goats' hair. Rams' skins dyed red, *tachash* skins and *shittim* wood. Oil for the light, spices for the anointing oil and for the spicy incense. *Shoham* stones and stones to be set for the *ephod* and for the breastplate. They shall make Me a Sanctuary that I may dwell in their midst. According to all that I show you, the form of the Dwelling Place and all its accessories, so shall you build it.
>
> (Ex. 25, 1–9)

ועשו לי מקדש

"You shall make for Me a Sanctuary;" with these words God formulates the concept of the Tabernacle and its accessories. ושכנתי בתוכם "so that God may dwell in their midst." This, we are told, is the purpose and the result of the entire ordinance, and for this purpose the Sanctuary is given the designation of משכן "Dwelling Place." The construction of this Sanctuary has been prescribed and shown by God with detailed specifications.

The Dwelling Place of God in our midst is dependent on factors entirely different from the mere physical construction and maintenance of the Sanctuary, and this structure as such must have a symbolic meaning representing the very conditions we must fulfill in order to bring this Sanctuary to its real purpose which is twofold. The Sanctuary will be the place where our assigned task—קדושים תהיו—will find its purest expression. Thus it will be a מקדש for us. God, fulfilling His promise—ושכנתי בתוכם—will then choose our מקדש as His משכן.

Three times did God Himself reject the Sanctuary, although constructed and maintained for Him in accordance with His commandments; once in Shilo and twice in Jerusalem, and He has also made
known to us the reasons for the destruction of these Sanctuaries. It
was not imperfections or negligence in the construction or maintenance of the Sanctuaries and their furnishings that brought about the
destruction. Rather, it was other requirements which should have been
fulfilled by and through the Sanctuaries but with which Israel did not
comply. Indeed, one glance into the Word of God in the Torah and in
the Prophets would enlighten us as to the requirements that had to be
met as essential prerequisites for God's Sanctuary.

"Stand in the gate of the House of God," was the word that came
from God to Jeremiah.

> Stand in the gate of the House of God and proclaim there
> this word. Say: Hear the Word of God, all of Judah that
> enter these gates to bow down before God. Thus . . . has
> the God of Israel spoken: Amend your ways and your
> deeds, and then I will allow you to dwell in this place. Do
> not trust in the words of falsehood, saying: Temple of God!
> Temple of God! They themselves are the Temple of God.
> For if you amend your ways and your deeds, if you practice
> justice between one man and another, and do not oppress
> strangers, orphans and widows, and do not shed innocent
> blood in this place and do not follow other gods to your
> detriment, I will allow you to dwell in this place in the land
> that I gave to your fathers, from eternity to eternity.
> Behold! You rely on words of falsehood that are of no
> avail. Will you steal, murder, commit adultery, swear false-
> ly and offer sacrifices to Baal and follow other gods that
> you do not know—and then come and stand before Me in
> this House that bears My Name, and say: Now we are
> saved! So that you may continue to practice all these
> abominations? Is this House that bears My Name a den of
> robbers in your eyes? And I, truly I, have also seen it, says
> God. For go now to My abode in Shilo, where I first
> wished My Name to dwell, and see what I have done to it
> because of the wickedness of My people Israel. And now,
> because you practice all that, says God, and I spoke to you

incessantly, but you did not listen, and I called you, but
you did not answer, so I shall do to this house that bears
My Name, in which you put your trust, and to this place
that I have given to you and to your fathers, as I have done
to Shilo, and I shall cast you out, far away from My Countenance, as I have cast out all your brethren, the whole seed
of Ephraim . . .

Thus . . . the God of Israel has spoken: Place your
burnt offerings with your meal offerings and eat meat! For
when I brought your fathers out from Egypt I did not
speak with them nor command them for the sake of burnt
offerings and meal offerings. But I did obligate them concerning the Word: Hearken to My voice, then I shall be
God to you and you will be My people, and walk entirely in
the way that I shall command you, so that it may be well
with you.   (Jeremiah, Chapter 7)

We deliberately chose a passage from the Prophets in order to
expose the perfidious lie with which people nowadays seek to deceive
themselves and others: that the prophets had emerged as the first
"reformers" in Judaism, disseminating more "refined concepts" of
Temple and sacrifices than those taught by "Mosaic Judaism."
Strangely enough, this falsehood is being spread by the very same
leaders who in our day have made a travesty of the synagogue and the
synagogue service, and see in the synagogue the whole of Judaism.
Their ancestors, treating the Temple in the same fashion, earned the
well-deserved rebuke of the Prophets.

But in no way is the word of the Prophets ever "on a different
level" from the Word of God's Law. That which Jeremiah and the
other Prophets "preached" during the period of ruin is nothing else
but that which has been "preached" in the Word of God's Law from
the very beginning.

Consecration of Sanctuary and Life

The Book of Leviticus, תורת כהנים, describes the consecration of the
Sanctuary, the consecration of the sacrifices and of the priests, but also
the sanctification of our own lives and the priestly dedication of all of
Jewish existence. It concludes with a view of the future that is in store
for Israel. This view does *not* read: If you will build Me the Temple and

observe the sacrifices and attend to the sacred objects, I will take up My residence in your midst and bless you. But if you will despise My Temple and neglect My sacrifices, I shall turn My anger against you and destroy your Temple and disperse you into exile. Rather, it reads as follows:

אם בחקתי תלכו *If you will walk in My statutes and will keep and fulfill My commandments,* I shall give your rains in their season, and the earth will give its produce and the tree of the field its fruit. Your threshing shall extend until vintage, and vintage until sowing; you will eat your bread until you are satisfied, and dwell securely in your land. I will give peace in the land, you will rest, and none shall disturb you. I will banish the wild beast from the land, and no sword shall pass through your land. You will pursue your enemies; they will fall before you to the sword. Five of you will pursue a hundred; a hundred of you ten thousand, and your enemies shall fall before you to the sword. I will turn toward you and make you fruitful and multiply you, and I will maintain My covenant with you. You will enjoy yesteryear's harvest and give away the old to store the fresh. *Then I will establish My Dwelling Place in your midst and My soul will not despise you. I will walk in your midst and I will prove Myself to you as God, and you shall be My people.* I, God, your God, Who brought you out from the land of Egypt, so that you should no longer be their slaves. And I broke the bars of your yoke and taught you to walk upright.

ואם לא תשמעו לי *But if you will not hearken to Me, if you will not fulfill all these commandments, if you will despise My laws and disdain My ordinances, so that you will not fulfill all My commandments,* so that you will destroy My covenant, then I, too, shall do this to you. . . . I shall turn my anger against you, you will be smitten before your enemies. . . I shall break the pride of your power, I shall make your sky as iron and your land as brass; you will spend your strength in vain. . . . My soul will despise you, and I shall make your cities a shambles, *lay waste your sanctuaries, and shall not accept the fragrance of your offerings.* . . . and I will disperse you among the nations. . . .

(Lev. 26)

Solomon was still engaged in the building of the First Temple when the word of God came to him: "As for this house that you are building, if you will walk in My statutes and fulfill My ordinances and keep all My commandments, then I will uphold with you My word that I have spoken to your father David, and I shall dwell in the midst of the sons of Israel and will not abandon My people Israel" (I Kings 6, 12–13).

When the magnificent structure had been completed and dedicated in a splendid celebration, God appeared to Solomon a second time, even as He had once appeared to him in Gibeon, and said to him:

> I have heard your prayer and your supplication. I have sanctified this house that you have erected, to establish My Name there forever. My eyes and My heart will dwell there always. And as for you, if you will walk before Me as your father David walked before Me, with dedication of all his heart and with uprightness, to act exactly as I have commanded you; *that is, if you will observe My statutes and ordinances,* then I shall maintain the throne of your dominion over Israel. . . . *But if you and your sons will withdraw from Me, if you will not observe My commandments, My statutes that I have laid down for you,* if you will serve other gods and bow down before them, then I shall destroy Israel from the soil that I have given them, *and shall remove this house, which I have sanctified for My Name, from before My countenance. . . .*
>
> (I Kings 9)

The Prophets did not utter so much as one word that was not already contained in the Word of God's Law. And whatever they said regarding the Temple and the offerings during the period of corruption, and when God's promise of doom came to pass, was exactly that which God had established as truth in Israel from the very beginning.

From all the foregoing, we find the following:

God's dwelling in our midst extends beyond the narrow confines of the Temple. His dwelling in our midst means that His beneficent and protecting Presence will be felt in every aspect of our lives.

Moreover, God's presence in our midst is not dependent on the existence of the Temple, but, in the final analysis, solely on whether we will sanctify and dedicate all of our lives to the fulfillment of His holy will, to the fulfillment of His Law.

ושכנתי בתוכם

All of the blessings and all the protection that were promised to us on every page of God's Law if we observe that Law, represent confirmation of the one idea: ושכנתי בתוכם I shall dwell in your midst, והתהלכתי בתוככם and I shall walk in your midst. The entire Law, with all its "testimonies, statutes, ordinances and commandments" is simply a consecration and devotion of all our lives and existence on earth which will make all of our life a sanctuary elevated toward God. We will then be worthy of having the glory of God enter into our earthly surroundings and having Him walk among us again, as once He walked with the first man in the Garden of Eden.

The fulfillment of God's Law is a precondition for God's nearness. Transgression of God's Law removes God from our midst. This has been stressed especially in connection with the most extreme transgressions of the Law in these three categories: the recognition of God, morality and social justice, expressed by the acts of idolatry, unchastity and murder.

Of the one who gives his children to the Moloch-idol it is said: "I shall set My Countenance against that man and destroy him from the midst of his people, for he has given of his children to the Moloch, to defile My Sanctuary and to profane My holy Name" (Lev. 20, 3).

The chapter on murder and manslaughter concludes with the words: "Do not defile the land in which you dwell, in the midst of which I dwell, for I, God, dwell in the midst of the sons of Israel" (Numbers 35, 34).

The chapter dealing with the purity of family life ends with the warning: "Keep away the sons of Israel from their impurity so that they will not die because of their impurity, by defiling My Dwelling Place which is in their midst" (Lev. 15, 31).

And even "when you go forth in camp against your enemies," we read, "keep yourself from every evil word. . . . For God, your God, walks in the midst of your camp, to save you and to give up your enemies before you; therefore your camps shall be holy, that He may never see a nakedness on you and withdraw from you" (Deut. 23, 10, 15).

It is therefore quite certain that God has appointed the Temple as the particular abode of His Presence, because He has said: "I will appoint My meeting with you there (i.e., I will meet you there; you are to wait for Me there) and I will speak with you from above the כפרת, from between the two cherubim . . ." (Ex. 25, 22). Nevertheless the concept of "His dwelling in Israel's midst" comprises the blessing and protection that His Presence will bestow on every aspect of Israel's life. His Presence is not limited to the Temple and its confines. It can only be the site from which His Presence flows out to spread over all of Israel.

It is equally certain that the Temple as such, and all that comprises its service and rituals, cannot be considered as being exclusively instrumental in bringing about the blessings and protection of God's Presence. The Temple should rather serve as the inspiration for the multifold activities of the nation to consecrate every aspect of Israel's life as a Sanctuary of God.

Hence, in seeking to establish the symbolic significance of the structure and the utensils of the Temple as a מקדש and a משכן, we believe we are not wrong in adhering to the following principle: The significance of the whole and of its details must be sought exclusively within the sphere of ideas relating to the task of the Jew (=מקדש), and to the promise of God (= משכן).

Meaning of the Materials

We will now attempt to ascertain the significance of the materials used in the manufacture of the sacred utensils and the construction of the Tabernacle in the sequence in which these are presented in Exodus 25.

The metals and fabrics comprise gold, silver and copper; sky-blue, purple and crimson wool; linen and goats' hair, also rams' skins dyed red, *tachash* skins and *shittim* wood.

Metals

Gold, silver, copper. Apart from their practical use, we find metals mentioned in Scripture metaphorically used in three distinct contexts; with reference to (a) their material density (b) their material value and (c) their metallurgical properties.

Qualities of strength, invincibility and indestructibility are generally equated with iron and with copper. Jeremiah 1, 18 refers to "a pillar of iron and walls of copper." In Job 40, 18 the bones of the behemoth are compared to ducts of copper, and in Job 41, 19 Leviathan is said to disdain iron as straw and copper as rotten wood. In 6, 12 Job complains: "Is my strength the strength of rocks, or is my flesh of copper?" In Lev. 26, 19 and Deut. 28, 23 the rigid heavens and earth are likened to copper and iron. In Isaiah 48, 4 the House of Jacob is rebuked with these words: "Because I knew that you are obstinate, and your neck is an iron sinew and your brow copper." In this last instance, obstinacy and stubbornness are described by the metaphors of iron and copper. In general, however, Scripture uses the metaphors of iron and copper to describe qualities of firmness and strength.

One telling example of the symbolic character of the whole structure, is the commandment that no stone in the Sanctuary may be cut or even touched with an iron tool. Every iron tool is suggestive of the sword, whereas the purpose of the Sanctuary in general and of the altar in particular is to bring peace; ". . . for you have swung the sword over it and thus desecrated it" (see Ex. 20, 25, Mechilta).

Elsewhere we find metals used as symbols with regard to their value. Gold and silver are considered the most precious of all material possessions and most eagerly sought by man. Thus Isaiah (60, 17) was promised a betterment for his people with these words: "For copper I will bring gold; for iron I will bring silver; for wood, copper; and for stones, iron." These metals are also used in Scripture to reflect the high regard for spiritual values. "If you seek it—wisdom—as silver, and search for it as for hidden treasures" (Proverbs 2, 4); "the laws of God are to be desired more than gold" (Ps. 19, 11); "kindness is more desirable than silver and gold" (Proverbs 22, 1); "the value of wisdom cannot be weighed in silver; gold cannot be compared to it" (Job 28, 15, 19).

The most frequent use of metals as metaphors relates to their metallurgical properties. The more precious metals are found in a pure, unalloyed state but often with mixtures of non-precious ores and residues. Yet, even in this impure state, such metals can be refined. The refining process, in which the pure is separated from non-precious and non-recoverable metals, is effected by means of fire. Moreover, alloys of precious and non-precious metals produce manifold grades of purity and impurity, ranging full cycle from the original state of perfect purity to an equal degree of purity regained by and after repeated refinings. The intermediate degrees of purity can be determined by tests and experiments, but even in the poorest mixture, the smallest granule of precious metal is not lost but can be recovered. Finally, the capability of a precious metal to endure is in direct proportion to its preciousness and purity, and the purest and most precious gold is also that which offers the most lasting resistance to the corroding action of time and the elements.

Thus, metals represent the best symbols for all things good and true in every mixture with elements of evil and falsehood. The concepts of purity, impurity and fineness in metals need only be taken in their symbolic meaning to express the best in ethics and moral truths.

"Test me," says Job (23, 10), "and I shall come forth as gold." Two thirds of the people of Israel will perish, we read in Zechariah 13, 8–9. "And I will bring the third part through the fire and will refine them as silver is refined, and will test them as gold is tested." In Malachi 3,2–3, "the messenger of the Covenant is "like a refiner's fire and like the launderers' cleanser." He is portrayed "sitting as a refiner and purifier of silver, purifying the sons of Levi and purging them as gold and silver." "The refining pot is for silver, and the crucible for gold," we read in Proverbs 17, 3. Isaiah reminds us (48, 10) that "I have refined you, but not in silver; in the crucible of affliction have I chosen you!" In Proverbs 25, 4, 5 dross is separated from silver, and thereafter the vessel goes to the refiner; in this manner evil is eliminated from before the king, and then "his throne shall be established in righteousness."

Scripture also speaks of "choice" silver, "worthless" silver, "drossy" silver and "refined" silver. "The tongue of the righteous is as choice silver" (Prov. 10, 20). "Burning lips and a morose heart are like an earthen vessel overlaid with silver dross" (Prov. 26, 23). God says to Jeremiah (6, 27–30): "In order to test My people, I have placed you among them firm as a fortress. You are to know and therefore to test their ways. They are all dross of the renegades, slanderers, copper and iron; they all create corruption. The bellows have ceased to glow, the lead has been consumed by fire; the refiner has refined in vain, for the wicked have not been separated. They are called worthless silver, because God has scorned them." In Psalm 119, 119 we read that God has condemned the wicked of the earth to destruction "like dross." In Psalm 12, 7 the promises of God are characterized as "pure promises; they prove themselves as refined silver on earth, refined twice sevenfold." Isaiah rebukes the corrupt nation of Judah: "Your silver has become slag" (1, 22). "How has the gold become dim! How has the best metal changed!" Jeremiah laments (Lamentations 4, 1).

The Word of God came to Ezekiel (22, 18): "O son of man! the House of Israel has become dross to Me. Tested in the crucible, they all turn out to be copper and tin, iron and lead; they are dross that only looked like silver. Therefore thus says God, the Lord: Since You all have become dross, I will gather you all into the midst of Jerusalem. As one gathers silver, copper, iron, lead and tin into the crucible to fan a flame around it, to melt it, so will I gather you in My fury and put you down, and melt you. As silver is melted in the crucible, so will you be melted in it and you will know that I, God, have poured out My fury upon you."

Isaiah complains, (1, 22) that Israel's silver had become tarnished and concludes with these words: "I will turn My hand upon you again and will purge away your dross as with lye, and will remove all your tin: and I will restore your judges as before, and your counselors as at the beginning. Only then shall you be called the City of Righteousness, the faithful city . . ."

The message to Daniel concludes (12, 9–10): "Go, Daniel, for the words are locked up and sealed until the time of the end. Before that, many will have to cleanse and purify themselves, and many must become refined and condemn the guilty. . . ."

It is clear from all the passages that in each case the metals are used as symbols characterizing varying degrees of moral purity and truth. While copper represents an impure metal, still unrefined, silver and gold represent varying degrees of purity, moral nobility and constancy.

Some final remarks concerning the relationship between silver and gold. Even though Scripture makes reference to various types of gold; i.e., זהב טהור ("pure gold"—Ex. 25, 39), זהב סגור ("refined gold"—I Kings 6, 20), זהב מופז ("finest gold"—I Kings 10, 18), זהב פרוים ("genuine gold"—II Chronicles 3, 6), we find that gradations of refinement are found only in silver. Indeed, the text speaks of smelting and refining, צרף (an intensified form of שרף—fire), only in the case of silver, while the term בחן, testing, occurs primarily in relation to gold. This may be due to the fact that gold occurs usually in the pure state but can also withstand the most rigorous tests, whereas silver must always be refined to varying degrees.

Finally, consider that metals in general combine malleability with firmness. Under the impact of the hammer or of fire, they will adapt to any desired shape, but once they have assumed the new shape they will maintain it persistently, yielding only to the destructive power of some superior force. Thus, metals demonstrate the qualities which we ourselves should show with regard to the performance of our duty, but especially our attitude toward the will of God as it has been revealed to us. Given all these facts, we should understand all the better why metals lend themselves so well for use as metaphors symbolizing what our moral attitude should be toward our calling.

In view of all the above, copper would correspond to nature in its still unrefined state; silver to the purity and goodness that can be acquired by refining; and gold to that pristine, perfect purity and goodness which can withstand any test.

Wool and Linen

In our essay on the symbolic importance of *tsitsith* we have noted the significance of clothing for man's moral calling in general, and the symbolic use of clothing to relate a person's appearance to his moral character. Threads of wool and flax are elevated to symbolic reminders of our vocation as moral human beings, and particularly the thread תכלת—a reminder of our purpose as Jews. In that connection we also noted that the prohibition of שעטנז—the mixture of wool and flax— occupies a very prominent place in the Law.

This prohibition is presented to us in two distinct contexts. In Levit. 19, 19 it is cited together with the prohibitions against cross-breeding of animals and plants. "Keep My statutes! Do not breed your animals in mixtures of species; do not sow your field with mixtures of seed; neither shall there come upon you a garment made of mixtures of materials—*shaatnes.*" In Deut. 22, 11 it is set forth together with prohibitions against mixing plant and animal species to include כלאי כרם (forbidden mixtures of seed in the vineyard) as well as the prohibition against using animals of different species to work together under one yoke. It is important that the prohibitions against these mixtures are immediately followed by the commandment of *tsitsith,* with which the *shaatnes* prohibition is closely associated in halacha (Yebamoth 4b).

This is not the place to go into greater detail regarding these prohibitions against mixtures of species. We will note here only in general terms that they have a dual purpose. One function is to prevent an arbitrary interference on our part with the laws established by the Creator and Regulator of nature. The other is to impress upon us the respect to God as the Lawgiver and Regulator of the universe, and our duty to observe His laws and ordinances in general, and His law of species in particular.

One glance at these laws is sufficient to substantiate the above. Graftings of trees and matings of animals in the sense of the כלאים-law would constitute a wanton interference by man with the God-given laws of nature. In such mixtures, energies and organisms would be forced to unite with, and to devote their strength to, organic groups which, if left in their natural state, would remain completely alien to each other, and which the Creator and Regulator had in fact designated as separate and mutually exclusive (כלאים—כלא).

However, כלאי זרעים, the prohibition against sowing two different species of seed next to one another, cannot have been intended to forestall an actual interference with the laws of nature by unnatural combinations of species, because it is permitted to sow two species of seed in immediate proximity to one another as long as the beds are separated by a clearly visible division (see משניות כלאים II,7; III,1). Even כלאי כרם can be sowed and planted side by side as long as they are separated by a proper fence (IV,3). This fence separates the two species only in a superficial, symbolic manner. No mixture and no interaction is possible between plants even if they are sown together. Hence the purpose of this particular prohibition may demonstrate and illustrate the deference to the lawgiver's natural order in the arrangement of fields and meadows. By showing to man that all living things forge ahead and develop in perfect obedience to His Law, they demonstrate God's great call to order: למינהו! "Each to its own species!" Each to its own purpose and task! Each group of men, and especially the Jew, must remain true to his own kind and species. For the Jew, this means that he must remain true to his vocation both as a human being and as a Jew. He must function and develop only in a manner worthy of a human being and of a Jew, and move only within the parameter of the Law that desires to make man aware of the command למינהו, which dominates the entire organic world but which man must accept and observe of his own free will in order to fulfill his purpose.

We encounter this admonition in all our contacts with the organic world, in agriculture, in cattle-breeding, in putting animals to work for our purposes, in the animal products we eat, and in the clothing we wear. These encounters come to the forefront particularly as we make increasing use of the organic world.

Shaatnes

Let us consider the prohibition against mixing wool and flax in our clothing in this context. By no means does this prohibition include all mixtures of materials in our clothing. It forbids only mixtures of wool and flax. Thus its meaning must go beyond the general lesson imparted to us in the law of the species. The mixture of these two particular substances must have a very special relation to our purpose, must be especially relevant to our own "law of species;" i.e., our purpose as human beings. As we have already demonstrated in our essay on the *tsitsith* commandment, this assumption becomes increasingly plausible the more closely the garment, in its dual function of concealment and protection, relates to our human vocation and its fulfillment, the more our clothing, in its physical makeup, marks the distinction between the human species and animals, and the more this relationship is stressed by the halachic connection between the commandments of *tsitsith* and *shaatnes*.

Wool and flax are not different kinds of one and the same species; they are not even different species of one kingdom. They are substances from two distinct kingdoms, and their relationship to one another is the same as that between plants and animals. Flax is specifically a vegetable product; wool an animal product. Thus, nothing seems more obvious than that, in symbolic terms, any combination of flax and wool would denote those characteristics which the human body has in common with plants and animals.

Essentially, the physical nature of man consists of two elements, the plant element and the animal element. Nourishment and procreation, and all the phenomena associated with these functions, comprise the plant element. Perception, will and motion form the animal element which, however, functions only in the service of the plant element: feeding and reproduction. In the animal, both elements are intertwined; the vegetative creates and preserves the animal element, and the animal element serves and promotes the vegetative. Both elements together comprise the total animal: a creature whose faculties of perception, volition and motion are devoted solely to feeding and procreation. Wool and flax, plant and animal are inseparably צמר ופשתים יחדו (Deut. 22, 11).

The species known as "man" was assigned a higher calling. In man the plant element must not dominate the animal element; the animal element must not receive its sole purpose and stimuli from the needs of the plant element; the animal element must not be subservient to the plant. Rather, both elements—separately and together—must serve the invisible godly element which, as the reflection of God in the human being, represents the third element through which alone man becomes a human being. To be human means not to employ one's faculties of perception, will and motion solely to feed and reproduce oneself, but rather to eat and to reproduce for the purpose of placing one's faculties of perception, will and action at the service of God.

Plant, animal, man, God: these are the stages which, in ascending order, lead man to perfection. Plant—animal—animal—plant: that is the narrow, closed circle within which the concept "animal" is confined. The control of the vegetative by the animal element, and the subordination and readiness of both elements to the service and the purpose of God, are defined as התקדש, "to make oneself available to God." (See our observation on the concept of קדוש in our essay on *tsitsith*). Conversely, the subordination of the animal forces to the demands of the vegetative stimuli, the placing of human nature, which should look up toward God, at the disposal of base physical stimuli that should be subordinated, is called השתקץ ("to make oneself an abomination"), שיקוץ נפש ("abomination of the soul"), תיעוב נפש ("abhorrence of the soul"), טומאת נפש ("uncleanness of soul"); in short, it is the alienation of man's soul from God. The surrender to a higher purpose is called קדוש; the surrender to a lower element is קדש.

We therefore believe we are not in error if we view the law against the intermingling of wool and flax in our clothing as a symbolic admonition not to permit our animal element to surrender to our vegetative stimuli, not to allow the former to be chained to, and interwoven with, the latter. Rather, we should let the vegetative element of our bodies uphold the animal element, and our animal element in turn uphold our human spirit, so that all three together, our human nature in its upward striving, may be perfected as the bearer of the Divine on earth, as truly "human." The separation and coordination of the three elements in man—the plant, the animal, and the godly element—are expressed in the halachic admonition: לבו רואה את הערוה אסור (ברכות כ״ד), the requirement that ערוה, representing the most intensive form of vegetative life—reproduction and feeding—must be covered over to separate it from לבו, representing the center of our animal element, the element of movement and will. This should also support the statement of R. Shimeon ben Eleazar (כלאים IX, 8) and his treatment of the word שעטנז. He explains שעטנז as נלוז ומליז הוא את אביו שבשמים עליו, "he is detached and detaches himself from his Father in heaven;" literally, "his Father in Heaven Who rests upon him." בני אל ילוזו מעיניך (Mishle 3, 21).

A man who meets the requirements of his calling is "אדם," he is הדום רגלי שכינה, a bearer of God's glory on earth. He performs this function as long as he remains holy to God, as long as his natural drives are subordinated to the vital energies within him, and both his physical drives and vital energies in turn subordinate themselves to his free-willed human essence; and his free-willed human essence, together with all his physical drives and his vital energies subordinate themselves to God, for the fulfillment of His holy will. But if he is שעטנז (ניז denotes something entangled or twisted within itself; hence something isolated), if he "wraps himself in self-entwined isolation"; if he does not see the goal and the direction of his endeavors above and beyond himself in God, but makes his energies subservient only to himself, if he links צמר downward with פשתים, then he has removed himself from his purpose and thereby causes his Father in heaven to move away from him; ולא יראה בך ערות דבר ושב מאחריך. נלוז ומליז "that He see no nakedness in you and turn away from you"—Deut. 23, 15.

Once all the aspects of our lives have been placed within the bond of God's Law, once we employ even our basest vegetative drives of food-getting and reproduction not for selfish pleasure but solely for purposes sacred to God, and our entire being is consecrated to these purposes in priestly holiness, then even the most physical aspect of our vegetative existence becomes as sacred, pure and godly as the most spiritual attainment of the Divine, free-willed aspect of our lives. Once we have attained that level, the dichotomy and conflict in our character will be resolved, and all the directions of our lives will range themselves before God, in perfect harmony with each other. Thus, the

תכלת of the ציצת, the vestments of the כהן גדול and (according to רב, Yoma 12b) the belt worn by the כהן הדיוט, representing the purest symbol of man's call to holiness, are thus logically exempt from the prohibition of שעטנז.

We will now return to the significance of the wool and the flax as substances used in the Sanctuary.

Wool: The animal aspect of our nature as human beings; life with all its vital fores of cognition, will and striving.

Flax: The vegetative aspect of our nature as human beings; nourishment, procreation, and all the stimuli, drives and actions associated with these.

Consequently, it is not particularly striking that these same substances convey both the idea of God's gift and man's consecration, both משכן and מקדש. For indeed we can offer to God only that which we ourselves initially received from Him. All God's gifts are received by us so that we may consecrate them to Him and employ them in His service, in His Sanctuary. This thought was already expressed by Jacob who laid the first cornerstone for all future houses of God. When he dedicated the stone beneath his head as a house of God, he said: וכל אשר תתן לי עשר אעשרנו לך (Gen. 28, 22). And after David had handed over to his son all the treasures he had gathered for the construction of the Temple, he turned to God and said: ממך הכל ומידך נתנו לך, (I Chronicles 29, 14).

Colors

The textiles used in the Sanctuary are also differentiated by color. We may assume that these colors serve to elaborate still further on the concepts symbolized by the materials as such. The color of fine linen would represent one particular aspect of the vegetative element of life, while the three distinct colors of wool would symbolize three distinct aspects of the animal element.

שש, the linen thread, is white. Tradition always identifies garments made from this material as בגדי לבן. White is considered, both in human terms and in the Scriptural text, as the color of purity. בכל עת יהיו בגדיך לבנים "Let your garments always be white," Koheleth declares (9, 8) when he seeks to impress upon us the need to cultivate our physical and moral purity. תחטאני באזוב ואטהר תכבסני ומשלג אלבין "Clear me of sin with hyssop, so that I may become pure; wash me and I will be whiter than snow" (Ps. 51, 9). אם יהיו חטאיכם כשנים כשלג ילבינו אם יאדימו כתולע כצמר יהיו "And even if your sins were as scarlet, they shall be as white as snow" (Isaiah 1, 18). In Daniel 12, 10: יתבררו ויתלבנו ויצרפו רבים "Many will have to cleanse and purify themselves, and many must become refined." The Hebrew term for "purify themselves" is derived from התלבן, literally, "make oneself white."

We are therefore justified in interpreting the white color of linen as a symbol of purity; שש, then, does not symbolize man's "vegetative" life in general, but quite specifically the *purity* of man's vegetative life. We see that in the Law of God, moral purity refers mainly to the forces of vegetative life and its stimuli. The Law views depravity as the gravest defilement of the pure in man. "Conceived and raised in purity" and "pure in nourishment and in family life"—these are the primary and indispensable conditions for all spiritual perfection and elevation toward God; hence the reason why precisely the שש appears as the color of purity. *Purity characterizes the level of moral elevation required by God particularly for the vegetative aspect of the human being.* The laws that form a hedge around the physical, sensual aspect of our lives shield the human being from substances and impulses that the Lawgiver has declared incompatible with his purity and his godly purpose. תולעת שני scarlet, ארגמן purple and תכלת (blue-violet) are the three colors in which the woolen thread occurs as a component of the Sanctuary. If we look at the sequence in which the textiles תכלת ארגמן תולעת שני ושש are named alongside the metals, זהב וכסף ונחשת, we will note that both textiles and metals are listed in a descending order. Just as זהב represents the highest form of metal and נחשת the lowest, so, too, we must consider תכלת as the highest color of all, their ascending order being: שש, תולעת שני, ארגמן, and תכלת.

We have already considered שש and its symbolic value. Next to it we note תולעת שני, followed by ארגמן. We believe that we must consider these two colors together because both of them are shades of red, and hence appear to be progressive nuances of one and the same level.

Having interpreted the white linen as symbolizing the vegetative aspect of life in terms of its particular characteristics, we understand the woolen threads of three different colors as symbolizing the animal aspect but in three gradations, signifying three distinct types.

תולעת שני and ארגמן are both wool dyed with red coloring matter.

Like the substance itself, the coloring matter, too, is an animal product.

If we scan the Scriptural text for references to the color red, we will see that red is used frequently in connection with abundant, exuberant vitality. David as a~youth is described as אדמוני, reddish, having the complexion of vitality and good health (I Samuel 16, 12). Esau came forth from his mother's womb "reddish" and consequently becomes known as "Edom" (Gen. 25, 25, 30). "The virtuous youth of Israel was brighter than snow, purer than milk and more reddish of complexion than corals" (Lamentations 4, 7). "What is your beloved more than another beloved?" the nations ask Israel (Song of Songs 5, 9). "My beloved is pure and reddish," Israel replies, "like a banner, surrounded by myriads." Here we have brightness and reddishness, purity and life!

However, in Isaiah 1,18, the color red appears as the color of guilt. In Verse 15, the prophet's accusation is summarized with the words, "Your hands are full of blood." Verse 16 then bids the guilty to "wash yourselves, make yourselves clean. . . ." Clearly, then, the color of blood in these passages signifies crime. The Scriptural use of scarlet in the literal sense as the color of blood is illustrated in Nahum 2, 4 מגן גבוריה מָאֳדָם—"the shields of his mighty men is colored in red", and Isaiah 63,2 מדוע אדם ללבושך—"why are your garments stained red". The interpretation of red as a sign of vitality derives from the original meaning of the color: blood as the bearer of life; כי נפש כל בשר דמו בנפשו הוא (Levit. 17, 14).

Consequently, if wool as a fabric represents the "animal" aspect of human nature, then wool dyed red represents the animal factor in its full vitality.

However, this vitality occurs in two degrees of intensity, as symbolized by תולעת שני and ארגמן. We have already deduced from the comparable sequence of זהב כסף ונחשת with תכלת ארגמן ותולעת שני, that תולעת שני is one step below ארגמן. A survey of the Scriptural text will lead to the same conclusion. ארגמן occurs only in descriptions of the garments of idols, kings and lords. In Jeremiah 10, 9 the idols made of gold or silver are clad in תכלת וארגמן. According to Judges 8, 26, the Midianite kings wore garments of ארגמן. In Esther 8, 15, Mordecai departs from the presence of King Ahasuerus clad in royal apparel, which includes a mantle of linen and ארגמן. In Proverbs 31, 22 the mistress of the house is dressed in garments of linen and ארגמן, while her household is clothed in שני. In general, שני occurs in Scripture as the color of ordinary finery. King Saul clothes the daughters of Israel in שני. In Jeremiah 4, 30 we read: "And even if you clothe yourself in שני." The Book of Lamentations (4, 5) describes the over-indulged in Judah as having been "brought up in תולע."

Thus, we see the two shades of red, scarlet and purple, representing a lower and higher level of life, the former referring to the vital forces and actions of the animal and the latter to the vital energies and endeavors of the human in man. Certainly man is called אדם, the "red one" *par excellence.* We have already noted in our essay on *tsitsith* that red is the least refracted ray in the spectrum, the ray closest to the pure light; hence it is a most appropriate metaphor for man, the creature closest to God, the image of God; ותחסרהו מעט מאלקים (Ps. 8, 6).

We have noted that תכלת is the color indicating the limits of our horizon, the invisible world that lies beyond our physical field of vision; i.e., the Divine. Therefore, a תכלת-colored thread of wool in the human garment is the color representing the Divine that has been revealed to us; it is the color of God's covenant with man, the symbol of the Divine that unites with the pure human being, permeating and shaping every aspect of his life.

Thus the four colors would parallel all the aspects of human nature, in ascending order, as follows:

שש:	the vegetative
שני:	the animal
ארגמן:	the human in man
תכלת:	the Divine in man

The use of עזים, goats' hair, in the making of garments was restricted to mourning and penitential garb; שק, sackcloth, and אדרת שער, the hairy mantle, in which the false prophets cloaked themselves in order to deceive—למען כחש (Zechariah 13, 4). Apparently this material was not really suited for garments designed to cling to the body, but must have served very well as material for protective coverings. For this reason, goats' hair was used predominantly in the making of sacks. Rizpah, daughter of Aiah, spread a cloth of such material upon a rock to protect the slain bodies of her loved ones over a period of many months (II Samuel 21, 10).

We will discuss the rams' and tachash skins when we study their use in the Sanctuary. (See Commentary, Exodus 26).

Shittim Wood

At this point, we have only the שטים wood left to consider. עץ, the tree, is the one species among all organic creations that develops before our eyes from the smallest of beginnings, takes the longest to complete its process of maturation, proliferates and expands the most in its development, and at the same time becomes taller and reaches a greater age than any other living thing. עץ, the tree, is consequently the most natural metaphor for any long-continued, steady process of maturation. It symbolizes hope that will find its realization over a long period of time and through dedicated effort. However, the blossoming, the progress and the life span of the tree are dependent on external factors, particularly the availability and proximity of water, and whether the tree can absorb that water in sufficient quantities. There-fore the tree becomes an apt metaphor for the righteous man, who is firmly grounded in God and His Word, from which he derives his development and prosperity. God and His Law represent the well springs of living waters and man is the tree that draws from them his strength, his substance, his life and his good fortune, without which he would wither and die.

Thus, כי יש לעץ תקוה "there is always hope for the tree if it is cut down, it will regenerate itself and will not cease to draw water into its trunk and branches. Even if its roots in the ground grow old and its trunk should die off, the strength of the water will cause it to bud again and to yield fruit like a young plant. Should then a man die when he becomes weak? Should man indeed pass away and exist no more?" (Job 14, 7–10).

In Jeremiah (17, 5–13) we read: "He who trusts in men, who allows flesh to be his arm, and whose heart departs from God shall be like one alone in the desert, living on heat-parched soil that offers no habi-tation." However, והיה כעץ ברוך הגבר אשר יבטח בה' "he who trusts in God שתול and he shall be like a tree planted near the water, that spreads out its roots to the water's branch; he shall not feel it when heat comes; his leaf shall always be fresh; and he shall not be anxious at the time of drought; he shall never cease yielding fruit." For מקוה ישראל ה' "Israel's wellspring is God; he that forsakes Him shall wither and go to ruin; he shall be marked as a deserter even on earth because he has forsaken God, the fountain of living waters." In the same spirit, Psalm 1 describes תורת ה׳, the Law of God, as the wellspring through which he who dedicates himself to it with all his thoughts and energies, והיה כעץ שתול על פלגי מים אשר פריו יתן בעתו ועלהו לא יבול וכל אשר יעשה יצליח, "will become like a tree, planted by rivers of water, that yields its fruits in due season, and whose leaf never withers; whatever he sets out to do will prosper."

In chapter 65 of the Book of Isaiah, in which the prophet depicts the restoration of Eden-like conditions on earth, and with it the restoration of human longevity, we read כי כימי העץ ימי עמי ומעשה ידיהם יבלו בחירי (Verse 22), "for as the days of the tree, so shall be the days of My people, and My chosen ones shall endure beyond the work of their hands."

In Proverbs 3, 18, wisdom itself is compared to a tree: עץ חיים היא למחזיקים בה "It is a tree of life for those that cling to it." In Chapter 11, 30 we read פרי צדיק עץ חיים, "the fruit of the righteous," that for which the righteous man aspires and which he achieves is not self-serving or sterile but "a tree of life." The "tree of life" is a metaphor (15, 4) for מרפא לשון עץ חיים "whatever brings healing to the *speech* of man," for what makes his word good and true.

While עץ, the tree in general, is a simile for growth and development, ארז the cedar, is a symbol of strength and height. According to Rosh Hashanah 23a, there are ten kinds of cedar; one of these is שיטה, the wood that was used in the construction of the Sanctuary and of its furnishings. The cedar generally is used as a simile for conspicuous power. The cedar's special characteristic is its ability to blossom and grow with ever-renewed vigor, and so this tree becomes the best example for growth. In Amos 2, 9 the power of the Emorites, whom God drove away from before Israel, is described as having had a "height like the height of cedars." In Song of Songs 5, 15, Israel's beloved is described as "excellent as the cedars." According to Psalm 80, 11, Israel, the vine planted by God, had "branches like the cedars of God." In depicting the rise, the arrogance and the fall of the Assyrian empire, Ezekiel (Chapter 31) uses the metaphor of a cedar that thrived under conditions most favorable for its growth, reaching the greatest height and beauty, only to be destroyed in the end. Similarly, (Chapter

17) the story of the ill-fated attempt of the last Jewish prince, who had been put up as a puppet of Assyria, to gain independence for his country by an alliance with Egypt, is told as a parable of the branch of a cedar. The prophet then uses the sprig of a cedar planted by God as a metaphor to foretell the future glorious restoration of the Jewish kingdom.

In Psalm 92, 13 the cedar symbolizes the Divinely blessed, satisfying life of the righteous: "The righteous shall flourish like the palm tree; he shall grow like a cedar in Lebanon, planted in the House of God they shall flourish in the courts of our God. They shall still bring forth fruit in old age; they shall be full of strength and vigor." In Numbers 24, 6 Balaam, the non-Jewish seer, whose eyes have been opened, described the huts and the dwellings of Jacob-Israel as spreading blessings "like brooks," as blessed "as gardens by the riverside," as "aloe trees planted by God," as "cedars beside the waters; the water flows from God's sources, and its seed is by many waters." In this passage it is not the individual but the institution of the family, מה טבו אהליך יעקב, the home, that is likened to a tree which has been blessed by God. The source of growth and blossoming of this tree is the fountain of God's blessing, and the development of this tree is like that of the cedar, vigorous and enduring.

Thus, עץ שטים is used in the construction of the Sanctuary and of its accessories as the symbol of a vigorous, enduring, ever-renewed and continuous development.

The Vessels—כלים

Having specified the materials which Israel as a national entity is to accept from its individual members of a freely given "uplifted offering for God," and having stated the purpose of these denominations with the words: ועשו לי מקדש ושכנתי בתוכם, the Scriptural text proceeds to give detailed specifications for the construction of this משכן—מקדש.

In the reference to the plans shown to Moses (Ex. 25, 9), the משכן is mentioned first, followed by כלים. This is only natural, for when viewing the completed Sanctuary one sees first the structure and then its contents. However, the detailed specifications that follow are given in reverse order; they begin with the preparation of the כלים and then proceed to the משכן itself. The intention here, it would seem, is to impress upon us that we must not regard the כלי מקדש as we would the contents of an ordinary building. The כלים of the Sanctuary are not intended as mere "fittings" for the structure. The כלים are the essentials; the משכן serves as their repository.

Earlier in this study we derived from the verse ועשו לי מקדש ושכנתי בתוכם the idea that the physical structure of the Tabernacle would symbolize its two distinct functions: מקדש and משכן. מקדש: dedication and sanctification, hence, the elevation of all our earthly concerns toward God, and, as a consequence, משכן: the entry of God's glory into our earthly sphere, the promised beneficent and protective Presence of God, His "dwelling" in our midst.

The order in which the construction of the Tabernacle is presented readily suggests to us that we should see the כלים as expressing the idea of מקדש, the establishment of a way of life on earth that is dedicated to God, while we would see the משכן as expressing the idea of God's dwelling in our midst.

ארון—*The Holy Ark*

The first of the כלים specified for the Tabernacle is ארון, the Ark of the Testimony. It is the only כלי concerning which the wording of the text implies that it must be prepared by the entire nation. As in Ex. 25, 8 ועשו לי מקדש, the verse pertaining to the Ark ועשו ארון עצי שטים is phrased in the third person plural. However, the detailed instructions that follow, ועשית, וצפית, up to the completed preparation of all the כלים, the משכן and the חצר are addressed to Moses in the second person singular. It almost appears as if the entire task implicit in the command ועשו לי מקדש is concentrated in the command ועשו ארון עצי שטים and that everything that followed was intended only as an elaboration on the ארון.

The ארון consists of three basic parts: the Ark itself, the cover bearing the cherubim, and the carrying poles. The two carrying poles are not meant to be required only when the Ark traveled. They were not to be removed from the Ark at any time; לא יסורו ממנו, והמסיר בדי ארון לוקה (Yoma 72a). (In fact, תוספות suggests that the Ark had two pairs of carrying poles. One pair had to remain in place at all times; they were never to be removed from the Ark. However, they were not used for carrying the Ark; hence their purpose was exclusively symbolic. The Ark was carried on a second pair of poles that were used only for this purpose and were put in place only when it was necessary to transport the Ark. (שם ד"ה בטבעות הארון)

ארון, כפורת and בדים, the basic components of the Ark, correspond to the three functions of the Ark with regard to the לוחות הברית: receiving, protecting and carrying. Together with their contents, the Testimony of the Law, these components present to us the Law of God, received, protected and carried aloft through the ages.

The Ark of Wood and Gold

ארון, derived from ארה, to gather for one's own enjoyment (Song of Songs 5, 1; Ps. 80, 13), like שאן from שאה, describes a container that does not serve as an accidental, temporary receptacle of certain objects, but receives its contents in such a manner that the latter are accepted and retained for all time. The only other connotations, aside from the Ark of the Testimony, in which the term ארון occurs are those of coffin in Genesis 50, 26 and treasure chest to receive the monetary donations for the Sanctuary in II Kings 12, 10 and II Chronicles 24, 8. By making an ארון to receive the Testimony of the Law, Israel signifies that it has accepted the Law and has taken it as its very own. The coffin receives the remains; the chest receives the donations for the Sanctuary, and the Ark receives the Law on behalf of Israel.

The ארון of the Law was a chest composed of three layers; a chest of שטים wood, enclosed between two receptacles made of gold. ועשו ארון עצי שטים. The Law itself is not meant to "progress" or "develop," having been given in its final form, engraved on tablets of stone. Not the Law, but we ourselves are the tree that can and should develop in never-ceasing progress and self-refinement. The Law is the fountain of living waters near and through which we mature and flourish. The meaning of בפקודיך אשיחה ("I will meditate upon Your mandates"—Ps. 119, 15) is, I grow spiritually in Your laws. Israel accepts the תורה so that through it, it will become כעץ שתול על פלגי מים וגו', "like a tree, planted by rivers of water, that yields its fruit in due season, whose leaf does not wither, and whatever he does he will complete successfully." (Ps. 1, 3)

וצפית אתו זהב טהור ("And you shall overlay it with pure gold"—Ex. 25, 11: However, the receptivity and the capacity for development which Israel brings to its observance of the Law must be paired with firmness, perserverance and constancy toward everything noble and good and true. The wood must be joined by metal; the tree by gold. The acceptance of God's Law requires a capacity for development coupled with constancy, a noble constancy that must prove itself both within and without; מבית ומחוץ תצפנו ("within and without shall you overlay it"). Purity and firmness everywhere in life, free from all baseness and evil, free from meanness and falsehood, the ability to resist corruption and distortion—these are the prerequisites, these the golden limits within which life, like a tree, must continuously grow and unfold from the soil of the Law. Impervious to everything evil, predisposed to everything good: this is the dual character which makes Israel fit to be a receptacle for the Law of God. The avoidance of evil in private and public life and the achievement of all that is good—this is the sum total of the purpose for which Israel has received and accepted the Law.

ועשית עליו זר זהב סביב (and you shall make upon it a circlet of gold around it"): The Ark is surrounded by a band or "circlet" formed by the edge of the golden outer wall of the Ark protruding slightly above the corner of the Ark. זר, "circlet," is derived from זור, "alien" and implies the natural distance from others. Thus, by virtue of its shape as well as by its linguistic definition, the circlet signifies the sanctity and inviolability of the sacred utensils. It is therefore related both etymologically and objectively to the term נזר, "crown" and "diadem."

Note that this circlet is not a separate piece of gold attached to the Ark but is formed by a protruding part of the Ark itself. Therefore, its message to us may well be as follows: If Israel will only devote itself to proving its firmness and strength by preserving the purity of its life, it will become immune to any attack. וראו כל עמי הארץ כי שם ה׳ נקרא עליך ויראו ממך ("all the nations of the world will see that the Name of God has been pronounced over you, and they will be afraid of you"—Deut. 28, 10), and קדש ישראל לה׳ ראשית תבואתה כל אוכליו יאשמו רעה תבא אליהם ("Israel is God's hallowed portion, The first fruits of His crop. All that devour him shall be held guilty; evil shall come upon them"—Jeremiah 2, 3).

If we summarize the thoughts expressed by the form of the Ark and by the materials used in its construction, we will find that they present both aspects of the fulfillment of God's Law, with עצי שטים symbolizing the observance of the positive commandments and זהב טהור, the observance of the prohibitions.

כפורת—כרובים

כפורת. All other connotations of the root כפר—pitch, frost, village, head of a pride of lions, atonement—converge on one basic concept, that of covering, protecting and preserving. Consequently, כפורת is simply a cover to protect and preserve. Upon this cover were two כרובים which were not separate pieces imposed upon the cover but were מקשה of one piece, hammered out משני קצות הכפורת shaped from the two ends of the cover. Thus, the *cover itself develops into cherubim at both its ends*.

כרובים: Cherubim in Scripture have two distinct functions: they act as *guardians* or *protectors,* and as *bearers of the glory of God.* In Genesis 3, 24 cherubim are appointed to guard the way to the Tree of Life. אַתְּ כרוב ממשח הסוכך, is the word to the king of Tyre (Ezekiel 28, 14). "You are a cherub, having been anointed as a protector." The king is also described as a כרוב הסוכך "protecting cherub." Thus there should be no doubt that the cherubim are assigned the role of guardians and protectors. They also serve as bearers of the glory of God. In Ps. 18, 11 God is described as rushing to David's aid borne upon cherubim. In the ninth and tenth chapters of the Book of Ezekiel cherubim occur as the bearers of God's glory. This function of the cherubim is confirmed particularly by the attribute of God as יושב הכרובים (Ps. 80, 2; Ps. 99, 1; I Samuel 4, 4; II Samuel 6, 2; II Kings 19, 15; I Chronicles 13, 6 and Isaiah 37, 16).

Note that the term used by Scripture in each instance is neither יושב כרובים nor על הכרובים, but יושב הכרובים. This implies not a transient, temporary sojourn but a steady, lasting presence; God does not "sit" upon the cherubim, but rather "dwells" upon them. Compare יושב הארץ and יושב בארץ and all passages where יושב is used with reference to a place, with or without a preposition.

In the Sanctuary, too, cherubim occur in this dual meaning, as expressed in the description of their position (Ex. 25, 20) "The cherubim shall spread out their wings upward"—(למעלה, "upward," and not מלמעלה "over it")—"covering, סוככים, with their wings above the cover, their faces turned one to another; toward the Ark cover shall the faces of the cherubim be turned." The covering and protective function of the cherubim is explicitly stated; it is clearly expressed by the term סוככים applied to the wings, and by the specification that the faces of the cherubim must be turned toward the Ark cover. However, the words פרשי כנפים למעלה seem to imply the additional function of the cherubim. The wings that were to spread upward above the Ark-cover performed both functions: they protected the Ark-cover and at the same time they bore the glory of God. However, the function of guarding and protecting was predominant because the protector and the object they protected were both visible. The other function was indicated by the outspread position of the wings bearing an invisible object resting above them. The bearers and their act of carrying were visible but the "object" that they bore could not be seen because it was the glory of God, which cannot be contained in any image.

However, the fact that the cherubim of the Ark-cover were indeed meant to bear the glory of God is documented not only by the expression יושב הכרובים which we have cited but also by the passages we have quoted from the Book of Ezekiel. The ninth and tenth chapters of the Book of Ezekiel describe סילוק שכינה, the withdrawal of the glory of God from the Temple that has been doomed to destruction. It is obvious from these passages that, prior to that time, the glory of God had indeed rested above and upon the cherubim of the Temple. Therefore, though Psalm 18, 11 portrays a cherub in general as the bearer of a manifestation of God, the relevant passages in the Book of Ezekiel would justify our associating the attribute of יושב הכרובים with the specific cherubim on the Ark of the Covenant in the Holy of Holies, since this attribute is mostly used in Scripture with reference to the closest bond between God and Israel. See Psalm 80, 2 II Kings 19, 15, Isaiah 37, 16. Moreover, in I Samuel 4, 4, II Samuel 6, 2 and I Chronicles 13, 6 the expression also occurs in association with the Ark.

This protecting and guarding function of the cherubim seems to us so identical with the function of the כפורת that we are led to consider the cherubim as linked conceptually with the כפורת. We have seen that the role of the כפורת is clearly that of a guarding and protecting cover. The cherubim are of one piece with the כפורת, the end of the Ark cover rising to form them.

To be precise, the cherubim are not described as the direct guardians and keepers of the Testimony itself (the Tablets) but as guardians and keepers of the כפורת. אל הכפרת יהיו פני . . . סככים בכנפיהם על הכפרת הכרבים. Their actual guardianship and their spiritual attention are both directed initially to the כפורת. *The Ark cover protects the Testimony, and the cherubim protect the Ark cover.* Yet, the cherubim are part of the cover itself. Having accomplished the task of protecting the Testimony—משני קצות הכפרת "at the two ends of the Ark cover"—the cover rises above itself and turns into its own pair of cherubim, as it were, which will protect it and bear the glory of God. This structural arrangement expresses a most significant thought:

By keeping the Law of God, he that keeps it becomes his own cherub and also the cherub of the glory of God. His guardianship of the Law of God becomes his own protection and at the same time makes him a bearer of God's glory of earth.

The ארון [which is made of golden and wooden parts] symbolizes the spirit with which Israel should *fulfill* the Law of God. It shows that Israel should synthesize gold-like pure constancy to resist all evil and tree-like vigorous activity for all that is good סור מרע ועשה טוב. To these aspects of fulfillment symbolized by the Ark, the כפורת adds the concept of *"guarding,"* guarding and preservation, thus encompassing what the Word of God expects of us as regards the שמירה of the מצות. ושמרתם ועשיתם—that is what God expects of Israel with regard to His Law.

As we have seen, the position of the cherubim demonstrates their "guarding" of the כפורת. Their faces turned toward the Ark cover express the idea of spiritual protection, and the wings spread over the Ark cover symbolize physical protection. In a similar vein, our Sages have perceived the שמירה of the מצות, which is required of us, side by side with עשיה, fulfillment in practice and concentration; a constant directing of the mind toward the Law of God, and *actual "guarding"*: keeping the Law of God safe from transgression and also taking active steps to promote its observance.

Fulfillment requires תלמד, the comprehension and grasp of the Law. "Guarding" or "keeping" entails סייגים ותקנות, fences around the Law and other ordinances which Israel itself has instituted as משמרת around the Law. Sifra א״מ offers the following explanation to the verse את חקתי תשמרו ללכת בהם, תשמרו זו המשנה ללכת בהם זה המעשה, תשמרו ללכת בהם נגוד (לא המשנה נגד אלא המעשה נגוד)—intention derived from נגד—towards); עשו משמרת למשמרתי and ושמרתם את משמרתי שמרו לי משמרתי.

Thus ארון and כפורת symbolize the dedication of all our mental and physical forces to the "guarding" and fulfillment of the Law that Israel has accepted from the hands of God. The cherubim, which are formed by the ends of the כפורת, symbolize the reward for Israel as a consequence of their "guarding" and fulfilling the Law. Every time Israel "guards" or fulfills one of the laws of God, it ensures its own survival, promotes its own welfare and prepares itself to become a dwelling place for God's glory on earth. The concern and the care which Israel extends to the "guarding" and fulfillment of the תורה become the "cherubs," which will guard and preserve Israel and invite the שכינה, the glory of God, to rest upon it.

The description of the golden Ark of the Testimony which encloses and protects the Law of God in receptacles of gold and wood, with a golden cover that culminates in cherubim performing functions of protection and carrying, expresses the words with which God charged Joshua, the leader of Israel: רק חזק ואמץ מאד לשמר לעשות ככל התורה אשר צוך משה עבדי אל תסור ממנו ימין ושמאול למען תשכיל בכל אשר תלך, לא ימוש ספר התורה הזה מפיך והגית בו יומם ולילה למען תשמר לעשות ככל הכתוב בו כי אז תצליח את דרכך ואז תשכיל, הלוא צויתיך חזק ואמץ אל תערץ ואל תחת כי עמך ה׳ אלקיך בכל אשר תלך "Above all, be firm and strong to guard as well as to practice according to the entire Teaching that My servant Moses has commanded you. Do not deviate from it to the left or to the right, so that you may act prudently in all wherein you walk. The Book of this Teaching shall not depart from your mouth, and you shall meditate in it day and night, so that you will guard it to act in accordance with all that is written in it. For then you will cause your ways to prosper and you will act prudently. Behold I command this to you. Therefore be strong and firm, do not fear and do not be afraid, for ה׳, your God, is with you wherever you go" (Joshua 1, 7–9).

The Ark conveys to us that which God has promised to our entire nation as a consequence of our "guarding" and fulfilling His Law: והיה עקב תשמעון את המשפטים האלה ושמרתם ועשיתם אותם ושמר ה׳ אלקיך לך את הברית ואת החסד אשר נשבע לאבותיך ואהבך וברכך והרבך וגו׳ "If you will hearken to these ordinances and you will guard and fulfill them, then ה׳ your God, will guard for you the covenant and the love He has sworn to your fathers; He will love you, He will bless you, He will multiply you . . ." (Deut. 7, 12–13).

And finally, the Ark teaches us what God's Law proclaims with regard to itself for all to hear: By "guarding" and fulfilling the Law, Israel simply lays the foundation for its own survival and welfare and preserves for itself the rewarding bond and nearness of its God.

Two Cherubim—Two Tablets
Study and Fulfillment

Why שני כרובים—why *two* cherubim? The כפורת that rises at either end to form the cherubim; the "guarding" of the Law, whose consequence for Israel is God's protection and rewarding nearness; Israel, which by "guarding" the Divine Testimony entrusted to it, becomes its own cherub and at the same time the cherub of the Divine Presence on earth—all these ideas really form one single concept. Hence one cherub would seem sufficient to symbolize them all.

The cherubim turned not only toward the כפורת but also toward one another: ופניהם איש אל אחיו. Consequently, the cherubim must represent two distinct functions. *Together,* as one, they perform the task of "guarding" the כפורת, the Ark cover which in turn guards the Law. But while they do so, they regard one another, each complemented in its mission by the other. They work together to "guard" the cover that guards the Law. For it is written: והיו הכרובים פרשי כנפים וגו' ופניהם איש אל אחיו אל הכפרת יהיו פני הכרבים.

Every component of the Ark presents a dual aspect. The Testimony, the object of the "guarding," consists of *two* tablets. The Ark itself, which is the receptacle of the Testimony, is composed of *two* substances. The "guarding" itself, as we have already noted, has *two* aspects: the theoretical and the practical. These repeated dual factors complement one another. Consequently, they appear as two cherubim, their faces turned toward one another, but both their faces are turned also *toward* the כפורת which they are to guard.

The Testimony consists of two tablets that are equal to one another in every respect: לחת כתיב שני לחת העדות. The one tablet carries the basis מצות שבין אדם למקום, for our relations with God, and the other, מצות שבין אדם לחברו, the basis for our relations with our fellow men. Both are equal components of God's Law. Neither can do without the other; neither can replace the other. If the "guarding" of the Law is to "guard" its "guardian," Israel, and Israel is to be perfected so that

it can become a bearer of the glory of God, then this "guarding" must
become applicable in equal measure to the contents of both tablets,
each complementing the other, each seeing its own purpose in the
other. And so this "guarding," must emerge not in the form of *one*
cherub, but in the symbolic form of a *pair* of cherubim, each paying
heed to the other, each seeing its own purpose in the other. And by
working together to guard the cover that guards the Law, this pair of
cherubim offers itself as the abode for the glory of God on earth: משני
קצות הכפרת שנים כרבים פורשי כנפים למעלה—סוככים בכנפיהם על הכפרת—
פניהם איש אל אחיו

The fulfillment of the Law, as symbolized by the ארון, is to be
accomplished in two directions: the commandments and the prohibitions, the accomplishment of good and the avoidance of evil. Both
these forces and both these aspects are of equal rank. Neither can do
without the other. Neither can replace the other. Each complements
the other. They do not relate to one another as two distinct stations,
with the lower stage to be discarded once the higher station has been
attained. Rather, both of them are part of the fulfillment of the Law,
and hence indispensable to the "guarding" of the Law. Only when the
"guarding" of the Law attends to both aspects of the fulfillment of the
Law with the same concern and the same care; only when Israel will
devote its energy and strength to accomplish all that is good and noble
and avoid and combat all that is base and evil—only then will both
aspects of Jewish life blossom into a pair of cherubim, with each seeing
its own worth and significance in the other; cherubim beneath whose
wings Israel itself will rest securely, preparing an abode on earth for
the glory of God: שני הכרובים משני קצות הכפרת—סוככים בכנפיהם על
הכפרת—אל הכפרת פניהם—פניהם איש אל אחיו—פורשי כנפים למעלה

The "guarding," the כפורת itself, which culminates in the cherubim,
the שמירת המצות, develops in *two* distinct aspects: תלמוד, spiritual
"guarding," and משמרת למשמרת, "guarding" in practice. In the spiritual
"guarding," both mind and spirit are dedicated to the constant and
ever-deeper understanding of God's Law, so that Israel may ever be
aware of the Law and its requirements, and ever see before it the ideal
it is to attain, shining in unclouded truth and clarity. In the practical
aspect of "guarding," the realization of this ideal is seen as the consummate good; as the sum total of life's purpose, so that no sacrifice is
considered too great to this end. In this aspect of "guarding," Israel

will gladly take upon itself any obligation that might bring it closer to the fulfillment of this ideal. These two aspects, theory and practice, indispensably complement each other, and as cherubim protect and preserve Israel so that it can be bear God's glory on earth. שני כרבים משני קצותיו, פרשי כנפים למעלה.

Thus, the pair of כרובים represent the   aspect of the Law (מצות עשה ואל תעשה), its fulfillment (מצות בין אדם למקום ובין אדם לחברו) and its "guarding" (תלמוד ומשמרת—practice and theory). The כפורת, with its cherubim at *both* ends, symbolically demonstrates that there must be no one-sidedness in the fulfillment and "guarding" of the Law, and that survival, Divine protection and God's rewarding nearness will come only if Israel fulfills and "guards" the entire Law in all its aspects—תורת ה' תמימה. The warning לא תסור ימין ושמאול, which recurs so often in Scripture refers to this total observance and fulfillment of the Law.

An analysis of the קרבנות צבור, the prescribed offerings made by the nation as a whole, shows that the collective character of the nation is symbolized by two distinct expressions: the number "one" and the number "two." The Scriptural text also employs two distinct terms to describe the nation as a unit: גוי and עם. גוי designates the community as a *nation,* a single closed unit in its relation to the world outside, while עם (עמם) defines it as a *society,* in terms of the multiplicity of individuals joined together. In the same manner, the nation is represented in the Sanctuary in two distinct terms: as one united whole, symbolized by the number one, and as a multitude of individual members, symbolized by the number two, the minimum of the many.

The Nation and the Holy Ark

If we perceive the ארון as representing Israel as it accepts the Law of God in order to carry it out with vigor and steadfastness, and we see in the כפורת a symbol of Israel's constancy as a keeper of the Law, then the pair of cherubim that emerges from the כפורת at either end may be taken to symbolize Israel fulfilling its mandate to guard the Law. If Israel, with the constancy symbolized by gold, watches faithfully over the consummate fulfillment of the entire Law entrusted to it, then it will not only become a גוי קדוש, a united national entity, but will also be a ממלכת כהנים, a society in which every single member performs a three-

fold function, namely to promote the personal happiness of his neighbor, to guard the welfare of the community as a whole, and to be one
of the bearers of God's glory on earth. Then all of the people of Israel
will become cherubim bound to one another by mutual respect, turning toward one another as brothers, supporting one another, answer-
ing for one another, open to one another. They will act as brothers to
guard the community that keeps the Law, working together to
become, in a figurative sense, a throne for the glory of God on earth.
Israel will be likened to שנים כרבים משני קצות הכפרת—two cherubim at the
two ends of the Ark Cover, פניהם איש אל אחיו—with their faces one to
another, פרשי כנפים למעלה—spreading out their wings on high סככים
בכנפיהם על הכפרת—screening the Ark cover with their wings, אל הכפרת
פניהם—their faces toward the Ark cover; ישב הכרבים—He Who is enthroned upon the cherubim (Ps. 80, 2) will be one with יושב תהלות
ישראל—He Who is enthroned upon the praises of Israel—Ps. 22, 4.

If we conceive of Israel itself—here, and particularly in this last
interpretation—as a cherub, we might note that in Ezekiel 28, the king
of Tyre is described in some detail as כרוב סוכך, the guarding cherub. If
the king was called a cherub because the resources and the culture of
nations had been entrusted to Him, then surely the metaphor of
cherub may be applied all the more to Israel, a people that had been
placed on earth לשמר את דרך עץ החיים ("to guard the way to the tree of
life"—Gen. 3, 24) and to whom God had said: ועשו לי מקדש ושכנתי בתוכם
("and they shall make Me a Sanctuary so that I may dwell in their
midst.")

A choice from among the various possible interpretations can be
made if we use the hermeneutical rules that are applied also in explain-
ing a Scriptural passage which is subject to several interpretations.
One would have to consider which interpretation would be the most
relevant and most natural to the passage—or, in our present case, to
the symbolic objects and their contexts—under study. If we would
have to make our decision at the present stage of our study we would
choose only between the first and the last of the interpretations we
have proposed for the meaning of the כרובים. One argument in favor of
the first interpretation would be the fact that there the object itself,
whose duality is to be symbolized by the paired arrangement of the
two cherubim, is most obviously recognizable in the form of the two
Tablets, the primary, essential contents of the Ark. This object could

be brought to mind most readily by the sight and the obvious interpretation of the cherubim. This claim cannot be made with equal certainty for the second interpretation and even less so for the third. Yet, precisely this consideration should speak even more decisively in favor of the third interpretation because it does not require any assumption or any object or point of reference outside of the כפורת. It clearly expresses the idea which results from a direct impression of the כפורת and the cherubim:

> *By keeping the Law of God, he that keeps it becomes his own cherub and also the cherub of the glory of God. "Guarding" the Law of God assures his own protection and at the same time makes him a bearer of the glory of God on earth.*

We have already seen the same idea conveyed by the cover of the Ark where the cherubim stand spreading their wings over the cover and, at the same time, outward and upward. This is further emphasized by the presence of not merely one cherub rising from the Ark cover but two cherubim, facing one another and, at the same time, facing the Ark cover.

> *The "guarding" of the Law of God produces not only one individual but a whole community whose members turn their faces toward one another, and at the same time toward the principle of the keeping of the Law and toward the community which indeed keeps the Law and of which they themselves are an integral part. Thus they stand guard over both the principle of the keeping of the Law and over the community of custodians of the Law on earth below, while at the same time they act as bearers of the glory of God from heaven above.*

Indeed, a final reflection upon these thoughts might reveal that the first and the last interpretations are basically identical. The two Tablets of the Testimony contain the very dual relationship which is shown by the direction in which the faces of the cherubim are turned and the directions in which they spread their wings. The cherubim turning their faces toward one another and their wings covering the entire community that guards the Law, symbolize the מצות שבין אדם

לחברו that are engraved on the second Tablet of the Law and that must be observed in both thought and deed. The cherubim turn their faces also toward the כפורת that guards the Law, and they spread their wings also toward the glory of God above, symbolizing the מצות שבין אדם למקום that are engraved on the first Tablet and that must be observed in both thought and deed. Thus, the Ark and its cover with the cherubim symbolize the realization of the entire Law of God in its purest, most perfect fulfillment.

The Carrying Poles

We have already noted earlier that the provision, as stated in Ex. 25, 5: "The poles shall remain in the rings of the Ark and shall never be removed from it," designates the carrying poles as important symbolic fittings on the Ark. In the case of the other objects in the Sanctuary, carrying poles were inserted only at the time when they were actually required for transporting these objects. The Ark, by contrast, was never permitted to remain without its carrying poles. As we have already noted, תוספות (Yoma 72) goes so far as to suggest that the function of the poles permanently fixed to the Ark was merely symbolic and that another pair of poles was attached for its actual transportation. This assumption is supported by the wording of Exodus 25, 12 (ויצקת לו וגו') and Numbers 4, 6 (ושמו בדים) but not by Exodus 25, 15 לא יסורו ממנו which indicates their permanent position alongside the Ark. In any event, the Scriptural specification that, unlike the carrying poles of the other objects in the Sanctuary, the carrying poles of the Ark must never be removed, assures these poles a place of basic significance in relation to the Ark. In I Kings 8, 8 we are told that the front ends of the poles caused the Ark curtain to bulge out so that they were noticeable to the outside even though they were covered by the curtain—ויארכו הבדים ויראו ראשי הבדים מן הקדש על פני הדביר ולא יראו החוצה.

Obviously, the בדים, the carrying poles of the Ark symbolize: it is Israel's purpose and mission to carry the Ark and its contents away, if need be, from one place to another. Thus, the specification that these carrying poles must never be absent from the Ark confirmed from the beginning, and for all time to come, the basic concept:

That this Law and its function are not confined to the soil
on which the Temple and its Sanctuary stand at any given

time. Rather, the Law is ready at all times to accompany the people of Israel wherever their God may lead them. Wherever they may have to travel, it is their mission to take their God-given Law with them, and to build a home for it in their own lives, seeing in the preservation of this Law the sole guarantee of their own survival, and to be bearers of the glory of God wherever their destiny will find them.

The function of the permanent בדים on the Ark as a reminder that God's Law is not bound to any one place is stressed even more by the distinction between the Ark and the remaining objects of the Sanctuary, particularly the Table and the *Menorah*: unlike the Ark, these objects do not have permanently attached carrying poles. This fact expresses the thought

> *that the Table and the Menorah of Israel are bound to the soil of the Holy Land; the Torah of Israel is not dependent on time or place.*

Conversely:

> *Though the people of Israel will take their Torah with them everywhere, they will find their Table and their Menorah only on the soil of the Holy Land.*

Let us assume that our late study will show us the Table as the symbol of the material life that is to flourish in abundance under the protection of God, and the *Menorah* as the symbol of the spiritual life that is to grow in full bloom toward God. We could then say:

> *The abundance of Israel's material life and the flowering of its spiritual life is bound to the soil of the Holy Land.*

And conversely:

> *Though the people of Israel must take their Torah with them everywhere, and the fulfillment of the Torah will be the purpose of Israel's life at all times, it is only in their own land*

*that God's promise of material and spiritual blessing to be
bestowed upon Israel as a result of its loyalty to the Torah
will become a reality.*

In Yoma 72a the Text is quoted: בטבעת הארן יהיו הבדים לא יסרו ממנו
"The poles shall remain in the rings of the Ark and shall never be
removed from it." This statement would imply that the poles should be
permanently fixed to the Ark by means of the rings. However, it is
stated also והבאת את הבדים בטבעת על צלעת הארן לשאת את הארן בהם: "And
you shall place the poles in the rings on the sides of the Ark, with
which to bear the Ark," even as is specified (Exodus 27, 7) with reference to the Altar והובא את בדיו בטבעת והיו הבדים על שתי צלעת המזבח בשאת אתו
"its poles shall be placed in the rings, so that the poles shall be upon
the sides of the altar *when it is carried.*" It is clear that this turn of
phrase can refer only to poles that were kept completely separate from
the altar and were placed in the rings only at the time when the altar
had to be moved, for the poles were not permanently attached to this
altar. (See תוספות). Hence from the similarity of phrases, the poles
perhaps should not be permanently affixed to the Ark. This apparent
contradiction is reconciled by the following comment: מתפרקים ואין
נשמטים. According to Rashi, the thickness of the poles at the ends was
greater than in the middle. The poles were initially forced through the
rings and thus could only be removed from the rings by force. This
explanation of the term מתפרקים appears to correspond to the Scriptural text לא יסורו ממנו as well as to the prohibition המסיר בדי ארון לוקה for
it connotes permanence while Rashi's explanation הולכין לכאן ולכאן, that
the poles were movable within the rings allows for a temporary role
for the poles as in the case of the Altar's poles.

Thus, the בדים were not irrevocably attached to the Ark, but had to
be placed into the rings. The Ark is conceivable even without its carrying poles. It is not permitted to remove the poles from the Ark
although it is possible to do so since they can be torn from the Ark by
force. However, separated from its poles, the Ark would remain intact
and would simply await its new bearers! The implications of this idea
are self-explanatory.

The שולחן—The Table
The Structure

The command to make the Ark is followed by the command to make a table from *shittim* wood. The top of this table is to be covered with a layer of pure gold and surrounded by a rim of gold. Furthermore, the table is to have a מסגרת. According to Menachoth 96b this was either a perpendicular border that surrounded the top of the table and extended above it, or a frame that bracketed the legs of the table underneath the top. The term מסגרת from סגר, "to enclose"—would speak in favor of the first interpretation. The making of the rim is mentioned twice in the verse (Exodus 25, 25); its position was למסגרתו, around the border or frame.

The accessories of the table were bowls, spoons, supporting side frames, and half-tubes to preserve the loaves of bread that were to be placed on the table. All these objects were of pure gold. The function of the table was לחם פנים לפני ה' תמיד, to bear the showbread together with frankincense before God at all times.

According to Menachoth 94b these loaves were flat with upturned ends ⌴;* the two sides that were bent up covered a surface equal to that of the base of the loaf. ** According to Leviticus 24, 5, there were a total of twelve loaves to be arranged on the table on stacks of six loaves each. The base of each loaf covered the entire table, and the two sides of each loaf rose to support the loaf directly above. According to ר"י, the two stacks, placed side by side, covered the full length of the table.

The bowls were so formed that they preserved the loaves in their proper shape until they could be place upon the table. The spoons were vessels for the incense that was added to the bread. The side frames were supports that were placed on either side of the table and rose to the height of the stacked loaves. These supports held the half-tubes that occupied the space between the loaves. The half-tubes

---

* According to the tradition of ר' חנינה which is most plausible, it was כמין תיבה פרוצה ("like a perforated box"). See תוספות. According to ר' יוחנן, the loaves were shaped כספינה רוקדת ("like a rocking boat"); i.e., the base was only one inch wide, with the sides slanting outward.

** According to ר' יהודה. According to ר' מאיר the two sides together covered a surface equal only to two-thirds of the base of the loaf.

served two purposes: to protect each loaf from the pressure of the loaf directly above and to protect both loaves from mold; their semi-tubular structure permitted the free circulation of air between the loaves.

The word שולחן, "table," as used in Scripture does not primarily denote a fixture upon which work is performed, a "work table," but rather—as indicated by the etymology of שולחן, from שלח, "to send," "to hold out," or "to offer"—one that "holds out to us" objects for our personal use and enjoyment. Scripture employs the word almost exclusively to denote a dining table, even as we associate tables primarily with the act of eating. Thus, the table becomes a metaphoric expression for nourishment, enjoyment, material plenty and prosperity. During their arduous journey through the wilderness, our ancestors wondered whether God could לערך שלחן במדבר—"prepare a table in the wilderness" (Ps. 78, 19). David declares תערך לפני שלחן נגד צררי "You do prepare a table before me despite my oppressors" (Ps. 23, 5). Those who forsake God, who forget His holy mountain, הערכים לגד שלחן והממלאים למני ממסך "set a table for Fortune and fill the cup for Destiny" (Isaiah 65, 11). ואף הסיתך מפי צר רחב לא מוצק תחתיה ונחת שלחנך מלא דשן "And though He has saved you from the confinement, the broad space still has no support beneath, even if that which is set upon your table were full of bounty," Elihu warns Job (Job 36, 16).

Food—Enjoyment

The table was laden with bread and frankincense. Obviously, bread represents nourishment. The connotation of scent or odor in general connotes pleasure and comfort (or displeasure). We need only recall the Scriptural phrase הבאשתם את ריחנו ("you have brought us into bad odor") (Ex. 5, 21). Thus, a pleaseant scent would signify pleasure or satisfaction. Inasmuch as the relationship of frankincense (one sole ingredient of incense) to קטורת (the full, completed incense) equals that of a single essence to a complex compound, then frankincense as such, particuiarly לבונה זכה, pure frankincense, should symbolize pure, simple, natural well-being.

If the table represents food and enjoyment, if it bears, or rather "holds out" to us, that which we call material prosperity, we can interpret the table as symbolic of that which grants prosperity; that aspect of national life which creates prosperity, the development of the economy of the state.

Therefore, the table is made of עץ, in particular עצי שטים representing an ever-vigorous, continuous development, with only its natural innate limitations. The מסגרת, too, was made of עץ. The table retains this character even though its top is covered with a layer of gold, which symbolizes constancy and strength. This metal has minor significance in the general character of the table: שאני שולחן דרחמנא קריי׳ עץ ("this table differs from other vessels because it is called "wood"). The gold was inconspicuous in appearance; it was צפוי שאינו עומד ("an overlay not solid enough to stand by itself;") not thick enough to be used as a tabletop by itself. (See Menachoth 97a and 96b).

But while the activities that create prosperity are symbolically expressed by the ever-thriving wood, a basis of solidity and purity must be established for this prosperity. Prosperity must be presented to us on a foundation as pure and solid as gold, on צפוי זהב טהור (an overlay of pure gold). It requires forms and standards. Therefore the table's supports and purifying ventilation devices—קערתיו, כפתיו, קשותיו, מנקיותיו ("its dishes, its spoons, its side frames, its half-tubes")—are of pure gold and symbolize the idea that the national prosperity must be supported and encased by accurate and durable principles.

The Show-Bread

Menachoth 97a: ועשית קערותיו אלו הדפוסים; the golden bread forms must be made first. The bread of "Jewish prosperity" was baked in metal forms of specified dimensions and then placed into golden forms to maintain its shape until it could be set out upon the table. By virtue of this shape—כמין תיבה פרוצה—each loaf offered as much space, or, according to מ״ר, almost as much space, for supporting the loaf immediately above as it occupied with its own base! Clearly, here we have the basic condition for all prosperity: brotherly devotion and the total elimination of egotism, with each individual acquiring and possessing wealth for the sake of his fellow man no less than for his own sake, extending to his fellow man as much, or almost as much, of the bounty that he has gathered on his own table (Also according to the tradition that the form of each loaf was כמין ספינה רוקדת, "like a rocking boat," each loaf formed a base one inch wide; its walls slanting outward and up toward the loaf resting directly above.)

The trait of brotherly love was symbolized so prominently in all the aspects of the bread that we must consider it the basic condition for Jewish prosperity.

Each loaf was made from two עשרונים, one tenth of an *ephah* each. One עשרון was the amount needed by one person for his minimum requirement in the Chapter of the *Omer* (Ex. 16, 16 and 36). One עשרית האיפה, עשרון, corresponds to the עומר, the daily ration bestowed by Heaven for every individual, עמר לגלגלת. Thus, two עשרונים constitute twice the daily requirement for one individual; the individual's own daily requirement and the daily requirement of his fellow man. Furthermore, in addition to being baked in specific forms, the loaves had to be baked in pairs: נאפות שתים שתים ובדפוס (ibid. 94a). A total of twelve loaves (corresponding to the twelve tribes of the Jewish people) were prepared and then arranged on the table in two stacks of equal height, side by side, in pairs (ibid. 98a). Consequently, the substance, shape, mode of preparation and arrangement of the loaves all expressly symbolized the trait of brotherly love—man and his brother.

It is clear from Menachoth 96a that elevated corners similar to the high corners of the Altar protruded from the four ends of the perpendicular sides of each loaf (קרנות). But unlike the straight vertical corners of the Altar, these were bent over horizontally to support the loaf directly above. קרנות לגוויה דלחם כייף להו ולחם עלייהו נח ליה. The קרנות of the מזבח symbolized man's striving toward God. The presence of similar corners upon the bread of Jewish prosperity would thus convey the thought that a Jew must make his prosperity available not only to his fellow man but also to God. That which he offers to God is put to its intended practical use by having it benefit his fellow man.

By being thus directed toward God, brotherly love becomes sacred duty; the duty of love becomes a duty of justice. חסד (loving kindness) becomes צדקה (righteousness). Whatever our fellow man can only hope to receive from us, God has a right to demand from us, and God will indeed demand it from us on behalf of our fellow man!

The Supports

כפותיו אלו בזיכין (Its spoons: These are the special censer-bowls) (ibid.). The frankincense was prepared in these censers, to be offered to God. (According to Tamid V,4 and VI,3, בזך was also the receptacle ordinarily used for the daily קטרת.) If frankincense symbolizes pleasure, gratification and contentment, which alone can turn bread, basic food, into real prosperity, then the censers in which the frankincense, symbolizing man's contentment, is prepared would express the following thought: One's own pleasure must be identified completely with what is pleasing to God. We can enjoy our prosperity only to the extent that our pleasure is pleasing to God. Our own pleasure must be ready, in a censer of purity, for God's approval.

The בזיכין, like the stacks of bread, were also two in number. This paired arrangement was a specification just as essential as the pairing of the stacks of bread upon the table: מעכבין זה את זה—"the omission of the one invalidates the other" (Menachoth 27a). If, then, the shape and the paired arrangement of the loaves and of the incense proclaimed brotherly love as the first condition for prosperity, the בזיכין, the censers in which the incense was prepared, proclaimed that the second condition for prosperity was the approval of God.

קשותיו אלו סניפין ומנקיותיו אלו קנים אשר יוסף בהן שמסככין בהן את הלחם (ibid.). It follows from the Mishnah (96a and 94b ibid.) that each stack of loaves was supported by two posts of gold. These posts had small פיצולין, protrusions to support the half-tubes that were placed between the loaves to preserve them. The very fact that these posts are described elsewhere in Scripture (Numbers 4, 7) as קשות הנסך, "the bearers of the covering," shows that they belonged to the half-tubes, אשר יוסך בהן, that were laid upon the loaves. They primarily served as supports for these half-tubes. This would clearly speak in favor of Rashi's interpretation (ibid.), as opposed to that of תוספות, according to which the posts were meant to support only the bottom loaf, when in fact that loaf rested directly on the surface of the table and was therefore hardly in need of a support. Also, the interpretation given in תוספות would make it difficult to explain the term קשות הנסך. The proposition that the half-tubes did not rest solely on the loaves (as תוספות would have it) but were held by the supports is confirmed by the tradition (ibid. 97a), according to which the four middle loaves of each stack were borne by the three half-tubes, while the top loaf was borne by only two because לפי שאין עליה משאוי, as it had nothing further to bear, and the bottom loaf required no half-tubes at all since it rested directly on the surface of the table. Accordingly, it is clear that if (94b), the סניפין, the supports, are described as holding up the loaves, סמכה ליה ללחם, so that the loaves would not break as the result of pressure from the upper loaves, אגב יוקרא דלחם תלח, the supports performed this function by means of the half-tubes that rested upon them. If, as תוספות has it, the half-tubes had rested only upon the loaves, they would only have added to the pressure instead of alleviating it by helping to carry the loaves. On the other hand, the half-tubes did not support the loaves by themselves but jointly with the loaf directly below; otherwise there would have been no difference in this respect between the top loaf and the middle loaves. Rather, the larger part of the half-tubes was pressed into the perpendicular sides of the bread which were grooved for that purpose. The supports held them only lightly above the sides of the other loaves, so that their part in keeping the loaves from contact with one another was hardly perceptible: שקועי משקע להו, ומגבה להו פורתא (ibid. 96a).

Thus we consider קשות and מנקיות, the supports and the half-tubes that covered the loaves, as having an inner connection. The golden half-tubes that were held in place by the golden supports keeping the loaves separate from one another had a twofold purpose: אגב יוקרא דלחם תלח, to protect the loaves against breakage due to pressure from the loaf immediately above, and משום איעפושי to protect the loaves against spoilage from too close contact with one another. The קערות (bowls) shaped the loaves and kept them in that shape which was necessary for their purpose, namely that the loaves should support one another. Thus, the bowls helped to form a brotherly union, as it were, of all the loaves. The קשות הנסך, (half-tubes or) "bearers of the covering," ensured that separation which is essential for the fully developing undisturbed existence of each individual. The former made certain that, despite this separation, each individual supported the other; the latter, that, despite this physical closeness, none of the individuals should injure or corrupt the other. Each individual unit was guaranteed independence and the atmosphere it needed for its own well-being. The ever-present conflict between man's acquired possessions and his responsibility for his brother's welfare need an overall regulatory norm: justice. The principles of justice are symbolized by the golden, unchangingly firm posts which uphold the unchanging demarkation lines separating the individual personalities who must remain united in brotherly love. Justice, symbolized by these posts, protects the independence of each personality within this bond of brotherhood. The basic principles of justice are symbolized by the קשות הנסך, the קשות and the מנקיות, the supports and the elements that preserve purity. These principles alone make free-willed brotherly love possible. Without the justice that supports each individual but also provides the needed inter-space between himself and his neighbor, society would collapse into a faceless mass, stunted by violence and corruption. Justice alone makes possible the free-willed bestowal of loving-kindness. Only justice can create individuals with wealth of their own who will then freely give of their wealth for the survival of their fellow man, doing so out of that love which God had elevated to the level of sacred duty. It would be difficult to symbolize justice more cogently than by the ספינים and קנים in all their delicate nuances.

The ideal of brotherhood, imprinted so firmly upon the bread of Jewish prosperity by its substance, its shape, its mode of preparation and arrangement, is joined by the ideal of justice, which alone assures support, permanence and indeed the survival of God's nation.

The Golden Rim

זר, *the rim*. Like the ארון so the table, too, was provided with a זר, with the difference that the rim on the Ark rose above the Ark cover, resting upon the Ark, as it were. Indeed, the Scriptural specification for the rim on the Ark reads: ועשית עליו זר זהב סביב "and you shall make *upon it* a gold rim, round about" (Exodus 25, 11). With regard to the rim on the table the Scriptural text states: ועשית לו זר זהב סביב "and you shall make *for it* a gold rim, round about" (Exodus 25, 24). This directive is repeated (in Verse 25), the rim being assigned a position more specifically on the border above the top of the table, or upon the frame that bracketed the legs of the table together underneath the table top: ועשית זר זהב למסגרתו סביב—"and you shall make a golden rim for its border round about."

The fact that the text reiterates the directive for the golden rim of the table, and the difference between the position of this rim and the place of the rim on the Ark, call for special consideration. We have already noted that, by virtue of its shape and the term denoting it, the rim symbolizes the idea that all alien and profane elements (זר =

strange, alien) must be kept away from the object which the rim encloses. Thus, a rim expresses the sacred and inviolable character of the object.

In the case of the ארון we believed that this sign of sanctity and inviolability was to be understood in relation to the outside world. The rim of the ארון does not surround the Ark but merely constitutes an extension of the golden Ark cover; the rim rises from the Ark itself and then extends above it. In the case of the table, the table itself—made entirely of wood except for a thin overlay on top—was surrounded by a golden rim. The rim relates to the table expressing the idea that the use and the purposes symbolized by the table must be guarded from all impure and unholy elements coming from the outside—a protective fence.

The rim around the table was assigned a special position on the מסגרת. We have already noted that tradition is uncertain regarding the character of this מסגרת. According to Menachoth 96a, it was either a perpendicular border that surrounded the wooden top of the table, or a frame bracketing the legs that supported the table top. According to the former interpretation (Sukkah 5), the מסגרת was only a הכשר כלי, an addition to the top of the table, so that it had no independent significance from the table. According to the latter interpretation, it was a distinct part with a significance of its own. According to the former interpretation, which views the זר around the מסגרת as a golden rim surrounding the edge of the table top, the זר would symbolize sanctity as a special condition for the basis of prosperity to be gained by physical activity, especially for the preservation of that prosperity. But according to the latter interpretation, which views the זר as a golden rim surrounding the frame that bracketed the legs of the table, the זר would convey the thought that this sanctity is a condition for attaining the objectives of all the physical material endeavors of life. The essential feature of the actions that create prosperity is primarily a vigorous, progressive unfolding of energy, as was already indicated to us by the substance from which the table was made. The essential component of the table was שטים wood. Thus, the sanctity and purity of all physical endeavor was stressed all the more, and repeatedly, as the universal basic condition for prosperity. Precisely because material, physical aspirations hold the greatest danger of defilement and desecration for the purity of human life, it was necessary to voice repeatedly the warning that these aspirations must be "surrounded" by the זר זהב סביב, the golden rim of pure, hallowing consecration. Indeed, purity in all its nuances—נקי, זך, טהור מנקיות, לבונה זכה, זהב טהור—is not stressed so emphatically in connection with any other part of the Sanctuary as it is in the case of the table. And although the "pure gold" occurred on the table only as an overlay for the top and as a rim on the table itself, this golden purity was so much the basic prerequisite for the "table" of Jewish prosperity that the entire concept of the table on which the bread was to be placed before God was summarized in Levit. 24, 6 by the designation השולחן הטהור, "the pure table." Only as a *pure* table can our table stand before God; השולחן הטהור לפני ה'. Only purity can make our מסגרת a true מסגרת, imparting strength to our endeavors and permanence to our achievements.

Summary

Human diligence, developing freely within the bounds of sanctity and purity creates the pure, golden foundation for Jewish prosperity:

שולחן עצי שטים

זר זהב טהור סביב

צפוי זהב טהור

The formative basis of prosperity is *brotherhood*: דפוס לחם הפנים כמין תיבה פרוצה.

Justice is the pillar that supports prosperity: קשותיו ומנקיותיו.

God's approval is the prime component of Jewish happiness: לבונה בבזיכין.

Thus, the categories of Divine Law that govern our activities may be similarly outlined:*

Bounds of sanctity and purity	=	חוקים
Brotherly love	=	מצות
Justice	=	משפט
God's approval	=	עבודה

* The author refers to division of the 613 מצות into specific categories in his *Horeb* (Ed. note).

It is such a table that will serve God's purpose, as it is written: ונתת על השלחן לחם פנים לפני תמיד "and upon this table shall you set the show-bread before Me always" (Exodus 25, 30). Only upon such a table and for such a table can the bread become לחם הפנים gained and enjoyed before God, protected and blessed by His Presence.

The Menorah

Components and Workmanship

The third כלי destined for the Sanctuary was the מנורה. The commandment pertaining to its construction specifies that it had to be מנורת זהב טהור, a *menorah* of pure gold, מקשה hammered out of one piece. It was to consist of ירך, a base, and קנה, a shaft, and it had to have גביעים, flower cups; כפתורים knobs shaped like apples; and פרחים, flowers. These ornaments were not to be soldered to the menorah but had to form one piece with it ממנה יהיו.

According to tradition there was a single flower at the base of the shaft; the base, together with this flower, accounted for one-sixth (i.e., three טפחים, handbreadths) of the total height of the candlestick. Above the base was a space of another two טפחים, followed by one flower cup, one knob and one flower in the sixth טפח at a point one-third of the total height of the menorah. These ornamentations were followed by three flower cups, along with one knob and one flower in the final three טפחים, immediately below the top of the shaft, on which rested the נר, the lamp.

The menorah was only the central shaft of the whole structure. From the shaft there came forth קנים, branches on both sides, three pairs, or altogether six branches. According to tradition these branches rose to the height of the central shaft, so that on top seven lights all burned in a *straight* line. The commandment states: "Six branches shall go out from the sides of the menorah; three branches of the menorah from its one side and three branches from its other side" (Ex. 25, 32). On each of these six branches there were three flower cups, one knob and one flower. The flower cups are described by the adjective משוקדים, which can mean either "almond-shaped" or "almond-like." According to Yoma 52a,b it is uncertain whether "almond-like" also refers to the knobs and the flowers (at least to those of the middle shaft; בית הבחירה פ״ג הלכה ב׳ מל״מ שם ״הל). The separating accent on the word גביעים would support this assumption.

On the menorah proper, on the middle shaft, there were thus a total of four flower cups, two knobs and two flowers. In addition, there was one knob under each pair of branches that came forth from the sides of the menorah; כפתר תחת שני הקנים ממנה "and a knob under two branches of one piece with it." Thus the menorah had a total of 22 flower cups, 11 knobs and nine blossoms. We learn from Menachoth 28 that all these ornamentations were indispensable so that the absence of even one element made the *menorah* unfit for use. גביעים מעכבין זה את זה כפתורין מעכבין זה את זה, פרחים מעכבין זה את זה גביעים כפתורין ופרחים מעכבין זה את זה—"The absence of one flower cup invalidates all the others; the absence of one knob invalidates all the others; the absence of one flower invalidates all the others; the absence of any flower cup, knob or flower invalidates all the other (ornamentations)."

However, the flower cups, knobs and flowers were required only if the menorah was fashioned of gold. If the menorah was made of another metal, the shaft and the branches could be made without these ornamentations; באה זהב באה גביעים כפתורים ופרחים אינה באה זהב אינה באה גביעים כפתורים ופרחים. The specification that the menorah, with all its parts, had to be מקשה, made of one piece, was only applicable if the menorah was made of gold; באה זהב באה מקשה. However, it was forbidden to make the menorah from גרוטאות, scrap metal, or from a substance other than metal. The menorah had seven lamps, (Menachoth 88b), one on the central shaft and six on its branches. The six lamps on either side were turned toward the middle lamp; the three lamps on the right side were turned to the left and the three on the left side to the right; אל מול פני המנורה יאירו שבעת הנרות והאיר אל עבר פניה מלמד שהיו מצדדין פניהם כלפי נר אמצעי (Menachoth 88b and 98).

If we reflect on the construction of the menorah, we note that the menorah consisted of two main components: מנורה, the candlestick itself, and קני מנורה, the branches of the candlestick. This distinction is clearly stated in the specifications for the construction of the menorah (Ex. 25, 31–36, particularly in Verse 34), and also in the passages giving the directions in which the lamps were to be turned (Exodus 25, 37 and Numbers 8, 2). The branches in turn are divided into two distinct groups, according to the sides of the candlestick from which they emanate—three branches on the one side and three branches on the other—and according to the different directions faced by the lamps they bear, the lamps on the right side of the candlestick turned to the left and those on the left side of the candlestick to the right.

The Lamp—The Light
נר—אור

The meaning of the menorah in the Sanctuary would seem obvious. Light symbolizes knowledge, and the candlestick, especially by virtue of its place opposite the table in front of the Ark of the Covenant would signify that spiritual enlightenment which, together with the table, the symbol of material prosperity, would symbolize the Jewish national life that stems from God's Law and remains consecrated to the Law forever.

However, thorough study of the pertinent Scriptural passages reveals a deeper meaning beyond this basic interpretation of the menorah.

True, נר and אור, "lamp" and "light," are not uncommon metaphors in Scripture for the source and the giver of spiritual enlightenment. There is the term האיר, "to give light," to denote the granting of light, enlightement and insight. "The Word of God is a *lamp* unto my feet and a *light* unto my path" (Ps. 119, 105). "For the Commandment is a *lamp* and the Teaching a *light*" (Prov. 6, 23). "The Commandment of God is clear, *enlightening* the eyes" (Ps. 19, 9). "The opening of His word gives *light,* affording insight to the most inexperienced (Ps. 119, 130). God has called Israel "in righteousness," has taken it by the hand "and preserved you and destined you for a covenant of the peoples, for a *light* of the nations" (Isaiah 42, 6). "For instruction shall go forth from Me, and I will create a quiet abode for My right, so that it may *shine* upon the nations" (Isaiah 51, 4). "O House of Jacob, come and let us walk in the *light* of God" (Isaiah 2, 5). For "behold, darkness shall cover the earth and gloom the peoples, but upon you God will *shine,* and His glory shall appear over you, and nations shall walk in Your *light* and kings in the ray of Your dawn" (Isaiah 60, 2). When society perishes through murder and misery, it occurs because "they rebel against the *light,* do not recognize the ways of God and never seek serenity in His paths" (Job 24, 13).

The Light—The Spirit

נר—רוח

Yet, equally beyond any doubt, and even much more frequently, Scripture uses נר and אור, "lamp" and "light," as metaphors for the source of growth and life, of unfolding and flowering, of undisturbed progress and happiness, joy and felicity.

Job laments: "Would that I had again the months of old, the days when God protected me, when His *lamp* shone above my head and I walked through darkness by His *light*"'s (29, 2–3). God says regarding Zion: "There will I cause the horn of David to grow; there have I ordered a *lamp* for My anointed" (Ps. 132, 17). "But how much longer until the *lamp* of the wicked burns out and calamity overcomes them" (Job 21, 17). Thus we note the extinguishing of a lamp as a metaphor for the end of happiness (Job 18, 5; Prov. 13, 9; 20, 20; 24, 20). Conversely, "*light* is sown for the righteous, and gladness for the upright" (Ps. 97, 11). "The *light* of the righteous rejoices, but the *lamp* of the wicked shall be put out" (Prov. 13, 9). "The *light* of the eyes gladdens the heart" (Prov. 15, 30). "*Light* is sweet" (Eccl. 11, 7). Job had looked for good, but evil came, "waited for *light* but there came darkness" 30, 26); (see also Isaiah 59, 9, Jeremiah 13, 16). "For the Jews there was *light* and joy, gladness and honor" (Esther 8, 16). God delivers from the path to the grave him who mends his ways, "so that his soul may yet look into the *light*," "that he may yet be *enlightened* by the *light of life*" (Job 33, 28,30). "Your dead will come alive again, My corpses shall rise—awake and rejoice, O sleepers in the dust! For the *dew of light* is your dew, while the earth will cast down the deceased" (Isaiah 26, 19).

If we summarize the symbolic significance of light in Jewish thought, we will note that to define light as representing merely "enlightenment" or "perception" would be a partial presentation of the over-all concept of "light" in the Biblical text. The other essential component in the symbolism of "light" is "movement," which must be joined to perception in order to achieve the desired effect and thus also to realize more fully the idea for which "light" stands. "Movement" in this context does not carry the purely mechanical connotation of a change of physical location. It is "movement" in that organic connotation which characterizes all processes of organic, vital and spiritual development. Light illumines life and also activates it; these two functions make light the metaphor of both cognition and the pulsating joy of living. For joy is essentially the feeling of awareness of blossoming life (compare שמח = צמח; שיש = ציץ).

The atmosphere impregnated by the ideas of Jewish symbolism in general, and the symbols of the Sanctuary in particular, contains the spiritual and moral human relationships that involve both the individual and the nation as its main focus. It leads to cognition and action, light and life, illuminating the mind and initiating movement. This powerful spark finds its beautiful symbolic meaning in the expression רוח, spirit. רוח grants enlightenment, insight and wisdom, and at the same time stirs man to moral volition and accomplishment.

Joseph, who was gifted with a higher level of perception, is described as a man in whom the *spirit* of God was found (Gen. 41, 38). Bezalel was filled with the *spirit* of wisdom, the *spirit* of God (Ex. 28, 3; 31, 3; 35, 31). The *spirit* of God came upon Balaam (Num. 24, 2). Moses was commanded to install Joshua as his successor because Joshua was a man "in whom the *spirit* dwells" (Num. 27, 18). Joshua was "full of the *spirit* of wisdom" (Deut. 34, 9). The *spirit* that was upon Moses came upon the chosen elders of Israel and Moses expressed the wish: "Would that all of God's people were prophets, that God would instill His *spirit* upon them" (Num. 11, 29).

The *spirit* of God spoke through David, and His word was on David's tongue (II Samuel 23, 2). The *spirit* of God rests upon Israel and the words of God are in its mouth (Isaiah 59, 21). God will pour out His *spirit* upon our children (Isaiah 44, 3) and ultimately upon all flesh (Joel 3, 1). Who could fathom the *spirit* of God? (Isaiah 40, 13). "The prophet becomes a fool, the man of the *spirit* a madman" (Hosea 9, 7). "My *spirit* began to search" (Ps. 77, 7). "It is the *spirit* in man and the breath of God that understands" (the experiences accumulated over the years) (Job 32, 8), and it is the *spirit* that answers Job out of his understanding (20, 3).

In other Biblical passages, however, "spirit" does not signify perception or cognition but the moral element which moves the human will to action, either good or evil. "Because there was another *spirit*" in Caleb and he "has followed Me fully" (Num. 14, 24). "Everyone whom his heart lifted up came, and everyone whose *spirit* moved him offered his homage to God" (Ex. 35, 21). God caused the *spirit* of Sichon to be hard and his heart to be bold in order to deliver him into the hand of Israel (Deut. 2, 30). God sent "an evil *spirit* between

Abimelech and the lords of Shechem" (Judges 9, 23). "Then the *spirit* of God came upon Jephthah, and he passed over Gilead and Manasseh" (Judges 11, 29). The "*spirit* of God began to move" Samson (Judges 13, 25). "The *spirit* of God clothed Gideon" (Judges 6, 34) and Amasai (I Chron. 12, 18). God "put a *spirit*" into the king of Assyria to make him return to his own land (II Kings 19, 7). God "stirred up the *spirit* of Cyrus, king of Persia" to permit Israel to return from exile (Ezra 1, 1). The "*spirit* of harlotry" led Israel astray (Hosea 4, 12 and 5, 4). God will remove "the *spirit* of impurity" from the earth (Zechariah 13, 2). David implores God to renew within him the steadfast, free-willed *spirit* (Ps. 51, 12, 14). God promises to put a "new *spirit*" into Israel (Ezekiel 11, 19; 18, 31; 36, 26; 37, 14).

Even in many passages where the word "spirit" is used to connote that aspect of our inner lives which we call "emotion," it simply describes the manner in which we express our attitude toward the outside world, our sympathy for, or antipathy to, an object, a condition or an act, and therefore designates that factor which prompts our decisions for good or evil. The wives of Esau were "a grief to the *spirit*" of Isaac and Rebeccah (Gen. 26, 35). Hannah was "of sorrowful *spirit*" (I Samuel 1, 15). God is near to those that are "of a contrite *spirit*" (Ps. 34, 19). "The offerings of God are a broken *spirit*" (Ps. 51, 19). See also the references to the "haughty *spirit*" (Prov. 16, 8), the "broken *spirit*" (Prov. 16, 19; 18, 14) and "the lowly *spirit*" (Prov. 29, 23). Thus, we feel justified in interpreting the light in the Sanctuary as a symbolic representation of the spirit in two distinct aspects—theory and practice, perception and volition, enlightenment and motivation for action.

The Spirit of God

The meaning of the Word of God itself is quite clear in the well-known message addressed to Zerubabel at the time of the return to Zion from Babylon. Zechariah, the Prophet, was the messenger of God to Zerubabel. The leader of the nation, Zerubabel, was about to lay the cornerstone for a new Jewish national life upon the ruins of the state that had perished. In this task he was to encounter large obstacles at every turn. The Prophet was shown in a vision the menorah with its seven lamps. When he asked the angel who had brought him this message from God to explain this vision, the angel replied: Zechariah, do you not know what these lamps signified? Upon Zechariah's answer, "No, my lord," the angel said to him: "This is the Word of God to be brought to Zerubabel: Not by armed might, nor by force, but with My *Spirit,* says צבאו' ה'" (Zechariah 4, 6). We are shown here that *this* spirit, meaning the spirit of God, is indeed the concept represented by the menorah that bears the seven lamps. And this symbolic connotation should be so obvious, so clear to everyone, that the question with which the angel counters Zechariah's inquiry: "Do you not know what these are?" sounds almost like a reprimand of the prophet for requiring an explicit interpretation of this symbolic vision. Let us note here also that, if the attention of Zerubabel is called to the spirit of God as the element with and through which he will accomplish his mission, "spirit" here, too, denotes not merely the means for attaining perception but also the motivation for action. For the word was addressed only to Zerubabel as the leader of his people, not as their teacher. He was not to teach his followers the will of God but to recognize it himself and to carry it out. He had been charged with the mission of laying the cornerstone for an edifice toward which the abundance of Divine Providence was directed.

Moreover, the Word of God itself has described for us elsewhere in Scripture the nature and the content of that spirit which God calls *His* spirit. ונחה עליו "and there shall rest upon him," we read in Isaiah 11, 2 concerning the shoot which is expected to grow from the stock of Yishai, רוח ה', and the term proceeds at once to explain the spirit of God as רוח חכמה ובינה, רוח עצה וגבורה, רוח דעת ויראת ה', "the spirit of wisdom *and* of understanding, the spirit of counsel *and* of strength, the spirit of knowledge *and* of the fear of God." Thus we should consider it certain beyond any doubt that the spirit which God regards as *His* spirit and which, as Zechariah teaches us, is symbolized by the candlestick with its lamps, is not a spirit of mere theoretical knowledge and perception, but one that bestirs both perception and practical action.

The Candelabrum

If the light borne by the *menorah* symbolizes the spirit of understanding and action granted by God to man, what is the relationship of the candlestick to the light that it bears?

If we reflect on the physical features of the candlestick, then its flower-shaft base (ירכה ופרחה), its shaft and its branches with their almond-shaped flower cups, knobs and blossoms (קנה וקנים עם גביעים כפתורים ופרחים משוקדים) recall to us a tree growing in a straight, upward direction from its root stock to become the bearer of the light.

The menorah was the only object in the Sanctuary that was made entirely of metal, namely, of gold. Thus, by virtue of the substance from which it ought to be made, the candlestick was intended to symbolize firmness, constancy and permanence, its appearance representing a process of unfolding and development.

Thus, by its physical appearance, the menorah represents the complete antithesis of the concepts symbolized by the table. The substance from which the table is made is predominantly wood, which although, like the menorah, the שולחן (wood) represents a process of continuous development, it derives, however, its limits, support, stability and permanence solely from its shape and its accessories. Thus it represents the material aspects of life which, by their very nature, are subject to constant change: germination and growth, blossoming and ripening, and eventually, death and decay. It is in the Divine Sanctuary, through the spirit and the order of God's Law, that the concepts symbolized by the table attain purpose and direction, stability and permanence, and a place in eternity. The menorah, by contrast, is made of gold throughout. Thus, by its very substance, it symbolizes precisely that element of constancy and timelessness which, as is implied by the form of the menorah, must be made to blossom and to develop in the Sanctuary of God through the spirit of God's Law.

The only firm, immutable and eternal element in man is the Divine spark within him, of which he becomes aware through his perception of truth and his desire to do good. These elements of cognition and volition in man, along with the aim of his actions—goodness and truth—are eternal and unchangeable, not subject to modification nor alteration. It might seem that the godliness of the mature man is infinitely richer than that which still lay dormant while he was young. The element of godliness that was latent in the child is no less pure and Divine than that which achieves full maturation in the adult. It is only the outward appearance that determines the measure of the difference in degree. Likewise, the simplest truths and the most common acts of goodness are just as true and as good as the most sublime truths and the highest, most profound manifestations of good. Whatever is genuinely true and good is simply—true and good. There can be no "more" and no "less" truth.

In the developmental stages of the physical world higher forms often grow only at the expense of a lower form. Lower forms die off so that higher, more developed forms may emerge. Each higher, more developed form may be a negation of the lower, less developed form that preceded it. But this does not apply to the spiritual realm of goodness and truth. Goodness and truth never lose any of their validity and justification. Whatever is good and true at one time remains good and true forever. All higher manifestations of goodness and truth represent not a negation but only a fuller realization of all the goodness and truth that have gone before. The old man, no matter how mature, cannot dispense with the virtues of his childhood; indeed, the most mature manifestations of his virtues are but the realization of his childhood virtues, now exercised under circumstances broader and more sophisticated than the narrower world of childhood. The most complex system of sublime, momentous truths cannot dispense with the simple, elementary truths that served as its starting point. It is precisely this solid inviolable treasure of elementary truths that provide the roots for the most advanced truths. In the final analysis these higher forms of truth cannot be anything else but the contents — explained and clarified—of that which, though still undeveloped and veiled from the conscious mind, had already been inherent in the original, elementary truths.

The Tree and the Branches

The tree of the perception and realization of goodness and truth, then, is a golden tree, made of gold from its roots to its flowers, golden in its every part and at every stage of its development. It is pure and genuine in its every particle and at every level, representing utmost perfection from root to flower, all of one piece, not pieced together but designed from the outset for utmost perfection. In short, this is the tree modeled for us in the מנורת זהב טהור מקשה תיעשה, ירכה וקנה גביעיה כפתוריה ופרחיה ממנה יהיו, with base, shaft, branches, flower cups, knobs and blossoms, all of *one* piece, of golden purity and consummate perfection.

Let us now examine the individual components of the menorah. First, the fact that there are seven lamps implies that the spirit nurtured here is not restricted, so that one lamp would have been sufficient to represent it, but that this spirit encompasses a great diversity of elements. If we recall the symbolic significance of the number seven, which we have already noted in the essay on *milah,* we will see at once that this is not simply a random number but is meant to signify the depth of all spiritual perception and moral volition. If we consider the lamps more closely, we will note that this character of diversity is joined by the ideal of utmost harmony and unity. We can see that the lamp in the center turns its light to shine upward, or straight ahead, while the lamps with their lights on either side, to the right and to the left, shine toward the center lamp. All the lamps are, accordingly, united in the same direction. Thus, the light in the center represents the ultimate goal of all the other lights on the menorah; or, that object upon which this central light shines is the goal common to all the other lights on the menorah. These lights, in turn, are borne by six branches. However, none of these has a separate base or shaft of its own. Rather, they all stand upon one base; they all have one root, and one shaft supports them all. Indeed, a more detailed examination will show that, as specified also in Scripture, the shaft on which the center light rests and which rises straight upward from the root stock, is the *menorah* itself, from which starting only at midpoint the other six branches sprout forth upward in pairs on either side.

Our attention is repeatedly called to the fact that these six branches emanate from the center shaft. Thus the light in the middle is not only the ultimate goal of all the lights, which serves to unite them all, but also the starting point from which all the other lights emanate. All the lights go forth from the one central shaft and all of them together strive toward the one central light. Thus we must interpret the presence of seven lights not in terms of simply seven, but in terms of *one* and *six,* as the single entity from which six lights come forth, and within which these six eventually come together again.

In our essays on *milah* and *tsitsith* we described the number six as symbolizing the physical world of creation, with the number one—the seventh—representing the One Being Who stands outside the physical world, yet remains linked to it. Thus the number seven stands for the One God and for the godly elements that emanate from Him. We would therefore have to interpret the *one* central shaft and its one central light as symbolizing the spirit of cognition and volition that aspires toward God, the spirit that strives to recognize and to serve Him.

As for the six branches with their six lights, we are to see them as symbolizing man's spiritual endeavor of cognition and volition that are directed toward the physical world. But then it is the *one* central shaft itself that branches out into these six lateral branches; the six lateral branches all emanate from the same central shaft and, with their six lateral lights turn in the direction of the one central light.

This teaches us that the concept of the recognition and service of God is not an abstraction, or a concept isolating us from the general knowledge and aspirations of the outside world. Rather, it is a concept that is fully activated in endeavors to understand and build the world. Thus, no motive of thought and deed is alien to God and His Service, because both source and goal are rooted in God and give basis and sanctity to thought and action. All that is truly moral and spiritual has only one base, one root and one goal: God is its beginning, God its end, תחלת חכמה יראת ה׳ (Prov. 9, 10) and ראשית חכמה יראת ה׳ (Ps. 111, 10): The fear of God is the beginning, and the crowning glory of all wisdom is the fear of God. The Text clearly stresses the distinction between the one central shaft—the candlestick proper—and the lateral branches; ועשית מנורת זהב—וששה קנים יוצאים מצדיה. But the Text repeatedly speaks of the lateral branches themselves, dividing them into two sections: "Three branches of the candlestick out of its one side and three branches of the candlestick out of its other side." This distinction is further defined by showing that two branches each project from the same point on the candlestick above one knob; וכפתור תחת שני הקנים ממנו וגו׳. In this manner the central seventh light, the light of Spirit, that is turned toward God also dominates the physical world (symbolized by the number six). By turning its light toward the physical world, it seems to support a dichotomy between the spiritual and physical, which, however, is reconciled by the harmonious reunion of all the lateral lights at their central point of origin.

We have already noted how רוח, the spirit, which is symbolized by the light of the menorah in the Temple, should be understood as that element which perceives, or even grants perception, as well as the element which is moved or makes movement possible. In man we have noted this duality in the form of cognition and volition. Spiritual perception and moral volition are the two phases which demonstrate the presence of the spirit. Thus, we can consider the two sides of the menorah as symbolizing this duality of spiritual knowledge and moral action. They are so inseparable in their origin and in their reality that each of necessity presupposes the existence of the other. True morality, the free-willed implementation of the good, presupposes the existence of perception, of cognition. Otherwise it would be a mindless action, rather than an act of free-willed morality. But merely perceiving the good presupposes the presence of moral volition because it demands that one's cognitive faculties should be directed, of one's own free will, toward the object that has been recognized as good. But then every conscious directing of a human faculty toward a desired end is in itself an activity arising from moral volition. Thus, essentially, the spirit inherent in man comprises both theoretical knowledge and practical volition. Volitional perception and perceptive volition spell out the life of the spirit. Only the abstract character of our understanding makes a distinction that labels the former as a manifestation of theoretical cognition and the latter as a demonstration of practical volition. This distinction depends on whether the goal of the endeavor is mental activity or physical action, which in turn both depend on the predominant purpose of a spiritual act. The difference lies in the result, not in the source, of the activity. At their root, both elements are in fact one, and they strive toward one another also in their objectives. Any perception of truth is of value only if it is directed toward the practical implementation of what is good; that is, if it ultimately serves to benefit the good. Also, every implementation of good must always be oriented toward the recognition of truth; only from the perception of truth can good derive its motivation and the assurance that it really represents a true, genuine value.

Each pair of the lateral branches emanates from the same point on the central shaft, and once they have reached the same level, the branches turn their lights toward one another, and thus at the same time toward the central point that is common to them both. This connecting point for the pair of lateral branches is part of the "seventh," thus symbolizing the spirit that strives toward God in the Sanctuary, the spirit nourished and fostered in the Sanctuary of God's Law. In this central point all perception and volition originate from one common root and then unite to aspire toward one common goal. For we can recognize the origin of our own spiritual life which aspires toward God only in the spirit that takes hold and refreshes and completes both mind and heart with the same pristine power and strength. Scripture defines this as יראת ה׳. The fear of God, יראת ה׳, constitutes the highest level of cognition which brings with it the highest form of morality. It is the spirit in which the perception of the highest truth is intertwined with the accomplishment of the consummate good.

The Emplacement of the Menorah

According to Menachoth 98b the tradition regarding the position of the menorah in the Sanctuary is uncertain. We know that the menorah stood at the south side of the Sanctuary, opposite the table. What is not clear is the direction in which the branches of the candlestick extended; whether from east to west or from north to south. If it was east to west, then the central light rose straight upward, continuing the direction of the central shaft, while the lateral lights inclined from west to east on the one side and from east to west on the other. If it was north to south, then the central light was directed toward the west, toward the Holy of Holies, while the lateral lights inclined from south to north on the one side and from north to south on the other.

We might point out that the sides of the Sanctuary derived their significance from the כלים that were placed nearest to them. On the west there was the Ark of the Law with its cover and the cherubim; on the north side was the table with the showbreads; on the south side the menorah with its lights. The east was the side facing the people. Here was the entrance and here, too, one behind the other separated by the enclosure of the Sanctuary stood the two altars that invited the people to dedicate themselves joyously to the Law of God that awaited them near the western side.

The western side symbolizes the centrality of the Law and of the nearness of God attained through the observance of the Law. The north side symbolizes the material aspects of life, the south side symbolizes the spiritual aspects of life, and the east side symbolizes the nation invited to elevate itself through its dedication to God and His Law.

If the menorah was placed in a north-south direction, then its central light was turned west toward the Ark of the Covenant which reposed in the Holy of Holies. The spirit granted by God and activated in His Sanctuary would have been defined more closely as the spirit striving to find God in His revealed Law and in the covenant which He established with Israel and which centers around the Law. Both of these aspects are symbolized by the Ark of the Covenant. The southern lights shining northward would then represent the nature of this spirit, the permeation of the material with the spiritual. The northern lights shining southward would symbolize the creation of that volition and accomplishment which implement the spiritual element within the material sphere. This spirit always returns, again and again, to its

source at its central point—to God, to His Law and to His covenant. The central light would be, at the same time, the נר מערבי, that נר
תמיד which was never extinguished but had to be kept burning at all
times, שממנה מדליק ובה היה מסיים, "from which all the other lights are
kindled and with whose tending each day ends." The permanence of
this light was to testify that the Presence of God dwelt in the midst of
Israel—עדות הוא שהשכינה שורה בישראל. Thus, by virtue of its physical
aspect and its care, the light would be consistent in every respect with
ideas we have already found embodied in the construction of the
central shaft of the *menorah* (see Sabbath 22b).

If the *menorah* was placed in an east-west direction, then its central
light would shine straight upward. In that case, the lateral lights from
the west and the east would define the spirit fostered in God's Sanctuary and turned toward Him as one deriving from the Law of God
and from the Divine covenant which was established around it and
which bears that spirit through history. This spirit is to permeate the
people of Israel, which yearns for sanctification and consecration. The
lights shining from east to west would symbolically offer up all of
Israel's volition and energy for sanctification and consecration to that
spirit emanating from the Holy of Holies. Both the spirit of the Torah
and the actions of Israel would then be brought together to rally about
the source and the ultimate goal that both have in common, around
the spirit that strives upward to God.

The Torah looks to the Jewish people for its realization, and they
look to the Torah for the content of their lives and both לימוד ומעשה
(study and action) have meaning only if both are לשם שמים, dedicated
to the attainment of one and the same objective: to strive selflessly
toward God and to find a common purpose in this lofty endeavor. If
the *menorah* were in this east-west position, the נר מערבי would not be
identical with the central light. The middle one of the eastern lights
that shines westward—the focal point for the cultivation of the
spirit—הטבה והדלקה—could then not be sought at the place where,
according to the construction and appearance of the *menorah,* the
origin and the objective of the spirit are located (meaning the central
shaft). If the central light of the lights shining from east to west were
that נר מערבי, which must be ממנה מדליק ובה מסיים תמיד לפני ה',
then the cultivation of the spirit would be connected with Israel's
innate, never-ceasing, ever-striving endeavor to come closer to God

and His Law. The very fact that this spark will never disappear in Israel, that Israel will forever remain God's, forever the people of His Law, that Israel will always turn toward the Shechinah which hovers above the Law, will be proof that the Shechinah is indeed enthroned in Israel's midst.

It might be difficult to establish on the basis of the extant traditional sources which of the two opinions regarding the position of the *menorah* is the correct one. רמב״ם in הל׳ בית הבחירה פ״ג adopts the first view; i.e., that the candlestick was placed in a north-south direction. ראב״ד ורש״י and most other authorities, on the other hand, favor the assumption that the *menorah* was placed in an east-west direction. (We follow the latter opinion and position the *menorah* in our synagogues on Chanukkah in an east-west direction.) (See Menachoth 97b, Sabbath 22b, Rashi ibid., כסף משנה on Rambam, מזרחי on Numbers 8, 2).

The Menorah of Zechariah

The Prophet Zechariah (4, 6) speaks of the significance of the *menorah* as a symbol of the רוח ה׳, and further comments are offered in Isaiah 11, 2 with regard to a more precise definition of the רוח ה׳. The Divine spirit resting upon man is described here in its most sublime form. We at once discern two distinct dimensions of this spirit, חכמה, עצה, דעת—wisdom, counsel and knowledge—on the one hand and בינה, גבורה, יראה—understanding, strength and fear of God—on the other; thus, there is theory and practice, perception and accomplishment. If we examine this passage from Isaiah more closely, we will find it consistent with all that we have noted as the construction plan of the *menorah,* a consistency so striking that we cannot help thinking that this passage is, in fact, an expression in words of the ideas symbolized by the *menorah.*

ונחה עליו רוח ה׳, רוח חכמה ובינה, רוח עצה וגבורה, רוח דעת ויראת ה׳ "And the spirit of God shall rest upon it; the spirit of wisdom and of understanding, the spirit of counsel and strength, the spirit of knowledge and of the fear of God." Here we see the spirit defined in its totality as one single entity which then unfolds into six distinct components. These form three pairs, and each of these pairs has one common bearer, for the text does not read רוח חכמה ורוח בינה וגו׳ but רוח חכמה ובינה וגו׳. This is

indeed a true replica of the מנורת הזהב which is described specifically in
the text: מנורת זהב ששה קנים יצאים מצדיה, שלשה מצדה האחד ושלשה מצדה השני
וכפתור תחת שני הקנים ממנה וכפתור תחת שני הקנים ממנה וכפתור תחת שני הקנים
ממנה לששת הקנים היוצאים מן המנורה

The passage in Isaiah continues: והריחו ביראת ה' "and he shall be
enlivened by the fear of God." According to all etymological analogies
הריחו can only mean to "permeate" a man with a spirit, to fill him with
a spirit, or to "spiritualize" him. Thus, the Divine spirit coming to rest
upon the "shoot from the stock" of Yishai is described in terms of the
sevenfold fullness of its many aspects, and one of these seven aspects is
singled out as the root of, and medium for, all this spiritualization.
Similarly, in the case of the seven lights of the *menorah,* there was one
light from which all the other lights were kindled and which was
tended at the end of each day: ממנה מדליק ובה מסיים. To make the
analogy complete, the bearer of this seven-rayed Divine spirit comes
forth as a shoot growing from one root; it is upon this bearer that the
one Divine spirit rests with its six parts. Thus, if we portray the passage in Isaiah graphically, we should have a diagram of the *menorah* in
terms of its symbolism as follows:

The Structure of the Menorah

Thus far we have considered only those features of the *menorah*
which are mandatory even in cases where the *menorah* cannot be made
from gold but through the pressing needs of the time must be made
from some other metal, We should stress here once again that the
menorah must never be made from מן הגרוטאות, scrap metal. This specification may well convey the message that the inclinations of man,
which are to be bearers of the Divine spirit, must be those original
unadulterated gifts with which man was endowed at the time of his
creation, but not elements acquired from other sources, artificially
grafted onto his personality. At the same time, however, it symbolizes
the truth that any man, not only the unusually gifted, is qualified to
strive for such a spiritual development. Even as the *menorah* need not
be made from gold, the most precious of all metals but, in the absence
of gold, might also be made from other metals, so, too, it could be
constructed piece by piece—not necessarily מקשה, hammered from one
piece. The spiritual development set forth by the *menorah* is by no
means confined to intellectual prowess and philosophical speculation,
but should provide the conditions for moral perfection. We will find
this idea expressed in the provision that every man is qualified by his
natural gifts to become a bearer of the light symbolized by the
menorah. Thus, every one must strive to reach this state. Any man, at
his own individual level and with the faculties bestowed upon him, is
capable of attaining that supreme objective of moral perfection
commensurate with his own level and with the aid of his own faculties.
In this manner, every man can reach the summit of his own spiritual
and moral calling. Every individual can obtain his own share of the רוח
ה', of רוח חכמה ובינה עצה וגבורה דעת ויראת ה', in direct proportion to his
individual efforts.

What is true for the individual applies equally to the entire Jewish
community. The possibility to aspire toward the spirit of God is not
restricted to a "golden age" such as that of a David or a Solomon.
Rather, independently of external circumstances, favorable or adverse,
even in "days of brass and iron," Israel remains bound to its Divinely-
ordained spiritual destiny and is expected to strive toward the height of
that vocation. Of course, it is true that the spiritual and moral goal
symbolized by the *menorah* is the highest level of spiritual and moral

perfection given to man and requires the service of the finest qualities in man. The very noblest there is in man must be dedicated to the Most High. But wherever this spiritual and moral development takes place under conditions symbolized by the purest gold and with the aid of the noblest human talents, this development is not only מקשה, fashioned all in one piece of material shaped by masterly craftsmanship from beginning to end, but becomes evident also in its many unique and meaningful details.

Only if the *menorah* was made from gold, then its base, shaft and branches had to have גביעים כפתורים ופרחים, "flower cups, knobs and blossoms." The position and number of these ornamentations were precisely specified and, as mentioned earlier, were so essential that not a single one could be missing מעכבין זה את זה.

Of these three ornamentations the symbolic significance of the פרחים—flowers—is the most obvious. פרח is the term commonly used for "flower" or "blossom," and פרוח the term commonly used for "flowering" or "blossoming." Hence, whęrever פרחים occur as symbolic ornamentations, we should not depart from the image conveyed by "flowers" and "flowering." Indeed, they will remain our point of reference when we establish the significance of the other ornamentations associated with them; in the present context, these are mainly the גביעים—flower cups—and כפתורים—the knobs.

The symbolic significance of גביע is also quite clear. The term denotes "chalice," or "flower cup." The use of this term in Jeremiah 35, 5 ("and I set before the house of the Rehabites *cups* full of wine, and goblets") seems to indicate that גביע refers not to the drinking cup but to a larger vessel in which the wine was brought to the table and from which it was then poured into כוסות—goblets. We are told that גביעים מלאים יין and כוסות were offered together. This explanation would be consistent with the connotations of the roots כוס and גבע. כוס derives from its relationship to כסס the connotation of apportioning, of "counting out" something to someone. כוס therefore denotes a vessel in which the individual who drinks from it is served a measure or portion specifically intended for him. Accordingly, it is used as a metaphor denoting man's destiny apportioned to him by God. The related roots of גבעה, גבע, גבח, גבה, גבא refer to an accumulation of matter. Hence, גביע would be that receptacle in which the entire amount of the liquid available for drinking is received, accumulated and held together.

כוס is the vessel into which the portion intended for the individual is poured from the גביע. Thus, the basic connotation of גביע would be the antithesis of פרח. For while גביע connotes an accumulation of matter, פרח, in all its related roots and derivatives—אפרח, פרע, פרא and the Rabbinic and Chaldean פרח, "to fly"—has the connotation of "becoming free," unbridled.

For the term כפתור, however, we find little linguistic analogy in Scripture other than Amos 9, 1 and Zeph. 2, 14. We must therefore rely on tradition, as taught in Menachoth 28b, according to which the כפתורים were shaped כמין תפוחי הכרתיים, like Cretan apples. Hence these ornamentations that protruded on the shaft and on the branches of the candlesticks were forms whose shape suggested a fruit.

If we review these ornamentations in their context and in the order in which they are consistently mentioned in Scripture, גביע, כפתור and פרח, they appear to be the components of one single system. The obvious connotation of פרח, "flower," "blossom," as well as the explanation of כפתורים as fruit-like shapes, which would fit into this context, indicates to us that we must turn to botany in our study of this system. The term משוקדים, "almond-like" or "almond-shaped," which Scripture adds as a more detailed characteristic of these ornamentations will also prove most significant in the total picture.

The structure of a plant as an organic system corresponds to the shapes we are now studying.

Normally a flower consists of three basic parts: (1) an outer covering, usually consisting of green leaves, the *calyx* or *flower cup*; (2) a capsule that contains the seed and collects the pollen (the fertilizing agent) through the *pistil* (which eventually becomes the fruit), and (3) surrounding the filaments, a *corolla,* which is the blossoming *flower.*

These parts correspond precisely to the three shapes on our *menorah*: the flower cup, the knob and the flower. We must therefore interpret these structures as symbols of a blossoming that bears fruit. We will then also understand why these ornamentations were indispensable parts of the *menorah,* particularly when the latter was made מקשה זהב standing before us in consummate purity, made of gold and fashioned all of one piece. This symbol was necessary precisely to show that this whole light-bearing tree, though made of one piece and representing perfection in all its parts, should signify not a rigid form of existence but a life of eternal, fruitful blossoming.

Now that we have flower cups, pistils (seed-bearing pods) and the corolla-flower, could the filaments and the pollen, that element which gives life to the whole, be lacking? We learn from Menachoth 28b that the flower cups, the pistils and the corolla-flower occupied the three upper טפחים of the height of the shaft. The shaft terminated in the פרח, the flower in which rested the vessel with the wick that bore the light. Mishnah Kelim XI,7 tells us that פרח came to be the term used for the depression on a lamp that held the actual light. If, therefore, the *menorah* culminated in flower cups, pistils and corolla-flower, and if the light that burned on the wick protruded from the corolla, then the burning wick on the *menorah* corresponded to the filament which bears the fertilizing pollen. It is the light itself, the spirit, the spirit of God, the fructifying element which, coming into existence upon the "tree of light," brings life to the seed which came into being upon that tree. The seed required stimulation and development. The spirit brings it to maturity as a ripe fruit.

We thus have the flower cup, the seed-bearing pod, the corolla-flower and the light, the fertilizing element on the filament. The flower cup, the seed-bearing pod and the corolla-flower surely represent specific concepts even as the filaments with their pollen obviously correspond to the fertilizing, life-giving element of the light and the spirit.

The Symbol of God's Spirit

We have noted earlier that Scripture itself defined the light of the *menorah* as symbolizing the spirit of God, and that the spirit has six distinct aspects. If we reflect more closely upon these six aspects of spiritual unfolding, we will find that they actually appear in three phases, or that the six aspects are stated in terms of three pairs:

חכמה ובינה
עצה וגבורה
דעת ויראת ה'

These three factors of spiritual development have possibly the same relationship to רוח ה'—representing both their source and their culmination—as do כפתור, גביע, flower cup, seed-bearing pods and corolla-flower to the נר, to the filament with its quickening and life-giving elements.

גביע, the flower cup, both etymologically and objectively, has been shown to connote a "collecting agent," a formative center for new plant growth.

כפתור, the seed-bearing pod is the place where the entire wealth of the plant in substance is transformed into seeds for the creation of new plants. All the other parts which, up to this point, have grown on the plant—stem or trunk, branches, twigs, and leaves—remain attached to the plant as dependent structures. But the function of the structures in the seed is to become independent, to detach themselves from the parent plant in order to begin a life of their own. There is latent within the tiny seeds an infinite wealth of formative charges and powers. But as long as these seeds remain inside the pod they are dormant, waiting to be released from their confinement for a life of their own. (Perhaps the etymological origin of the term כפתור is כפת, "to bind," plus פתר [פטר], "to release").

פרח are the plant's "wings of freedom," which strive upward with the spread of their blossoms to draw to their filaments the dust of life which in turn awaken the seeds within the pistil for growth, life, and freedom.

Let us see how the phenomena just described relate to the three aspects of spiritual life as it strives upward to the רוח ה'.

חכמה ובינה both figure in the recognition of goodness and truth. Truth includes all that is true and good, the former representing the truth that is, and the latter, the truth that should be. Truth is a given absolute, so that in the final analysis any perception of truth is only a gathering and accepting what has already been objectively, irrevocably stated. חכמה primarily denotes the intellectual perception; בינה denotes the productive aspect of cognition. חכמה may be the element in the perception, grasping, comprehension and retention of given truths, while בינה, as expressed in הבין דבר מתוך דבר, may be intellectual exercises and inferences to reformulate truths.

But all is not what it seems to be. Any "new" truth is "new" only when viewed in subjective terms. A truth seems "new" only in that it has not yet been consciously noted by the cognitive intellect. Moreover, it is "truth" only insofar as it was already inherent in given truths that had been recognized as such before. Credibility depends entirely on the extent to which it can be traced back to a premise already recognized as given truth in the past. The additional factor in בינה is that it affords a comprehensive view of every given truth in terms of all the inferences and conclusions implicit in that truth. Any "new" truth which.claims to be more than an aspect of, or a conclusion from, an "old" truth that merely had not yet been recognized by the conscious mind, ceases to be truth and moves off into the realm of fantasy and delusion. God has laid down in His world and in His Revelation all the truths that man is capable of perceiving and has given us the sum of all the truths within the reach of human cognition. חכמה ובינה only reclaim these treasures to gather and to comprehend them, to obtain from them a clearer and more perfect and detailed knowledge in terms of their remotest implications, and to retain this knowledge in the conscious mind.

The spirit becomes truly creative only in עצה וגבורה, in counsel and in that energy through which the knowledge gained through חכמה ובינה is shaped into planned action. This is the energy through which the individual, who until that point has only reflected, becomes ready to step outside of himself and to intervene actively in the world of concrete realities, injecting into this world of events, of cause and effect, his own free-willed activity as a potent seed to be brought to fruition by the future.

עצה וגבורה correspond to the seed-bearing pod that shapes within its womb resolutions and decisions as seeds for the future, and holds them in readiness for evolving into deeds.

The flower cup, at its best, opens to form the corolla to collect for the seeds the fertilizing element of the pollen. So, too, if resolution is to ripen into action, action that is right and hence the only genuine action that will truly reach into eternity, action that is vital, viable and life-giving, the noblest flower of perception, that is, דעת ה' ויראת ה' must strive upward to gain in רוח ה' the true spirit which alone can cause resolutions and energy to ripen and to culminate in the proper action.

If all knowledge does not lead us to perceive God in the world and to perceive the world as derived from God, if all the perception of Divine revelation does not inspire us with the fear of God, with the realization and acknowledgment of our own personal relationship with God, with the desire not to be anything else but a servant of God in this world of His, then the seeds that should build the world and eternity will lie dormant and there will be no resolution and no free self-determination. The seeds will atrophy, the noblest and godliest qualities in man will remain unborn, because all his knowledge and all his strength will lack the quickening, enlightening breath of God. The spirit of God descends only where all knowledge culminates in the recognition of Him and all strength in the fear of God. When the recognition and fear of God admit the spirit of God to enrich all human counsel and strength, when all counsel and strength are thus offered to the spirit of God, only then will life germinate and bear fruit.

In conclusion:

נר — רוה ה' = pollen
פרח — דעת ויראת ה' = corolla-flower
כפתור — עצה וגבורה = pistil; seed-bearing pod
גביע — חכמה ובינה = flower cup

As we have mentioned at the outset, tradition is uncertain whether, as indicated by the accentuation, the term משוקדים refers also to the shape of the כפתורים and the פרחים. The term שקד, both as a verb and as a noun שקד, "almond," is used in Scripture to describe a most intensive, single-minded concentration upon a subject or purpose. The almond tree is the earliest to blossom (as early as March in our part of the world) and sprouts flowers even before it grows leaves, so, too, the name of this tree, שקד, is generally used as a metaphoric expression for zealous, ceaseless mental activity, ever alert and diligent, striving steadily toward a speedy attainment of a goal. The term connotes that which we would call diligence and earnest study. "If God does not guard the city, then the watchman watches (שקד) in vain" (Ps. 127, 1); "Fortunate he who hearkens to Me, לשקד, watching diligently at My gates day by day" (Proverbs 8, 34); "Even as שקדתי עליהם I have watched over them diligently to ruin and destroy without cease, so אשקד עליהם לבנות ולנטוע will I watch over them diligently without cease to build and to plant" (Jeremiah 31, 27).

"What do you see?" Jeremiah was asked (1, 11) when he received his first call from God. "I see מקל שקד, the rod of an almond tree." "You have seen well," God replied, "for שקד אני על דברי לעשתו, I watch diligently over My word to fulfill it."

In Numbers 17, 23 the prince of the tribe was to be identified as chosen by God by the fact that his staff would sprout blossoms, and this staff was to be kept before the Ark of the Testimony as an everlasting memorial. We are told concerning the staff of Aaron, which, by bringing forth blossoms, reaffirmed that the tribe of Levi, and the family of Aaron within the tribe, had been chosen for the priesthood: ויגמל שקדים, "It brought forth flowers, sprouted filaments and grew almonds." We see here שקד, the earnest and unceasing dedication to one's calling, as that character trait which showed that the Aaronide family was indeed qualified for the lofty spiritual calling of Jewish priesthood. We believe we can interpret this as a substantiation of our view of the almond-like flower formations on the *menorah*. For the shaft and the branches of the candlestick bore those very symbols which identified Aaron's staff, reposing in front of the Ark of the Testimony, as the staff of a priest. In both instances we see almond blossoms ripening into almonds. We have rendered ציץ as "filaments," and we believe this interpretation is supported by other Scriptural passages; in Ezekiel 8, 3, ציצת describes a lock of hair — "I was taken by a lock of my head," and in Numbers 15, 38 ציצת denote the fringes to be placed on the corners of one's garments.

It is also significant that the idea of ceaseless diligence, expressed by שקד, is symbolized by the גביעים, the flower cups on the *menorah* which receive and gather knowledge, חכמה ובינה. It is interesting to note here that each כפתור and each פרח is preceded by a triple flower cup; שלשה גביעים משוקדים. Thus the function of the גביעים is singled out from among those of all the others both quantitatively (שלשה) and qualitatively (משוקדים). Therefore, the symbolism of the גביעים, the gathering, collecting and retaining of truths, reflects the activity we call לימוד, "learning," requiring our unceasing devotion יומם ולילה. The גביעים משוקדים on our *menorah* call out to us: הוי שקד ללמוד תורה (אבות פ"ב מש' י"ד); and שלשה גביעים משוקדים, the fact that the cups representing study were three-fold, with one כפתור and one פרח projecting from them, representing subsequent action teaches us that גדול לימוד שמביא לידי מעשה (קדושין מ')

We have drawn these parallels: flower cups = חכמה ובינה, pistil; seed-bearing pods = עיצה וגבורה, and flower = דעת ויראת ה'. Therefore, we have these same manifestations of the spirit in the three side branches of the menorah. They appear to be independently developed, while, on the shaft, they appear only as stages in the development toward the נר ה', which is the רוח ה'. These same flower cups, pistils and flowers also appear on the sides of the *menorah,* leading to the following thought: חכמה ובינה, עצה וגבורה, דעת ויראת ה' must be furthered to such a degree that they are inspired by the רוח ה'. This רוח ה' will enrich every phase of that spiritual development, and each of these phases will blossom separately as an independent achievement, as a fruit ripened by the spirit of God.

In order to reach the ultimate goal of perfection, חכמה no less than בינה, עצה no less than גבורה, and דעת no less than יראת ה', each one a level of intellectual and spiritual attainment, requires a most diligent search for truth as symbolized by the almond-blossom shaped flower cups, a molding of methodical intellect and creative energy, and a knowledge of God and fear of God that will seek their inspiration in the spirit of God.

Thus, the middle shaft of the *menorah*, the bearer of the spirit of God, provides one pistil for each of these levels; cf. כפתור תחת שני הקנים ממנה, because עצה וגבורה, mind and strength (the mind, עצה, that works deliberately toward a practical objective and the strength that will overcome all obstacles) גבורה the concentrated potency raised to intensified power, כפתור, are needed to attain these levels of the spirit in a state of godly purity and perfection.

Our attention is drawn also to certain other parts of this fruit-blossom ornamentation in two places on the shaft.

ירך, the base—the root stock from which the tree of light emerges has, at the place where the shaft begins, פרח, one single flower that has neither flower cup nor pistil. After a space of two טפחים we note, within the third טפח, the sixth in the total height of the shaft measured from the bottom, a complete flower structure including flower cup, pistil and corolla, but all on a reduced scale. While the flower structure at the top of the shaft measures three טפחים, with each part measuring one טפח, this flower structure in miniature—flower cup, pistil and corolla—is concentrated within the space of one טפח. (See תוס' מנחות כ"ח: ד"ה וטפח). Moreover, it has only one simple flower cup, while the formation at the top of the shaft has three such cups.

Flowers and Man—Four Stages of Development

If we study the *menorah*, we will see the flowers in four distinct stages of development: (a) פרח at the ירך; (b) גביע, כפתור and פרח in the sixth טפח; (c) שלשה גביעים, כפתור, פרח and (d) כפתור תחת שני הקנים ממנה in the last three טפחים at the top of the shaft.

It is interesting to note that this development of the flower begins at the lowest position with the same form as that with which it concludes at the peak of perfection. פרח, the corolla-flower, is the last sprout at the top of the shaft, but it is also פרח, a corolla-flower, that marks the beginning of the blossom at the lowest step. True, this latter formation does not emanate from a flower cup, nor does it bear seeds for which it would need the life-giving element of pollen as symbolized by the light. It is merely a blossom through which the trunk emerges from the roots. We have identified this flower upon the tree of the spirit as a symbol of the recognition of God and the fear of God, דעת ה' ויראת ה', forming the noblest, consummate flowering of spiritual life that can unfold from man and that is needed on the highest level if the spirit of God is to be won and the human mind is to be perfected as a bearer of the Divine spirit.

Are these not in truth the very same elements with which man's spiritual development must begin in earliest childhood, from the origin of spiritual life? These are truly ראשית דעת, in a double sense the earliest beginning and the consummate flower of human knowledge. The tree which symbolizes man's spiritual development in the Sanctuary of God sets forth the profound and unchangeable truth that if the knowledge of God and the fear of God are to reach the highest level in mature man, then this knowledge and fear of God must have been nurtured already at the very root of spiritual existence, in earliest childhood? It forms the basis for all spiritual development.

To be sure, at that level it is still only a blossom without a flower cup and without a seed-bearing pod. At this level it is דעת ויראת ה', a knowledge of God and a fear of God that has not yet emerged from cups that would already have gathered חכמה ובינה, and that it is not yet directed toward the production of fruit in the form of action, עצה וגבורה. Rather, it is a blossom of the knowledge and the fear of God that was given directly along with the origin of the human spirit—ירכה ופרחה—(Ps. 8, 3) מפי עוללים ויונקים יסדת עז, which can be awakened and trained from its deepest core even without the flower cup, i.e., without theoretical preparations.

A child's דעת ויראת ה' need not yet concern itself with sowing the seeds for עצה וגבורה, for that seed which stimulates action is not yet present at this point. Rather, דעת ויראת ה' in the child must arise out of an unconscious willingness to grow toward the light. Later, in his youth, there will begin to appear these three levels of spiritual life, and he will first exercise and develop the capacity for drawing חכמה ובינה, the capacity for the creation of עצה וגבורה, and the capacity for דעת ויראת ה׳ which begets action. In other words, the youth will then exercise and develop the natural tendencies toward all these qualities on a small scale.

Only in adolescence will the individual employ all his עצה וגבורה, all his energies of strength and resolve for the separate development of each of these three manifestations: כפתור תחת שני הקנים ממנה, וכפתור תחת שני הקנים ממנה, וכפתור תחת שני הקנים ממנה "one knob under the two branches that go out from it, and one knob under the second pair of branches that go out from it, and one knob under the third pair of branches that go out from it."

Then, finally, in manhood, he must turn all these three branches back to the one central point in order to develop from the wellspring of חכמה ובינה the דעת ויראת ה׳ that will know how to attain the light and the quickening spirit from above, in the נר ה׳ the spirit of God, for the quickening and maturing of the עצה וגבורה which results in all action: שלשה גביעים משוקדים כפתור ופרח ועליה נר ה׳.

שמונה עשרה

In all our liturgy, the spiritual legacy of our great past, no part plays a more important role than the prayer commonly known as שמונה עשרה, the core of our Divine Service. "One hundred and twenty elders of the nation, among whom many prophets" מאה ועשרים ובהם כמה נביאים composed and arranged these eighteen blessings (Megilla 17b). So that in this array of Berachoth we have in our hand a bouquet out of the hands of the spiritual elite of our nation with which they wished to ensure that the noblest, most far reaching views and thoughts be handed down to all the future generations of their people.

According to Berachoth 26b, תפלות אבות תקנום ואסמכינהו רבנן אקרבנות (our forefathers arranged the prayers and our Sages tied them to the daily sacrifice) or, as similarly expressed in the same context תפלות אבות תקנום, תפלות כנגד תמידין תקנום. Our three daily prayers were instituted by the Patriarchs as the spiritual sustenance of our lives: "תפלת עמידה," the prayer in the rays of the early morning sun, taught by Abraham (ואברהם ... עמד לפני ה׳ Gen. 18, 22); "תפלת שיחה," the prayer when the rays of the sun have reached their zenith and are turning towards the afternoon, taught by Isaac (ויצא יצחק לשוח בשדה Gen. 24, 63); and "תפלת פגיעה," after the setting of the earthly sun, taught by Jacob (ויפגע במקום Gen. 28, 11). The Sages of our people arranged and ordered the daily prayers in accordance with, and parallel to, the daily offering in the Sanctuary. These prayers, with the exact same text, must convey to our minds basic truths which are applicable to the three different stages of the day: the fresh morning awakening us to active life (עמידה); the day drawing to its close, inviting us to self reflection (שיחה); and at night, bringing one close to God (פגיעה). This prayer therefore forms the common source for our spiritual development bringing facts and ideas to us which enable us to attain our goals for every phase of our life.

Furthermore, our תפלה has a profound connection to the קרבנות so that the same rays of the rising and sinking day which marked the national offering in the Temple should touch every member of the nation standing in prayer in the wide expanse of the whole world. Our prayer is not a substitute—as some erroneously interpret—but has always served as an accompaniment to the offerings. The great Jewish leaders known as אנשי כנסת הגדולה who arranged our prayers lived just at the time of the Second Temple in the re-establishment of which they enthusiastically took part. The opinion of the Sages did not consider prayers or reading and studying the laws referring to the offerings as substitutes for the offerings (Taanis 27b). Prayer, and especially the one we are considering, was attached to the offering and ran parallel to it. Since the time of the first Prophets the whole nation, divided into 24 sections—מעמדות—took part in spirit in the offerings, some by taking turns in being actually present in Jerusalem, some by gathering for Divine Service in prayer in their home towns (Taanis 26a,b) simultaneously with the time of the offerings in the Temple. In the whole land, and even on the Mount of the Temple itself, there were synagogues (Yoma 68b, Rashi) in which parts of the daily prayers were co-ordinated to and coincided with the daily offering (Tamid IV).

The relation of our daily prayer to the daily offering must be more than a mere superficial one, just to be said at the same time. The phrasing of the sentence תפלות תקנום next to the other one תפלות כנגד תמידים תקנום אבות תקנום teaches us that the origin of this Tefilla stems from the actual offerings while its basic concept is rightly attributed to the Patriarchs.

מפני מה אמרו תפלת הערב אין לה קבע שהרי אברים ופדרים שלא נתעכלו מבערב קרבים והולכים כל הלילה הלילה (What is the reason that there is no fixed time for the evening prayer, its time is not limited like the other two? It is because any limbs or parts of the afternoon offering which have not been consumed by the fire on the Altar, may be placed back and go on burning all through the night.) This statement proves the inner connection between the prayer and the offerings. For if the אין לה קבע of our ברייתא is to be taken in the sense in which אין לה קבע of the משנה is explained in Berachoth 27b, namely that תפלת ערבית רשות the Shmone Esre of Maariv was not ordered as an absolute duty—then the reason given in our ברייתא would not lie so much in the positive fact that offerings were brought on the Altar during the night (שהרי אברים ופדרים וגו׳) but rather in the limiting circumstances expressed by the addition of שלא נתעכלו מבערב. It was only in occasional cases that sacrificial procedures were prescribed to be done after nightfall, if and when any parts of the offering had not been consumed by the fire on the Altar before nightfall. Thus the "non-obligatory" nature of the offering-procedure is transferred to the prayer which then has its origin in, or according to ר׳ יוסי בר חנינה, is founded on it. *The Shmone Esre is but a rendering in words of the procedures of the Tamid offering.*

The entire procedure of the morning and evening offering consisted essentially of three parts:—

(a) זריקת הדם—sprinkling of the blood on to the lower half of the Altar—with the preceding שחיטה, קבלה, הולכה—the ritual slaughtering, receiving the blood in a vessel of the Sanctuary, and taking it to the north-east corner of the Altar. דם, blood, the main object of this part, is repeatedly designated by the Torah as the symbolic expression of נפש as the personality of the human being. Thus blood is first surrendered (שחיטה), then accepted and gathered up by the Sanctuary (קבלה), brought near to its holy mission on earth (הולכה), and given over to striving with all its energy towards the heights starting with זריקה למטה sprinkling at the base.

(b) הקטרת איברים—burning all the parts of the animal—with the preceding הפשט ונתוח and הולכת איברים לכבש—removing the skin, cutting up into the prescribed parts and bringing them to the ramp. The objects of these procedures are the internal and external organs, corresponding to those which man uses to achieve those goals set by זריקת הדם with all of his mental and physical faculties. They are given over to the אש אוכלה representing what later is termed אש דת, to become לחם אשה ה׳ "food" matter and substance to keep the Law of God, the Torah, alive on earth. This הקטרת איברים took place in two procedures: הולכת איברים

לכבש, depositing the parts on the lower western (or eastern) half of the ascent to the Altar; העלת איברים מן הכבש למזבח in fact זריקת היאברים, consigning (by throwing, similarly to the blood) the parts to the fire on the Altar. קטורת and נרות as well as the recitation of certain prayers preceded these procedures.

(c) מנחה ונסכים, the flour-offering and the wine-offering which belong to every הלוע. They were attached to the חביתי כה"ג, the daily offering of the High Priest.

The Shmone Esre also consists of three parts:

(a) The first three Berachoth אבות גבורות וקדושה, which together form one unit (Berachoth 34a).

(b) The אמצעיות, the twelve (actually thirteen) middle ones which are all of a similar nature, all בקשות, requests, which in the specific meaning of ברוך dedicate God's gifts to God's service.

(c) The three last Berachoth רצה, מודים, שלום, which again form one unit (ibid.).

THE MIDDLE BERACHOTH

We now focus on אמצעיות, the middle part of the Shmone Esre and הקטרת איברים, the middle group of the תמיד procedure. This middle group of the offering-procedures deals with parts of the body the meaning of most of which leaves little room for doubt, and equally so the meaning of those middle Berachoth is also quite clear.

Concerning the parts, as well as the order in which they are to be brought to the Altar, Tamid III and IV, and Yoma 25 a,b are sources of reference. Regarding the division of the animal into fixed groups of parts there are no divergent opinions. But regarding the order in which these groups of the parts were brought we find five different opinions. The one generally accepted both in Tamid and in Yoma is the following:—

1. First: הראש עם הפדר ורגל הימנית וב' ביצים עמה—the head with the omentum (the fatty layer which covers the entrails like a cloth) together with the right hind-leg and the two testes—constitute the first group.

2. The second: שתי ידים—the two fore-legs.

3. The third: העוקץ עם ב' צלעות מכאן ומכאן והאלי" ואצבע הכבד וב' כליות עמו

ורגל השמאלית—the lower backbone with the corresponding two ribs on either side, together with the rump and the extension of the liver, the two kidneys and the left hindleg.

4. The fourth: החזה והגרה עם שתי צלעות מכאן ומכאן ובה הקנה הלב והריאה—the breast and the throat with the two upper ribs on either side and the trachea (and esophagus?), the heart and the lungs.

5. The fifth: דופן הימנית עם ב׳ צלעות דקות למעלה ולמטה והכבד תלויה בה ודופן השמאלית עם ב׳ צלעות דקות למעלה ולמטה והשדרה עמה והטחול התלויה בה—the flanks with the backbone and two ribs on either side above and below, the liver with the right flank and the spleen with the left. (According to the commentaries on Tamid these ribs do not seem to have remained on the flanks. This remains unclear.)

6. The sixth: הקרבים וכרעים על גביהן—The stomach and intestines together with the lower foot joints.

If we examine the first group, the head immediately presents itself as the organ of intellectual and mental perception. What one is offering is the dedication of our דעה, just as דעה, knowledge, is also the subject of the first of our middle Berachoth. But it is not just knowledge as a mere abstract function of the brain but also as its directing and guiding our spiritual and physical aims of life. The physical needs of our body, so central to our cerebral activity, are represented by חלב, the reserve saved-up stores of the body. Our "way through life" and our posterity are represented by the right leg and the two ביצים. In the first of the middle Berachoth, knowledge is depicted not merely as a theoretical abstract דעה but also as practical knowledge in its application: דעה בינה והשכל—בינה to discern (בין) and השכל—to apply wisdom (שכל) are the practical corrolates of acquired knowledge (דעה). The meaning and importance of the first group as offering our "head," our knowledge, to God is further enhanced by the הטבת ה׳ נרות which immediately preceded the severing of the head, or אליבא דרבנן הטבת ב׳ נירות which took place just before giving it over to the fire on the altar, thereby connecting the offering of the head with the מנורה, the symbol of spirit and clarity.

The second group: ידים, the fore-feet in animals, the leading limbs of movement (whereas the hind-feet are more the bearers of motion); transferred to the human body: the hands, accordingly, the instruments of the initiation of the action. So that what we are offering and handing over to God is the direction of our steps and actions, what we strive for and do. That is exactly the content of the second of the middle Berachoth, תשובה, which represents in its own specific way our "movement" back to God's Torah.

In the third group we first note the kidneys, כליות, which in Scripture is used as a metaphor for the "lower" physical urges and feelings. In this sense also the kidneys are prominent in אימורי חטאת וכו׳, and indeed are offered with a part of the liver: על הכבד על הכליות (—according to יותרת על הכבד the רמב״ם הקדמה לפירוש המשניות על סדר קדשים is nothing else but just the extension of the liver which occurs here too—)as well as in our כבש של תמיד, the האליה תמימה, is part of the third group. חז״ל teach: כבד כועס the liver-bile is the seat of anger. Anger, resentment against opposition, against that which is offensive or repugnant, is directed against (אצבע הכבד) the impulses which the כליות represent. כלה—yearning, desire. וכלות אליהם "and long for them" (Deut. 28, 32); כלו עיני לאמרתך "my eyes long for your words" (Ps. 119, 82). Altogether desires and anger may well form the positive and negative poles of our wishes. עוקץ is another part of this group. The word is synonymous with עָצֶה; thus לעומת העצה is the region of the כליות (כליות יועצות). Thus conceivably the leading right hind-leg is connected with the leading head whereas the trailing left hind-leg is brought together with these symbols of the lower instincts. The potential conflict between the above-mentioned human trends, movements and impulses justify the urgent need for סליחה and מחילה as expressed in the third of the middle Berachoth.

The trachea, and probably also the esophagus, (which is closely joined to it and which possibly could be included in the name גרה [מעלה גרה], unless it belongs to the sixth group in connection with the stomach), the heart and the lungs, together with the breast which covers them, and the upper ribs on either side, form the fourth group. Here we have together all the vital organs and their protective encasement, on whose unimpeded functioning the very existence of the living creature is dependent. Without the functioning of the esophagus — which, by bringing the food to be digested into nutritive substances distributed to the body in the blood stream by the heart pump — the body would become entirely impoverished; without the functioning of the trachea and the lungs the whole life-process comes to a deadlock, and the living individual falls as dead matter. The deliverance from all dangers to our existence (גאולה), the protection from impoverishment (עני) and all struggle (ריב) form the subjects of the fourth of the middle Berachoth which correspond to the organs representing the vital and indispensable requirements for our existence.

The fifth group, the two flanks, with the backbone and two lower ribs on either side and the liver on the right flank and the spleen on the left can only be characterized by considering the meaning these organs have for the whole organism. The liver and spleen are important organs in the metabolism of fats and for the formation and disintegration of the corpuscles of the blood. The importance of these organs for the general health of the body is self-evident. If, accordingly, we consider the liver and spleen, with their protective flanks, and add the spine and its system of nerves governing the entire body, then this group represents to us those organs and that system on whose undisturbed maintenance the health of the body essentially rests, and we have as the object of this fifth group the same idea which is also that of the fifth of the middle Berachoth: רפואה.

Finally, the sixth group shows us the stomach and intestines and the lower foot joint representing food and the search for food. Sustenance, פרנסה is the subject of the sixth of the middle Berachoth: ברכת השנים.

There seems to be a natural parallel between these six middle Berachoth and the six groups of the parts of the Tamid-offering that were offered twice daily. Not only does each one of these groups correspond to one of the Berachoth, but the sequence is completely identical in both cases. A conformity which, as we think, can well justify the conclusion that the fixing of the order of the one served as the model for the other, or that both owe their origin to being arranged at the same time. We shall have to consider this in connection with what is taught us in tractates Yoma, Megilla and Berachoth about the order in which the parts of the offerings were brought on to the altar, as well as the order of our prayers in general and of that of the middle Berachoth in particular.

We explained the parallels:

ברכת דעה =	the "head"-group.
ברכת תשובה =	the "forelegs"-group.
ברכת סליחה =	the "kidney"-group.
ברכת גאולה =	the "heart-lung"-group.
ברכת רפואה =	the "liver-spleen"-group.
ברכת פרנסה =	the "stomach"-group.

When we consider the remaining seven, originally six, middle Berachoth, we see that they are but a twice repeated expression of the Berachoth גאולה, רפואה, פרנסה.

קיבוץ גלויות, the seventh Beracha, represents the national גאולה, the ingathering of the exiled.

משפט, the eighth Beracha representing the regeneration of the Jewish society based on Torah Law—and למלשנים, the ninth Beracha which was added at a later date, to preserve the national integrity from slander express the need for a national רפואה.

על הצדיקים, the tenth Beracha is the prayer to preserve and strengthen Israel's spiritual leadership, its true sustenance and mainstay, our national פרנסה.

Thus, the seventh, eighth, ninth and tenth Berachoth represent for the nation what the fourth, fifth, and sixth Berachoth represent for the individual. The subsequent three Berachoth re-state the three themes גאולה רפואה פרנסה focusing on the central element for their realization for the nation.

בונה ירושלים, the eleventh Beracha, the rebuilding of Jerusalem represents the national גאולה centered on Jerusalem, the city of redemption for Israel's exile.

את צמח דוד, the twelfth Beracha expresses the revival of the "sprout" of David, the bearer of the national רפואה, the spirit of the Torah which will prevail and before which all opposing influences will disappear.

שמע קולנו, the thirteenth Beracha evokes God as the Ultimate Provider for the nation, the sole source for the national פרנסה. Jerusalem and David are the instruments for the dominion of God for the social and spiritual well-being of the nation, but all hopes for the flourishing and blessing of the nation remains for ever resting in God.

The theme of the first three of the middle Berachoth (דעה, תשובה, סליחה) are expressed just once. The other themes (גאולה, רפואה, פרנסה), are repeated, referring each time to a different relationship due to the nature of their subjects. The conditions for the "redemption," "healing" and "maintenance" of the nation differ from those facing the individual and are therefore described in distinctly different terms. However, the need for "knowledge," "repentance" and "forgiveness" is essentially the same for the nation as well as for the individual.

Accordingly the middle Berachoth appear to fit the following outline:

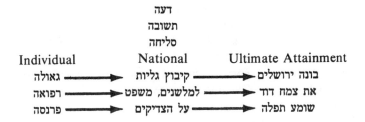

Individual	National	Ultimate Attainment
דעה		
תשובה		
סליחה		
גאולה ⟶	קיבוץ גליות ⟶	בונה ירושלים
רפואה ⟶	למלשנים, משפט ⟶	את צמח דוד
פרנסה ⟶	על הצדיקים ⟶	שומע תפלה

THE THREE LAST BERACHOTH

We have already remarked that the offering of the Tamid took place in two separate procedures. The parts were carried to the Altar in a fixed order of groups and deposited on the ramp leading up to the top of the Altar. There they were strewn with the salt which, in the order given in Levit. 2, 13, the Torah itself describes as the idea of renewing and consolidating the "lasting" nature of the Covenant of God—ברית מלח עולם (ברית אלקיך) Numb. 18, 19); thus salt transforms the offering from a fleeting gesture into a lasting expression of our Covenant with God—כורתי בריתי עלי זבח Ps. 50, 5 ("those that have made a covenant with Me by offerings").

Once the last group of the offering—which we have found to correspond to our שומע תפלה—had been deposited on the ramp (for the time being we take no account of the מנחות ונסכים, being subsidiaries to the Tamid, although by their nature representing פרנסה they correspond closely to the קרבים group) before they are given over to the fire as אשה ריח ניחוח לה', the leading priest directed the officiating priests to say and pray, אהבה רבה, עשרת הדברות, שמע, והיה אם שמוע, ויאמר, אמת ויציב, רצה, ושים שלום (Tamid V,1).

In the most direct connection with the offering-procedures, in the middle of which these passages of our prayers were introduced, רצה appears at once to us as a Beracha which accordingly is also called עבודה. It contains the prayers that the Divine Service in general, and those "given over to the Fire" אשי ישראל in particular, may achieve their purpose, namely, to be acceptable to God, and find רצון, to be pleasing in His eyes. It is remarkable that רש"י in Berachoth 11,b refers to this prayer as being said for the completed procedure of the offering בשביל העבודה שעשו היו מברכין אחריה. Indeed the real act which characterizes the הקטרת איברים, עולה, was only preceded by הולכת איברים לכבש. For even if כפרה is only contingent on זריקת הדם, nevertheless the text specifies אם אין בשר אין דם (Pesachim (Deut. 12, 27) and ועשית עלתיך הבשר והדם 77a) so that at least בשעת קבלה the burning of the whole of the parts, and בשעת זריקה a part of them must still be available to be burnt (Menachoth 26a, Zebachim 25a). In fact it is only by the הקטרת איברים that an עולה differs from an אשם and a שלמים, the זריקה being the same for all three. It is remarkable in any case that we find the place for the recitation of the Beracha רצה immediately after the middle Berachoth. This corresponds to its recitation by the priests after הולכת איברים לכבש which parallels our middle Berachoth.

Of the passages recited by the priests at that point it is only רצה which is really in relation to the עבודה. Consequently the significance of the other passages as an introduction to רצה must be explained.

The Jewish Sanctuary was dedicated to the תורה, to דבר ה' centered on the קודש קדשים which accordingly was called דביר, the "Home of the Word." The place for the שולחן מנורה ומזבח הזהב—all these כלים representing the dedication of our spiritual and material means to give satisfaction to God, as expressed by קטורת—was called the היכל, the "Home of Ability," (יכול), the means for the realization of the Word, of making it a reality. The theme of the first of the recitations that preceded the actual offering—אהבה רבה—preserved also in our present תפילה as part of the introduction to the שמע—is precisely אהבה—the unreserved dedication to the beloved one: God's love for His people—Israel's love for its God. Total dedication again expresses itself in the very nature of the offering: דם the essence of our personality; איברים—all our physical capabilities; מנחה ונסכים—all our possessions, our wealth. It is only through this total consecration of our existence to תורה that the Word becomes reality—the transition from the דביר to the היכל becomes a living truth—and thus our life gains God's approval לריח ניחוח לה' and the promise ועשו לי מקדש ושכנתי בתוכם attains fulfillment.

The מזבח was a "Mount of God" on a smaller scale, הראל—a replica of Sinai—ה' בם סיני בקדש (Ps. 68), perhaps also what is referred to in עולת תמיד העשויה בהר סיני (Numbers 28, 6)—hence the ultimate purpose of the מזבח was for Israel to dedicate every aspect of itself to the תורה.

The overall content of the passages: אהבה רבה, עשרת הדברות, קריאת שמע and אמת ויציב, the thought which they brought to the minds of the officiating priests when they laid the איברים on the Altar ramp was none other than:—תורה, the Word of God, the Divine Law and

Teaching, and the call to Israel to eternally bear and carry out this Torah of God.

Our תפלות—as arranged by the אנשי כנסת הגדולה—follow the exact order of the recitations as delineated in the Mishna (Tamid V,1) with the exception of the עשרת הדברות which according to Berachoth 12a was eliminated מפני תרעומת המינין to avoid even the slightest possibility to consider the "Ten Commandments" as the only authentic communication of God.

The priests recited שים שלום immediately after רצה. The Mishna says עבודה וברכת כהנים. Rambam, both in פירוש המשניות and in the יד החזקה, explains this ברכת כהנים as being שים שלום, since the actual ברכת כהנים took place later and not in לשכת הגזית. תוספות also (Berachoth 11b) concurs. Although תוספות explains that they only said the three verses without נשיאת כפים, "כמו שאנו אומרים," nevertheless תוספות could not have meant that they only said the three verses, for then the Mishna would hardly have designated that as a ברכה. Since the text of the Mishna reads ברכו את העם שלש ברכות אמת ויציב, ועבודה וברכת כהנים therefore ברכת כהנים is definitely described as a ברכה. Thus the explanation of תוספות may also well be taken to mean that these three verses were included in the Beracha שים שלום in the same way that our שליח צבור does in the repetition of the Shmone Esre. Consequently, for this reason the whole Beracha might have been designed as ברכת כהנים.

In our Shmone Esre מודים is inserted between רצה and שים שלום. In his Commentary on the Mishna, the רמב״ם actually includes מודים among the Berachoth recited by the priests. And indeed this seems to be a necessity if the ברכת כהנים mentioned in the Mishna does not refer to the Beracha שים שלום but only designates the three verses of the priestly blessing; then the three Berachoth would be:—אמת ויציב, רצה, מודים—and ברכת כהנים would be a separate independent recitation. The origin of מודים remains to be found. Only the פירוש המשניות refers to מודים (וזו לא ידענו מניין לו—תוס׳ יו״ט תמיד פ״ה משנה א׳) no other commentator, including the רמב״ם himself in his יד החזקה, mentions מודים. Therefore, it seems that the priests said only רצה ושים שלום at the offering, and thus a special reason must be found for the insertion of מודים in our Shmone Esre.

We have already stated that תפלות כנגד תמידים. We must find a procedure belonging to the Tamid-offering which could have its corresponding expression in the words of מודים, as does the offering of the parts in the middle Berachoth. If we do find such a parallel it would also explain why the priests did not say מחים. They did not need to do so—just as they did not say אמצעיות, the middle Berachoth, because what מודים expresses in words they expressed in deed.

The offering of the parts was followed by the offering of the מנחות ונסכים. Immediately after the (פרנסה) קרבים group they were deposited with it on the ramp of the Altar, and immediately after it given over to the fire. (See Tamid VI and VII.) They belonged essentially to every עולה או זבח (Numbers 15), and in accordance with all the regulations concerning them, they are to be taken as an essential complement of the Tamid-offering.

The meaning of the concept מנחה represents everywhere a paying of homage. מנחה, as a special form of gift, expresses acknowledgment to the one on whom he depends for his fate and whom he has to thank for his well-being. Thus we read of the Mincha-offering of Cain, Jacob's mincha to Esau, and the brothers' mincha-offering to Joseph in Egypt. A nation's tribute to its ruler is called מנחה (Judges 3, 64; I Samuel 10, 27). All these were the expresion of an obligation and the acknowledgment of dependence. מנחות as offerings have the same meaning. Thus, the expressions הגיש מנחה, נשא מנחה are used both in מנחות from man to man and at the Mincha-offerings. Therefore, הגשה is an essential procedure at the bringing of all מנחות, with the exception of מנחת נסכים (Menachoth 61a).

After the tragic and far-reaching episode of the sin of the spies, in an apparent un-connected order, the Torah commands (Numbers 15) that in future every עולה or שלמים must be complemented by מנחה and נסכים. That fateful error, as a result of which the Promised Land became lost to a whole generation, had its roots solely in the fact that they did not acknowledge God as the Master of their fate, as the One Who gave the Torah and Who would also give the Land for the Torah. "The Land is good," was the finding of the leaders of the community, "but we are too weak!" It is God, and only He, Who will crown our efforts with success. It is, however, up to us to undertake our tasks, as ordered by God, in full confidence in His protection and Supreme Might. We will never be "too weak" if we walk on the path of God's Torah, however difficult and how dangerous it might appear to us. Joshua and Caleb, the two who alone had remained faithful, said it precisely:—אם חפץ בנו ה' והביא אתנו אל הארץ הזאת ונתנה לנו ארץ אשר היא זבת חלב ודבש. Thereupon God's Torah commands: כי תבאו אל ארץ מושבתיכם אשר אני נתן לכם ועשיתם אשה לה' עלה או זבח וגו' והקריב המקריב לה' מנחה סלת

עשרון בלול ברבעית ההין שמן ויין לנסך וגו'. Henceforth, the dedication of our person and our limbs (דם ואיברים) represented by the עולה, or the dedication of our person and our impulses (דם ואימורים) represented by the שלמים, to God's Will must be accompanied by an expression of homage for providing the means for our existence. And so there is never דם and איברים or אימורים without שמן, סלת and יין. Our whole person is to be subordinated to God, affirming the dependence and obligation which one owes to the One to Whom one is dedicating one's whole personality for the maintenance, care and comfort which that person has already received from that same God and from Him alone.

Not only the national well-being in general is to be acknowledged to God, but God's השגחה פרטית for every home and every individual is to find its specific expression in חלה, the passage for which (Numb. 15, 17) immediately follows the passage on מנחות ונסכים. In the same vein, the Torah then goes on to ordain in v. 24 that if at any time the highest ecclesiastical authority, the Sanhedrin, should declare, through an error in decision-making that an act of עבודה זרה, idolatry, would be permitted, and thereby נעשתה בשגגה has resulted in actual sinful practice, then not only will a special חטאת have to be brought but the חטאת has to be preceded by an עולה with מנחה and נסכים. For, fundamentally, עבודה זרה is based on the erroneous conception that God Who dictates our duty is not the same God on Whom our fate depends. Hence such dualism must first be emphatically rejected before atonement for an aberration of that nature can be achieved (Zebachim 90b). Thus David, in Psalm 15 refutes the erroneous conception that God was only our Lord but not at the same time the Dispenser of our happiness [טובתי בל עליך, see Hirsch's commentary on that Psalm]. The conception of נסכים as we have taken it, gives the phrase בל אסיך נסכיהם מדם (Ps. 15, 4) still more meaning.

דגן תירוש ויצהר are the most notable gifts of the land which God has bestowed on us. Through them, God grants us, according to Psalm 104, 15, life, health and joy, ויין ישמח לבב אנוש להצהיל פנים משמן ולחם לבב אנוש יסעד—these important products of the land, and the most precious possessions of human life derived from them. do we lay on God's Altar daily together with our whole person, in the offering of סלת, שמן and יין. Thereby we acknowledge that it is the same God Who has given us the task of our life by the Torah, Whom we have to thank for the means which bring about the maintenance, the care and happiness of that life. Accordingly in fulfilling His Will, as expressed in זריקת הדם and הקטרת

איברים, we are only presenting to Him what we have received entirely and solely out of His Hands. מנחות הבאות בפני עצמן (such as: מנחת כהנים, גוים, נשים וכו') are set down by a special הגשה (being deposited on the southwestern corner of the Altar before being offered; note by Isaac Levy) before God. at מנחת נסכים such הגשה is not necessary, as they do not come for themselves independently, but by way of supplement and complement of the personality which in זריקת הדם has already rendered the expression of its total subordination to God. The idea of the Mincha had been already implicitly expressed in the זריקת הדם.

If we now look around for an expression in words which would correspond to the homage-paying acknowledgment of God as the guide, master, and ruler of our fate—which is expressed by the מנחת נסכים—our language offers us no better word than just הודאה. ועתה אלקינו מודים אנחנו לך says David in I Chron. 29, 13 and in this one word he finally summarizes all that he had previously said in the sentence לך ה' הגדולה וגו'. Everything great and glorious is God's and comes from Him; and whatever was received from Him we dedicate to Him. הודו לה' כי ממך הכל ומידך נתנו לך ("for all things come from You, and what we give You comes from Your Hand," v. 14). That is the great national summons to Israel to pay homage to God, to acknowledge and declare what we owe to God. Whereas הלל is the objective declaration of God's greatness and might, which the contemplation of His rule in nature and history brings forth, הודה is subjective, the expression of what God has become to us, and what thereby we are, and should be, to Him. (Thus הודה is also the confession of guilt; ידה the basic root of הודה is related to יד, the hand reaching out from within, exposing from within as it relates to someone). If we compare the expression הודה where it occurs in תנ"ך with reference to God we find it corresponding exactly to what is expressed in תנ"ך by the symbolism of the מנחה. For a similar reason, as being the most specific expression of paying homage, כריעה and השתחויה are also connected with הודאה. Thus the laying of our flour, oil, and wine on the top of the Altar, and giving the flour and oil over to the Fire of the Altar and the pouring of the wine, is the expression of our devotion to God for His granting our whole earthly existence with all its possessions, powers and joys. Indeed, this devotion could hardly find a better expression than is given in our מודים. In it we acknowledge God as צור חיינו מגן ישענו to Whose Hand the care of our lives and souls is committed and Whose wondrous kindness sustains us daily and hourly.

Accordingly, we believe we can see in our מודים, our הודאה-Blessing, the parallel expression for our מנחת נסכים which accompanied the Tamid-offering. In רצה we first pray that God may find satisfaction in dedicating our person with all its faculties to be acquired with God's help—corresponding to the actual offering itself—to be a bearer and preserver of godliness on earth. Then in הודאה we add—similar to the מנחת נסכים—the expression of our homage for all that had already been granted to us in our earthly existence, and express our readiness to strive for the future.

But with ברכת שלום we conclude in quite the same way as the priests in the Temple. It is the conception of שלום that is to be impressed upon us in this concluding Beracha as the highest form of blessing in all Divine Service and prayer. In words as well as in offering, it is not the individual, but the nation as a whole with all its members (כלנו כאחד) which renews its committment to God, the only basis of its very existence (באור פניך). Thereby the nation becomes the united people of God, all joined for the same pursuit. This union is expressed in actual life by living in שלום, in harmony, peace and friendship.

But, significantly all three: שלום, הודאה, עבדה form one complete, self-contained unit. שלום is not the first, שלום is the last prayer, and there can be no שלום without הודאה and עבדה, just as there can be no הודאה without עבדה. Our שלום is meaningful only if it is gained on the basis of our common homage of thanks and our common surrender to the service of God's Torah, and *every rendering of thanks to God is a denial of Him if it has not been preceded by surrendering to the service of God's Torah.*

THE FIRST THREE BERACHOTH

The parallelism of the middle Berachoth with the offering of the parts of the Tamid as well as that of the last three Berachoth with רצה and ברכת כהנים and the מנחת נסכים which accompanied the Tamid, has been clearly demonstrated.

But a parallelism similar to this includes also the first three Berachoth.

What is their common idea, and what is the relationship of the אבות, גבורות and קדושה to the middle Berachoth, and is there still a part of the procedure to the Tamid-offering which is similarly related to the

הקטרת איברים? It strikes one at once as a characteristic difference of these first three Berachoth that they are שבחות, praises of God, while the middle Berachoth are בקשות, prayers and petitions.

But exactly the same difference characterizes the procedure of שחיטה קבלה הולכה וזריקה which precedes the הקטרת איברים in relation to the subsequent offering of the parts. Whereas in the latter, the object to be offered appears in its separate groups, its physical elements, abilities and activities standing at God's disposition, here in the former, the procedures preceding the offering of the parts, the object of the offering appears primarily to be just the נפש, the עבודת הדם, the personality in essence, so that the parallelism of the first three Berachoth to this עבודת הדם is quite clear.

In comparing the first three Berachoth and עבודת הדם we must ascertain their precise relationship.

There are four עבודות: שחיטה קבלה הולכה וזריקה but there are only three Berachoth. Perhaps שחיטה could be disregarded since, to a certain extent, it is not considered an עבודה: שחיטה לאו עבודה היא (see Zebachim 14b). As a matter of fact, שחיטה is only an act of the denial of a life which hitherto had remained unaffected by the transforming power of the Sanctuary. שחיטה is the giving up of the animal life hitherto led, indeed it is the whole indispensable *preliminary* condition or prerequisite to surrender to the Sanctuary. Thus the positive activity of the Sanctuary only begins with קבלה, the taking up of the life (as represented by the דם, I.L.) into the sphere of the Sanctuary; that is clearly the reason why שחיטה כשרה בזר (may be performed by the non-priest). Only after this, מקבלה ואילך מצות כהונה (all procedures must be carried out by כהנים). Or from another point of view הולכה could equally be left out, as this is an עבודה which is not necessarily essential—עבודה שאפשר לבטלה (זבחים שם).

In a more profound sense the first three Berachoth basically need not be parallel to three of these separate first procedures of the offering.

For שחיטה קבלה הולכה וזריקה do not represent four different tendencies of the person who is striving to enter the sphere of the Sanctuary, but they are rather the progressive steps of one single procedure of the blood representing the life of the bringer of the offering: giving it up, having it accepted, taken towards the Altar and finally having it directed with all energy onto the four sides of the base (which is the beginning of the summit of the Altar). But the contents of the three Berachoth are not to be taken as merely a progression of one and the same idea but rather are three distinct facets of one task—ברוך which is the consequence of דעת ה'.

אבות takes the thought of God and how He appears to us in all His Greatness and Loftiness (הגדול הגבור והנורא) from the beginning, when He chose and guided the forefathers, till the most distant future, continuing the covenants of the forefathers, graciously and mercifully in the founding, unfolding and the final development of our national existence; but at the same time encompassing עוזר ומושיע ומגן in the concept of מגן אברהם all His Love, His helping sustenance to all, and demanding from us that we subordinate ourselves (by the concept of ברוך, I.L.) to Him: hence, God in His Love.

גבורות gives us the concept of God's Almightiness from the aspect of His Rulership overcoming even those powers which ordinarily hold sway over all strength, health, or even over life itself. This thought of God's Almighty Power overcoming even death is expressed in the concept of מחיה מתים and receives our dedication to God imbued with the thought of His Almighty Power to guide us beyond Death to Life: hence, God in His Might.

קדושה does not speak of God's Rulership and Guidance and turns our thoughts to the foremost attribute of God—קדושה. How can man attain קדושה—the supreme attribute of God and from which flows our entire and close relationship to God?—"He is קדוש, and all that we know of Him is קדוש. If we ourselves are קדושים then we make known His glory every day, every hour, in every situation of every moment of our lives," as He Himself has indeed declared: קדושים תהיו כי קדוש אני. But קדושה is simply the absolute, complete, unconditional readiness for everything that is good; it is the highest conception of a free-willed morality—a goal that man is able to achieve through his God-given בחירה; at that time man then shares in God's קדושה. This Beracha brings the highest attribute of God's Being to our minds, together with the awareness that we ourselves can strive to acquire this loftiest of qualities; we must offer absolute devotion and surrender to God: hence the Beracha expresses God in His Holiness.

From this summary of the contents of these three Berachoth, it seems clear to us that they do not contain a progression of one simple idea, as would have to be the case if they were to correspond to שחיטה קבלה הולכה וזריקה which are progressive stages towards the completion of one idea. But they each bring to our minds one and the same completed idea, the concept of the active furthering and achieving of God's Will that we designate in the one word of "dedication," ברוך, (ברוך from ברך move forward, to further God and His Will—Gen. 9, 26; 24, 11). And this is brought to us from three different points of view: in אבות, from the point of view of His Love helping and guiding us in this world; in גבורות from the point of view of His Almighty Power guiding us even beyond the grave; and in קדושה, absolutely—whether the direction of life seems to be ascending or descending—purely and solely from the point of view of our personal belonging to God, of our being unconditionally ready in all circumstances for God. Thereby ברוך is the consequence of דעת ה'.

If then, after all that has been previously elucidated, we are justified in assuming a parallel to the Tamid-offering in these three first Berachoth as well, there is only one more act that presents itself, and that is זריקה to which שחיטה, קבלה, הולכה are the only necessary preparatory steps. We now have to find whether זריקה, which represents the surrender of our נפש, our life, was performed in any such three differing and corresponding ways to which we could compare אבות, גבורות וקדושה as expressing them in words.

Whereas in the חטאת, the נתינת הדם באצבעו על קרנות המזבח was to preach to the חוטא בשגגה, to one who unthinkingly had carelessly committed a grave sin, that henceforth he must carefully maintain the moral height he had regained, in the case of עולה which was to be מכפר על עשה, on the other hand was to preach against an error of omission, being remiss in an undeserved feeling of moral accomplishment while we were to use all our powers to attain the heights which the Torah sets as the ideal for our lives. Hence it says of the עולה:—וזרקו הדם על המזבח סביב, the priest is to stand back from the Altar and throw the blood, which had been taken up in a basin of the Sanctuary, onto the Altar, and specifically on the lower part of the Altar (למטה מחוט הסקרא which in Ezekiel (43) is called the עזרה, similarly to the forecourt of the היכל, thus representing only a preliminary stage). Accordingly, the זריקת דם העולה represents the way we are to consider ourselves as being still far off from the very first stage of the summit for which we have to strive. But this זריקה, expressing the dedication of all our life, is to be made סביב, is to comprise every side of the Altar. It was made in מתנות שתים שהן ארבע, in two diagonally opposite throws, which touched all four sides of the Altar, מזרחית צפונית, on the northeastern corner and מערבית דרומית, the south-western one. But the שירים, the remainder of

the blood, as a third act, was poured out onto the base of the Altar, the
יסוד.

The surrendering of the blood of the Tamid to the Altar was thus
made in three distinct moves, זריקה מזרחית צפונית, זריקה מערבית דרומית,
ושפיכה כנגד היסוד throwing to the north-east, throwing to the southwest, and pouring on to the base.

These different directions represent phases of the day, of life:—
midnight to dawn, the rising rays of life, and mid-day to eve, the sinking rays of life. Our total dedication must dominate the ascending and
descending part of life. Still, the timeless שפיכה כנגד היסוד represents the
complete subordination without any consideration of life's course,
upward or downward.

Subordination to God when He leads our life in an upward direction, subordination to Him when He leads it in a downward direction,
complete subordination to Him on the base on which He has established our life without any consideration whether it leads upwards or
downwards—is this not exactly the pattern which we found to be the
contents of the Berachoth אבות, גבורות, וקדושה?

אבות is dedicating one's life to the guidance of God when He leads
us out of midnight to day; גבורות, from mid-day to darkness; קדושה the
complete consecration of our life to Him, regardless of our life's station. And just the last act, the שפיכת הדם was on the יסוד דרומי on the
"mid-day" side of the base. This is eminently characteristic of our
basic attitude toward God: the זריקות to the different directions representing the different stages of life, are transitory; the essence of our
personality joining the מזבח on its south side—the zenith, highest point
in the solar day—will thus always be spent in the bright sun of mid-
day, his whole life imbued with the absolute, קדושה.

We believe this comparison is quite clear.

The reason that the זריקה embracing all the four sides of the Altar
was done just on the northeast corner and the southwest corner, and
not on the southeast and northwest corners was because קרן מזרחית
דרומית לא היה לה יסוד the base was not built out at all on the southeast
corner. That corner was without a base and it marked the boundary
line between the territory of the tribe of Judah and Benjamin. Only this
small portion, the southeast corner, lay in the territory of Judah. But
the whole rest of the Altar stood on Benjamin's ground. Thus the base
did not extend into the domain of Judah. But all placing of blood of
the עולה-offering had to have the יסוד, the base of the Altar, beneath it.

Thus the prescribed סביב, the placing of the blood on all four sides of the Altar could not be effected on it because the southeast corner had no יסוד (Zebachim 53b, 54a, 51). (According to another opinion which, however is not the accepted one, the southeast corner did have a יסוד, but it was not מקום מקודש לדמים.) זריקה, that most essential procedure of the offering, was not allowed to be performed on the soil of Judah.

Not on the soil of Judah, the royal tribe, crowned with the glory of military success, but on that of the youngest and weakest one, did the Altar stand seemingly unfinished. Only in the territory of Benjamin, the weak one, it is completed. On that of Judah, the strong, it still awaits its completion. Is not this the lesson of all of our history, לא יסור שבט מיהודה ומחוקק מבין רגליו (Gen. 49, 10). The future of our nation was to be accomplished when the royal sceptor and law-inscribing style will be permanently the role of Judah, the Jewish kings. Just at the moment when the cataclysmic end seems near—עד כי יבא שילה (—שול, שוליים, extreme end) לו יקהת עמים nations will surrender to him. Experience has taught the truth of the words יאי עניותא לישראל ("poverty is good for Israel," חגיגה ט׳). For the rays of light rising up from the darkness of night to the brightness of morn, the bright rays of mid-day sinking to eve, even the dusk of evening sinking to the utter darkness of mid-night, all this we have learnt to know and to endure, have been able to keep our devotion to God and His demands in all the changing times of our fate; we have been able to overcome the trying times of being a "Benjamin." But that of a "Judah," the strong and powerful, the bright sun of life ascending from morn to mid-day has always proved to be a trial for us. That is why we have never yet been able to maintain that condition permanently. The whole of our historical education is to teach us to build our foundation to the "morn to mid-day Judah corner" on earth, and when the course of our lives soars from "morn to mid-day," to enable us to devote ourselves to the fulfillment of our duties.

In summary, our שמונה עשרה and the תמיד and their intrinsic link can be perceived as follows:

הפלה   תמיד

```
                          אבות ⎫                   מזרחית צפונית ⎫
          ראשנות ⎨         נבורות ⎬        זריקה ⎨   מערבית דרומית ⎬
                          קדושה  ⎭                 שפיכה כנגד היסוד ⎭

                          דעה                      ראש ורנל של ימין ⎫
                          תשובה                    שתי ידים          
                          סליחה                    עוקץ כליות ורנל של שמאל
   אמצעיות⎬  בנין ירושלים  קבוץ נליות  נאולה       החזה והנגרה        ⎬ איברים
           צמח דויד  מינים  משפט,  רפואה          דפנות כבד טחול      
           שומע תפלה  על הצדיקים  פרנסה            קרבים וכרעים       ⎭

                          עבודה                     רצה
                          הודאה                     מנחת נסכים
                          שלום                      שלום
```

TALMUDIC NOTES

תפלה במקום תמיד

Comparing the Shmone Esre with the various procedures of the Tamid-offering serves to facilitate the explanation of several passages in the Talmud which refer to the Shmone Esre.

In the first section we pointed out how our Tefilla was in no way to be taken as a *substitute* for the offering. Indeed, the origin of our Shmone Esre coincided with the establishment of the offerings in the Second Temple, and the duty of prayer in general is as old as the duty of offerings. In טור אורח חיים צ״ח we read: ולעבדו בכל לבבכם: איזוהי עבודה שבלב הוי אומר זו תפלה "and serve Him with all your innermost heart"; what Service is there which is performed with the heart? This is prayer. And the Sifri on Deut. 11, 13 concludes כשם שעבודת מזבח קרויה עבודה כך תפלה קרויה עבודה (just as the service on the Altar is termed "Service," so prayer is called "Service"). Thus Tefilla and offering can well be considered as mutually complementing each other, both together accomplishing the realization of the one purpose, עבודה, the submission, and the dedication to

God, for carrying out His will. This explanation is of great significance for the conception of Jewish offerings as well as for that of Jewish prayer. It is the inner man that is to be touched by the act of the offering and the act of prayer. The expression in the Gemara (Berachoth 26a) תפלה במקום קרבן היא (prayer is in the place of offering) can accordingly be taken only in the sense that תפלה—the prayer that is prescribed to be said thrice daily—is on the same level as that of the offering which it accompanied. This statement does not mean that the Tefilla is a substitute for the offerings since the Gemora is dealing there with the question of prayer as an obligatory duty, a question which is not relevant to the presence or absence of offerings. Rather our Tefilla is on an equal level with the offering so that certain rules for the offering apply to prayer as well. But if nevertheless it does say שתפלה היא במקום קרבן דכתיב ונשלמה פרים שפתינו (טור א״ח שם) pointing evidently to קרבן תשלומי, the reference must be to the time after the destruction of the Temple. In any case, until the rebuilding of the Temple, it is the only kind of עבודה which is left to us, which we thus have to hold dear since it constitutes the whole of our עבודה.

תפלת ערב אין לה קבע

Our interpretation of the ברייתא: ומפני מה אמרו תפלת הערב אין לה קבע, was that the שהרי איברים ופדרים שלא נתעכלו מבערב קרבים והולכים כל הלילה precise time during the night for תפלת ערבית was not fixed. This might resolve the difficulty which caused תלמידי ר׳ יונה to induce the רי״ף to take the אין לה קבע of the ברייתא to be only in the sense of זמנה כל הלילה. For if the אין לה קבע means that the evening Tefilla is not fixed as an absolute duty, and that the time for it is not limited, then both interpretations would be valid. It is רשות because only such parts which had not been consumed by day—which is the time when they should really be brought, and so were even שבת דוחה—were given a subsidiary permission to be offered by night; and זמנה כל הלילה because then such parts of the offerings קרבים והולכים כל הלילה. Furthermore, the תפלת ערבית רשות in itself gives the reason why זמנה כל הלילה, for if it were מן הבוח its time would be restricted, just as it is for קריאת שמע for reasons of גייס. (See צל״ח thereon.)

שמעון הפקולי הסדיר שמונה עשרה ברכות

In Megilla 17b, to explain the statement that "by reversing the prescribed order of the 'Eighteen Berachoth'—למפרע—the duty of saying
the prayer would not be fulfilled," one is first referred to the ברייתא,
שמעון הפקולי הסדיר שמונה עשרה ברכות לפני רבן גמליאל על הסדר ביבנה, so that
the existing order of the Berachoth is not arbitrary but rests on the
order which was fixed by Rabbi Gamliel in Yavneh. Then one is directed to the other ברייתא: מאה ועשרים זקנים ומהם כמה נביאים תקנו שמונה עשרה
ברכות על הסדר according to which the order was already fixed by the
Men of the Great Assembly who composed the Shmone Esre. Then the
question is asked, what was the reason for שמעון הפקולי, to establish an
order which was already long in existence. The answer given: שכחום
וחזר וסדרם, the original arrangement of the order of the Berachoth had
become forgotten, and שמעון הפקולי under the authorization of Rabbi
Gamliel re-established it. The difficulty in the assertion that the order
of the Berachoth in a prayer that had been repeated three times daily
for centuries could have become forgotten could well be solved by
what we have shown in the parallelism of this prayer with the Tamid-
offering. For, in our explanation, we remarked that there were five different traditions as to the order in which the groups of parts of the
Tamid were brought onto the Altar, while concerning the grouping
itself there was absolutely no question.

It was clear that there were no divergent opinions about the right
hind-leg belonging to the group containing the head or that the two
forelegs formed a group by themselves. But the opinions differed as to
the order in which the groups were brought to the Altar and consigned
to the Fire. If the idea which each one of these groups was to represent
was to be expressed in words in one of the middle Berachoth, if
there is a conflict in the order of the groups, then there could be the
same conflict applied to the sequence of the Berachoth. And so in
Rabbi Gamliel's time it became necessary to make a final decision as
to which order of the bringing of the groups was to be accepted as
Halacha. The sequence of the offering which we compare to the
sequence of the middle Berachoth is confirmed in Tamid and Yoma as
the accepted one. We may ascertain therefore that the acceptance of
both sequences was ascribed to the same time and the same authority.
The principle which was at the base of this prescribed order of the
sequence of the Berachoth was, as quoted by בתר עילויא, ר' יוסי הגלילי,
דבשרא determined by the choiceness of the various parts in question; ר'

יוסי takes that to refer to the greater or lesser excellence of the meat שמנא דבשרא; the prescription of the Mishna is איברא דבשרא. This איברא דבשרא is explained by Rashi as גודל איברים the size of the parts. We doubt that one can find anywhere else that size or weight is expressed by איברא. The number of priests, assigned to carry the groups, varied in proportion to the groups' weight (Yoma 26b) but the sequence was not determined by the relative size of the group starting with the heaviest and ending with the lightest. The איברא דבשרא means the anatomic importance of the parts as organs (the head the most important, not on account of weight, but as an organ, and hence its group comes first; I.L.) which decided its sequence, and it is not impossible that Rashi too wished to express this by גודל האיברים.

אמצעיות אין להם סדר

The statement in Berachoth 34a: אמצעיות אין להם סדר (the middle Berachoth have no fixed order of sequence) could also have resulted from the parallelism of these Berachoth with the groups of the offering. According to the way R. Hai Gaon (see בעל המאור) takes this dictum and according to one way that Rashi takes it (עיין תוספות שם) it would mean to say that a Beracha which had been mistakenly omitted could be said quite out of the prescribed sequence, wherever one remembered it, although thereby the whole sequence is out of order. For, as the sequence of the groups of parts itself, which these Berachoth represent, is not definitely certain, it can well be understood that although a sequence had been accepted as הלכה and in accordance with that prescription the order of the Berachoth had correspondingly been fixed, still בדיעבד, if such a mistake has happened, the keeping of that prescribed order need not be insisted upon. In any case we can see the reason why just the sequence of the middle Berachoth need not be as imperative as for the first and last Berachoth. Moreover, if our opinion that the arrangement fixed by שמעון הפקולי refers primarily to the middle Berachoth is not without foundation, and we call to mind that it is just to these middle Berachoth that we are referred (in Megilla 17b) for an explanation of the dictum וכן בתפלה לא יצא למפרע, this would confirm the opinion of רשב"ם ורב אלפס established as Halacha (see תוספות there) that, after the sequence had been fixed, even בדיעבד, for the middle Berachoth too, although perhaps not quite so strictly as for the first and last Berachoth, the correct sequence for them is obligatory.

הני י״ח כנגד מי

At first glance, the question posed in the Gemara (Berachoth 28b) הני י״ח כנגד מי why the Tefilla was composed of just eighteen Berachoth, seems contrary to our interpretation namely that כנגד תמידים תקנום the number corresponded to the procedures of the Tamid-offering. We have seen that for the offerings directly, only twelve Berachoth would be indicated:—three procedures of the זריקה; six groups of the parts, and רצה, נסכים, ושלום. The fourth, fifth and six groups of the parts were modified threefold, accordingly represented by nine Berachoth, thus giving us the total of eighteen. But such an explanation was not necessarily evidenced by the offering itself. It would be conceivable that, for instance, in the one Beracha גאולה, both קבוץ גלויות and בנין ירושלים would be expressed; in השיבה שופטינו, the מלכות בית דוד could be included at the same time; or, for instance, separate Berachoth could have been composed for צדיקים וחסידים, for זקנים וסופרים or for גרים. Accordingly, even accepting our parallelism, the question on fixing the Berachoth at just eighteen is well taken (Yerushalmi Berachoth IV,3).

מנין שאומרים אבות

In Megilla 17b there is a discussion as to the motives of the authors when they composed the Berachoth of the Shmone Esre. The questions are posed as follows: regarding the first three Berachoth—מנין שאומרים אבות and regarding the following ones—ומה ראו לומר בינה אחר קדושה. For the first three, reasons were sought for their essential origin, purpose and meaning but for the others, the subject of the Beracha is presumed to be known and only the reason for the sequence is sought. This striking difference is not at all surprising when we take into account the result of our investigations.

The middle Berachoth, בינה, תשובה, סליחה were the direct expression in words of the corresponding groups of the parts of the Tamid-offering. But the contents of the first three Berachoth are not so clearly seen in the three aspects of the זריקה. The שתי מתנות שהן ארבע and שפיכה כנגד היסוד represent the idea that it is God Who directs our fate and fortune not only when His guidance leads us on the upward path but equally so when it does the reverse; and finally we are taught that we must dedicate ourselves entirely to Him and His Torah as the basis of our life regardless of our material fortune.

This approach to God is formulated in our שמנה עשרה as:

אבות —the reality of God's guiding Hand in our fate in the history of our people.

גבורות —the basic concept of our trust in God's Providence and Might to raise us up from the deepest abyss.

קדושה —the bond that ties us closely to 'ה rooted in the Holiness of God, and our mission and ability to attain this relationship with God—קדושים תהיו כי קדוש אני.

The concepts expressed in the first three Berachoth are not easily appreciated from the general procedures of זרייקה and שפיכה, and hence the questions are valid: מנין שאומרים אבות, מנין שאומרים גבורות, ומנין שאומרים קדושות.